THE EAGLES OF BASTOGNE

THE EAGLES OF BASTOGNE

The Untold Story of the Heroic Defense of a City Under Siege

MARTIN KING

With Michael Collins, Patrick Seeling, and Ronald Stassen

CASEMATE

Pennsylvania & Yorkshire

Published in the United States of America and Great Britain in 2024 by
CASEMATE PUBLISHERS
1950 Lawrence Road, Havertown, PA 19083, USA
and
47 Church Street, Barnsley, S70 2AS, UK

Hardcover Edition: ISBN 978-1-63624-413-6
Digital Edition: ISBN 978-1-63624-414-3

A CIP record for this book is available from the British Library

Printed and bound in the United Kingdom by CPI Group (UK) Ltd, Croydon, CR0 4YY
Typeset in India by DiTech Publishing Services

For a complete list of Casemate titles, please contact:

CASEMATE PUBLISHERS (US)
Telephone (610) 853-9131
Fax (610) 853-9146
Email: casemate@casematepublishers.com
www.casematepublishers.com

CASEMATE PUBLISHERS (UK)
Telephone (0)1226 734350
Email: casemate@casemateuk.com
www.casemateuk.com

(All images from the Don F. Pratt Museum Archives, used with permission unless stated)
Cover image: the Don F. Pratt Museum Archives

Dear Mr. Martin King,

You have the admiration of the entire 327th Infantry Regiment, 101st Airborne Division. The word "Bastogne" is spoken daily at Fort Campbell, Kentucky, by the nearly 4,000 members of the modern-day 327th Infantry Regiment. To us, Bastogne is far more than a word. It represents the historic winter of 1944 and '45 where our reputation was built on the backs of brave men and women, soldiers and civilians. To a soldier, history is essential. Hearing the stories of the men and women whose shoulders we stand on commits us deeper to the missions of today's conflicts in defense of freedom. Please accept our deepest gratitude and respect for telling this important story and for your efforts to recognize and immortalize the battle for Bastogne, Belgium. The soldiers of the 327th Infantry Regiment send our love and respect.

Sincerely,
Robert C. Campbell (fmr) Colonel, U.S. Army, Commander,
327th Infantry Regiment, 101st Airborne Division

This volume is dedicated to all American war veterans past and present, and to Mr. Hans van Kessel and Mr. Johnny Bona at the 101st Airborne Museum Bastogne for all their kind assistance.

Contents

American and German Forces at Bastogne, December 1944–January 1945

American Forces

101st Airborne Division

501st Parachute Infantry Regiment
502nd Parachute Infantry Regiment
506th Parachute Infantry Regiment
327th Glider Infantry Regiment
321st Glider Infantry Regiment
907th Glider Field Artillery Battalion
377th Parachute Field Artillery Battalion
463rd Parachute Field Artillery Battalion
81st Airborne Anti-Aircraft Battalion
326th Airborne Engineer Battalion
101st Airborne Signal Company
801st Airborne Ordnance Maintenance Company
326th Airborne Medical Company
426th Airborne Quartermaster Company
1 Battalion, 401st Glider Infantry Regiment
327th Medical Detachment
58th Armored Field Artillery Battalion
482nd AAA (AW) Battalion
1st Artillery Battalion

Attached Units

Third Army, 10th Armored Division, Combat Command B
Team O'Hara
Team Cherry
Team Desobry
80th Armored Medical Battalion, part of Company B
420th Armored Field Artillery Battalion
796th Anti-Aircraft Artillery Battalion, Battery B

Additional Units

705th Tank Destroyer Battalion
755th Field Artillery Battalion
333rd Field Artillery Battalion
969th Field Artillery Battalion
109th Field Artillery Battalion
771st Field Artillery Battalion
687th Field Artillery Battalion
158th Engineer Battalion
73rd Armored Field Artillery Battalion
9th Armored Engineer Battalion, Company C
20th Armored Infantry Battalion
28th Infantry Division; 110th Infantry Regiment
9th Armored Division; 2nd Tank Battalion; 52nd Armored Infantry Battalion; 73rd
  Armored Field Artillery Battalion
Team SNAFU

German Forces

47th Panzer Corps
Panzer Abteilung 115
66th Infantry Corps
18th Volksgrenadier Division
62nd Volksgrenadier Division
58th Armored Corps
506th Volksgrenadier Division
116th Panzer Division "Windhund"
37th Armored Corps
2nd Panzer Division
Panzer-Lehr Division
26th Volksgrenadier Division
Führer-Begleit-Brigade
5th Fallschirmjäger Division
9th SS Division "Hohenstaufen"
12th SS Division "Hitlerjugend"
766th Volks-Artillerie-Korps
15th Volks-Werfer Brigade

It is only those who have neither fired a shot nor heard the shrieks and groans of the wounded who cry aloud for blood, more vengeance, more desolation. War is hell.

William Tecumseh Sherman

Foreword

The 101st Airborne Division's 1st "Bastogne" Brigade Combat Team can trace its lineage back to the 327th Glider Infantry Regiment, which earned the "Bastogne Bulldog" moniker after its dogged defense of the Belgian city during the Battle of the Bulge in 1944.

Today, I have the distinct privilege of leading the Bastogne Brigade, and with this privilege comes opportunities to visit the very battlefields where our forebears fought, bled, and died. As a brigade commander and novice historian, I now also get the privilege of enjoying Martin King's superb and holistic chronicling of the "Mighty 101" and its exploits during World War II. Martin's résumé, accolades, and depth of knowledge come together in *The Eagles of Bastogne*, beautifully written with the help of his long-time friends and co-authors Michael Collins, Patrick Seeling, and Ronald Stassen.

I have spent the past 20 years of my Army career as an infantry officer, five of which were spent in combat zones in the Middle East. One of those overseas tours included a deployment as the commander of the 327th Infantry Regiment's 1st Battalion. All of this to say I can attest to Martin's ability to illustrate the finer details of soldiering—details that bring a story to life and vividly depict the fortitude, grit, tenacity, and fighting spirit of the American soldier.

The "Screaming Eagles" of today's 101st Airborne Division (Air Assault) can be proud of this book knowing the honored legacy that inspires us every day is very much alive. With *The Eagles of Bastogne*, Martin has fully and poetically brought to life the extraordinary and heroic deeds upon which our military heritage is built. The current generation of air-assault soldiers will reflect on the valor of the glider soldiers that came before them and understand that the 101st has always solved the most challenging problems in the most lethal environments under the harshest conditions. I could not imagine a more fitting reminder to our nation, allies, and adversaries that we will always accomplish any mission, anytime, anywhere.

Thank you, Martin, for continuing to tell the indelible story of the 101st. "The Eagles of Bastogne" will not soon be forgotten.

Colonel Trevor S. Voelkel
Commander of the 1st Brigade Combat Team "Bastogne"
101st Airborne Division (Air Assault), United States Army
November 14, 2023

Prologue

There are few place names in the annals of military history that evoke such emotion, and in some cases controversy, as the small Belgian town of Bastogne. It was, after all, right at the heart of the largest land battle in American military history, which by default should put it right up there with Yorktown, Gettysburg, the Meuse–Argonne, and Iwo Jima. Many great books have already been written about this famous city in the Belgian Ardennes; many have focused on the exploits of "Easy Company" from *Band of Brothers* fame as if they were the only unit there.

It troubles me a little that some previous volumes on the subject refer to "mountains" in the Ardennes and the Schnee Eifel region of Germany. There are no mountains in either area, just rolling hills. While some other publications have an inane tendency to simply rehash the same widely available matter using the same protagonists, others simply exhaust every synonym for "freezing" and "fighting." Granted, certain names and details are inevitably unavoidable, but it should be noted that the 101st Airborne Division only constituted one third of the eventual force that helped to save Bastogne from annihilation. Hopefully this volume will dig a little deeper and reveal more details about those indomitable "Eagles" and the other units that stood with them during that punishingly bitter winter of 1944–45.

Although I don't regard myself as an expert on the subject of Bastogne or the Battle of the Bulge, a number of recent publications have referenced some of my previous books—*The Tigers of Bastogne*, *Searching for Augusta*, *Voices of the Bulge*, and *The Battle of the Bulge*. I openly admit some of the veteran accounts in this volume have been borrowed from my previous publications, but only the relevant ones.

When my dear friend Mike Collins (who also won an Emmy) wrote *The Tigers of Bastogne* with me some years ago, it was mainly because his grandfather had served with the 10th Armored Division (10th AD) in Bastogne, and because we concurred wholeheartedly with General Anthony McAuliffe's opinion that the 10th AD had been terribly overlooked by history. We wanted to put that right, and to some extent I think we succeeded. I cannot count the times we have filmed and interviewed veterans, attended ceremonies, campaigned for monuments, and simply met up in Bastogne to enjoy what this excellent town has to offer. To do this, I assembled a team of friends for this project that can only be described as "the best of the best." They are: Michael Collins, official historian of the 10th AD, and archivist extraordinaire;

Patrick Seeling, the official serving division historian of the 101st Airborne Division at Fort Campbell, Kentucky; Ronald Stassen, an incredibly knowledgeable expert, and battlefield tour guide, who almost knows everything about the 101st and has accompanied many veterans around sites in the Ardennes and the Western Theater; Bob Allen, who provided all the GPS coordinates for the "Tour" section; and Alex Khan, "Prince of Macedon," who contributed the "Gaming" aspect of the 101st Airborne in World War II for various platforms.

Bastogne really is a great town. Mike and I know it intimately. It has thrived and suffered throughout the centuries, and its story still lives on; it's indelibly engraved in its buildings and the ubiquitous local battle monuments. By fusing our collective knowledge, we hope we can provide a comprehensive and accurate account of this momentous battle.

I'm British; I have lived in Belgium for over 40 years and during that time have met many veterans of the 101st, both past and present, and toured extensively around all the relevant sites in the Ardennes, living just over an hour north of there. I have a very good knowledge of the topography of the Ardennes region and specifically Bastogne. This volume will attempt to relate the story of Bastogne, hopefully without lapsing into obsequious or sycophantic effusions about the heroic actions that occurred there in World War II. This is, however, a subjective appraisal that shouldn't detract from anyone's admiration and respect for the 101st Airborne Division, who deserve all the kudos they have accumulated over the years.

While Mike Collins and I were having an outrageously good time touring the east coast of the United States for *The Tigers of Bastogne*, we had the opportunity to sign copies of our book in the former office of "Easy Company" commander Richard "Dick" Winters, which had been relocated in its entirety (including the wallpaper) to the USAHEC, the U.S. Army Heritage and Education Center in Carlisle, Pennsylvania. I recall feeling profoundly honored to be able to see and browse through Major Winters's personal copy of Stephen Ambrose's bestselling book *Band of Brothers*, which was handed to me by his closest friend, Mr. Bill Jackson, the owner of the *Hummelstown Sun* newspaper.

As I browsed through the book, I couldn't help noticing there were remarks and observations in the margins of almost every single page, and some of these were not particularly flattering. Although the original book spawned many individual biographies, autobiographies, and reappraisals, none of these have actually covered the story of the 101st Airborne in its entirety. However, we can't detract from the fact that *Band of Brothers* made the 101st's E Company famous, and rightfully so. It's also fair to assume that without the inspiration of Ambrose's monographs, memoirs such as that of Major Winters would probably never have been published.

Regarding publishing, over the past 25 years I have published 14 books on the subject of military history. Six of them were co-written with Mike. *Searching for Augusta*, based on the life of Augusta Chiwy, a nurse born in the Belgian Congo who served with American forces, including the 101st Airborne at Bastogne, was the inspiration for the Emmy Award-winning documentary of the same name.

Mike and I decided it's time to tell the whole story of the events that directly involved the 101st Airborne and subordinate units in Bastogne in World War II, based on our own extensive research, and personal veteran archives accumulated collectively over the past 40 years. With this volume, we're not assuming we will present the definitive account of the momentous battle, because that would simply elicit too much outrage from historians, re-enactors, and ardent admirers, not forgetting the multitudinous fans (whose main knowledge of Bastogne is based on repeatedly binge watching the hit TV series *Band of Brothers*, taken from the book of same name), whom we have absolutely no intention of offending. We just want to present other perspectives.

Such is the power of contemporary audiovisual media. The resounding success of both forms of *Band of Brothers* definitely raised the profile of this remarkable division, and widened the audience demographic considerably, but it didn't impart the whole story, and, in some cases, wildly exaggerated other accounts for effect. There will indubitably be those who will dispute, disagree, and attempt to correct us, for which I have only one conceivable riposte: "Please feel free to write your own book, but thank you most graciously if you're contemplating the prospect of reading ours."

Many years ago, I travelled to the home of the 101st Airborne at Fort Campbell—it's where I gratefully received a certificate of appreciation—and since then have personally maintained good relations with both serving and former Airborne soldiers. I digress. It's still a challenge to bring something new to the table, but what's life without a challenge? Now it's time to include other protagonists, not just the ones mentioned in *Band of Brothers*.

The first few chapters of this volume will focus primarily on the German build up, and the opening assaults against the 28th Infantry Division and the 9th Armored Division that were directly in the path of those first devastating waves. It's a slow build, but hopefully it will set the stage and provide a solid foundation for the arrival of the 10th Armored Division's Combat Command B and the 101st Airborne.

The story of the battle for Bastogne is a compelling one of sacrifice, dedication, comradeship, and duty in the face of terrible adversity, but more importantly it's a human story, one that encapsulates the finest and worst attributes of humankind in the absolute direst of circumstances.

Martin King

Introduction

In the beginning, American Maj. William C. Lee said, "Let there be Airborne troops" and so the first U.S. Airborne force was created at Fort Benning, Georgia, in January 1940. It was there they developed the necessary accouterments and employed specific training that would be used as the solid foundation for all ensuing U.S. Airborne units. By the time of the attack on Pearl Harbor in December 1941, there were in effect three U.S. Parachute Infantry Battalions and one Airlanding Battalion (later to become a Glider Infantry Battalion). These formations were quickly used as the basis for expansion to four Parachute Infantry Regiments (PIRs) and Glider Infantry Regiments (GIRs).

Brigadier General Lee had visited British Airborne forces and discovered they were planning whole Airborne divisions. On his return to the United States, he recommended using the same model. Consequently, on August 15, 1942, the 82nd and 101st Airborne Divisions were activated:

SUBJECT: Activation of 82d and 101st Airborne Divisions
TO: Commanding Generals
Third Army,
Airborne Command.
1) Effective August 15, 1942, the 82d Division will be redesignated and its personnel and equipment will be utilized to form the 82d Airborne Division and the 101st Airborne Division. To accomplish this reorganization the War Department will publish instructions constituting, redesignating, and disbanding units as may be necessary.
2) Commanding General, Third Army will effect the reorganization of the 82d Division and will activate the 101st Airborne Division on August 15, 1942, in accordance with the provisions set forth herein.
3) The 82d and the 101st Airborne Divisions will be stationed initially at Camp Claiborne, Louisiana, and will be organized as indicated below:
  A. Administration and training: Effective August 15, 1942, both divisions are attached to the Third Army for administration and supply only. The Airborne Command will direct and supervise the training of these divisions, for which purpose direct communication is authorized.
  B. Organization: Pending approval of Tables of Organization, each airborne division is authorized a strength of 504 officers and 8,321 enlisted men. The attached chart, Inclosure 1, shows the general organization of the division. Approved tables will be furnished as soon as practicable.
  C. Source of personnel and equipment: The personnel and equipment of the present 82d Division will be utilized to organize and equip the two airborne divisions, exclusive

of the parachute regiment required for each. Detailed instructions will be issued by this headquarters at an early date relative to the selection and transfer of personnel and equipment.

The first commander of the 101st Airborne Division, now Major General Lee addressed the troopers of the division with these memorable words: "The 101st Airborne Division, which was activated on 16 August 1942, at Camp Claiborne, Louisiana, has no history, but it has a rendezvous with destiny." Prophetic words indeed.

The 101st Airborne Division was not originally nicknamed the "Screaming Eagles." Subsequent chapters will refer to the division as the "Eagle Division," a nickname submitted by Pvt. Jesse Willis. The nickname was originally attached to the 502nd PIR's boxing team which won multiple tournaments while the division was stationed at Camp Mackall, North Carolina. The nickname was later used by the division boxing team that fought at Rainbow Corner, and reporters from *Stars and Stripes* applied it to the division as a whole, ultimately leading to it being permanently associated with the unit.

By 1943, the 11th, 13th, and 17th Airborne Divisions had been activated. While this represented the first large-scale use of Airborne forces by the United States, the idea was far from new. Using parachutes to drop soldiers behind enemy lines was a 20th century creation, but the idea of transporting soldiers into combat by air dates back to the formation of the United States. In 1784, Benjamin Franklin witnessed a demonstration of the first hot-air balloon while serving as ambassador to France. Recognizing its potential, he remarked:

> Five thousand balloons capable of raising two men each could not cost more than five ships-of-the-line; and where is the prince who could afford to so cover his country with troops for its defense as that ten thousand men descending from the clouds might not in many places do an infinite deal of mischief before a force could be brought together to repel them?

While Franklin's idea did not become a reality in his lifetime, the Airborne landings in World War II demonstrated the utility of such a maneuver.

The actual concept of dropping infantry soldiers behind enemy lines by parachute was first envisaged and proposed in 1917 by Winston Churchill, who was serving as the Minister of Munitions in Prime Minister David Lloyd George's coalition government. Then along came William "Billy" Mitchell—a senior commander of the Air Service of the American Expeditionary Force during America's involvement in World War I and regarded as the father of the United States Air Force—with a masterful plan to provide elements of the American 1st Infantry Division with parachutes and drop them from converted bombers near Metz, France, as part of a larger offensive against German positions, but the Armistice was declared before his stratagem could be executed. Sadly, his career came to an ignominious end when he was quietly demoted for criticizing the American government. The situation came to a head in December 1925 when Mitchell was convicted of conduct that brought discredit to the military service and was suspended without pay. He resigned in February 1926 but continued to promote military aviation until he died in 1936.

In the early 1930s, military developers in the Soviet Union envisioned the concept of "sky soldiers," which entailed getting troops aloft inside hundreds of biplanes. The idea was that when the target area was reached, the soldiers would effortlessly slide off the wings, then their 'chutes would deploy and they'd land battle ready, albeit in many cases slightly bruised and even concussed. Soviet Army maneuvers in 1936 entailed the incorporation of over one thousand parachutists. Some Kremlin officials, unencumbered by rudimentary intelligence or basic common sense, even proposed the idea of parachutes was a symbol of Western decadence.

Throughout the 1930s, countries such as Japan, Germany, and Italy followed Russia's lead by pioneering indigenous Airborne forces, with the addendum that all the troops would be suitably equipped with parachutes. The United States, Great Britain, and France soon followed suit.

The German Fallschirmjäger (paratroopers) were the ones who made the first combat jumps during large-scale Airborne operations in World War II. In contrast to Allied Airborne units that were part of the Army, German paratroops were originally part of the Luftwaffe, the German air arm. Throughout World War II, their commander, appointed by Luftwaffe chief Hermann Göring, was the incredibly astute and capable Gen. Kurt Student, who joined the Luftwaffe in 1934 and subsequently introduced the concept of using Airborne infantry as additional forces to assist ground troops. He aptly demonstrated his capabilities at the onset of the invasion of the Low Countries in May 1940 when a mere 100 Fallschirmjäger soldiers overpowered and captured the mighty Belgian fortresses of Eben-Emael, located between Liège and Maastricht in the east of Belgium. Student rose to the challenge again with the subsequent successful Axis invasion of Crete in May 1941. Heavy losses suffered by the German paratroopers there prevented further large-scale Airborne operations by the Germans. Instead, the Fallschirmjäger were more often used as traditional infantry. It should be noted that Student was present at Arnhem during the specious Operation *Market Garden*.

As a precursor to the Battle of the Bulge, German paratroops would be dropped on December 15, 1944, for the abortive Operation *Stosser* ("Stosser" is German for an ejector pin), Operation *Hawk* in English. There were bad omens from the outset. Insufficient available fuel to transport the paratroops to the allotted airfield meant only a third of the battle group, around four hundred men, actually participated in the op. They were expected to secure vital crossroads along the flank of the German line of advance in the attack zone of the 6th Panzer Army, which was at that moment preparing to advance along the northern shoulder and block the movement of Allied reinforcements. The designated drop zone for Operation *Stosser* was poorly chosen. It was then, and still is, a region of steep hills, dense woods, and marshy valleys, with only one navigable north–south road that connected the town of Malmedy with the German-speaking Belgian city of Eupen. The crossroads at Belle Croix was the original target for the roadblock until the paratroopers were relieved by the 12th SS Division. Later on, during the Battle of the Bulge, another paratrooper unit, the 5th Fallschirmjäger Division, would be deployed when some of its battalions defended Remoifosse and Assenois (the anglicized version of this town was "Ass noise," which caused much jocularity), near Bastogne, with the 26th Volksgrenadier Division.

Over the past 30 years, perceptions of events that occurred in the Western Theater during World War II have changed dramatically. This renewed interest has been unassailably bolstered by a significant increase in public support for Airborne forces. Contemporary reappraisals, enhanced by the power of the popular media, have given the Airborne their rightful dues, and these opinions have definitely been enriched by numerous publications of private memoirs of paratroop veterans proclaiming the Airborne's heroics and efficiency.

In his personal memoir, *Beyond Band of Brothers, The War Memoirs of Major Dick Winters*, the eponymous major provided a relatively comprehensive account of his service with E Company, 506th Parachute Infantry Regiment, 101st Airborne Division. He began his career as a second lieutenant and was later, due to the death of his immediate superior, promoted to captain. Winters stated quite emphatically that some of the objectives attributed to his company were simply not accomplished. He was known as a quiet, unassuming man who seldom raised his voice or used foul language. Members of his unit claimed he had a way of getting his point across without shouting, and the men were more than willing to follow him. Although he was not loud or boisterous, it was said he could burn a hole through you with a glare.

Winters further insisted that the more challenging results achieved could not have possibly been delineated before his combat troops encountered them on the ground. The destruction of the German artillery battery at Brécourt Manor was one such instance. He recalled, "Even though Easy Company was still widely scattered, the small portion that fought at Brecourt [*sic*] had demonstrated the remarkable ability of the airborne trooper to fight, albeit outnumbered, and to win."

Available information about American Airborne divisions that parachuted into Normandy has been meticulously dissected, glorified and venerated to elevate the involved characters to the point of legendary status. But therein lies the problem. Thanks in some part to overzealous Normandy tour guides, some veteran stories have taken on a life of their own and, as the years pass, in some cases it has become increasingly difficult to decipher the facts from the numerous myths and legends.

The contemporary need to identify and empathize with the human aspect and the heroics of the Airborne often blur the reality of what actually occurred. This volume doesn't seek to detract from the incredible heroism, but memories fade and in the process personal accounts become distorted to satiate the public's capricious demand for identifiable heroes. Sadly, not many are still with us.

The actions of paratroopers of the Airborne divisions during the D-Day landings were initially regarded as a failure. According to some authors, they were too widely dispersed, unable to regroup, and, in many instances, completely missed their primary objectives. Military historians previously studying the Airborne engagements on D-Day argued convincingly that, due to their prominent high casualty rate, the paratroopers squandered both men and materiel to little avail. Bastogne would be a different matter entirely.

At Bastogne, the 101st Airborne Division, the "Eagle Division," wouldn't only contribute, it would command and control the situation and, with the invaluable assistance of other units such as the 10th Armored Division (the "Tigers"), they would stoically meet every challenge, and weather all adversity, with courage, tenacity, and almost immeasurable fortitude. However, while many veterans of that battle would remain silent and take their story to their graves, others would, over time, reveal their experiences, experiences that in some cases blighted the rest of their lives. Such was the magnitude and impact of those who knew Bastogne. Mike, Patrick, Ronald, and I have been lucky to have known so many of them. We hope that you enjoy this as much as we enjoyed writing and assembling it.

CHAPTER ONE

Setting the Scene

It was bitterly cold, and there was no heating in our halftrack, so we did as best we could to keep warm.

HANS HERBST, 116TH PANZER DIVISION

By December 1944, both the 101st and the 82nd Airborne Divisions were being held in reserve. Both had actively participated in the ill-conceived Operation *Market Garden*, but this sojourn was to be a temporary respite because, when the call to arms arrived, both units were ordered to head north as fast as possible. Precisely which division would go where would be clarified later, but Bastogne, which was roughly at the center of the 90-mile German attack zone, was going to play a key role in the coming battle.

Since its conception, the Belgian city of Bastogne has been a strategically important town in the Ardennes, primarily because it rests on a high plateau where seven roads converge. There are still a few planted woodlands near the city, as there was in 1944–45, and there's still a lot of arable farmland in the region. These days, Bastogne is situated in the province of Luxembourg, which is irrefutably Belgian territory, not to be confused with the independent Duchy of Luxembourg a few miles south and east of the historic city.

SHAEF (Supreme Headquarters, Allied Expeditionary Force) first heard about Bastogne in early September 1944. It was at precisely 11:45 am, September 10, 1944, when Pfc. Ernest Gessener, 110th Infantry Regiment, 28th Infantry Division, became the first American soldier to be killed there; sadly, he wouldn't be the last.

The following morning, September 11, Gen. Norman "Dutch" Cota, who had led the 29th Infantry Division on D-Day, and was now commanding the 28th Division, ordered his men to attack the city. While visiting the front, he came across a group of men laying on the ground outside their foxholes, near a group of Germans, roughly one hundred fifty yards away, doing the same. Neither group showed any real interest in continuing hostilities.

At 11:00 am, the advance guard of the 2nd Battalion arrived at the perimeter of the tiny hamlet of Marvie, about two miles east of Bastogne along the main

Bastogne–Wiltz highway. The Germans made a hasty retreat after a short skirmish; the 3rd Battalion, 110th Infantry, went into action west of Bastogne aided by resistance fighters, many of whom were Belgian veterans of the praiseworthy 2nd Chasseurs Ardennais Regiment, which was one of several similar units that countered the German invasion in 1940. The battalion unit insignia remains a wild boar's head and the motto translates as "Resist and bite." The veterans proudly donned their old uniforms and supported the action in its entirety. By noon, they were marching through the town followed by vehicles of the 28th Division. After four long years of punitive German occupation, Bastogne had been released from the Nazi yoke. The local people heartily welcomed their American liberators. At one point, fraternization reached such epidemic proportions that curfews were imposed, but rarely observed. That was the fun time to be in Bastogne; the liberation would prove to be an all-too-brief hiatus.

After the Normandy breakout, SHAEF commander Gen. Dwight D. "Ike" Eisenhower and his generals initially concurred that victory was in sight, and there was a pervasive, almost palpable, feeling disseminating throughout the ranks of "We've got them on the run." As enemy resistance dissipated and Allied momentum increased, parts of Europe were finally beginning to emerge from over four long years of castigatory Nazi rule.

At this juncture, the Allies still hadn't prioritized their schedules. Considering the logistical problems they were encountering in the field, opening Antwerp docks should have been paramount to all other considerations because the harbor was of great strategic importance, particularly for recently promoted Field Marshal Bernard "Monty" Montgomery's 21st Army Group and the rest of the Allied advance in the north. Despite the city being taken with the docks more or less intact, the estuary was still not secured, which in effect rendered the harbor inoperable and inaccessible. Moreover, Monty had persistently deflected the need to open the harbor and had argued for the introduction of an alternate strategy that would allow him to focus on other objectives. Eisenhower, under some duress, approved the field marshal's audacious idea to launch an Allied air assault deep into enemy territory, to use the Airborne forces to seize the bridges over the Maas (Meuse), the Waal, and the lower Rhine. The 101st Airborne Division was originally earmarked to go to Arnhem, but was replaced by the British 1st Airborne Division, apparently because it had conducted prior reconnaissance of the area. Even if the 1st Airborne had captured the bridge at Arnhem, it's highly unlikely Monty would have been able to progress into Germany, as he had insisted to Eisenhower.

Montgomery and Eisenhower were men from such profoundly contrasting backgrounds that their relationship was always bound to be fraught and, on occasion, even tempestuous. Monty was an undeniably difficult man, a World War I veteran and a product of a privileged background, whose aspirations, after El Alamein, were not always equaled by his achievements in the field. Ike was the son of a penurious

Midwestern farmer, an even-tempered, charismatic, and modest person. They had both graduated from elite military academies—Sandhurst and West Point respectively. There was one occasion, during a heated debate concerning the notorious "Broad Front Strategy," when Ike decided that Monty's condescending attitude towards him was going a bit too far. He placed his hand on Monty's knee and said, "Steady, Monty, you can't speak to me like that, I'm your boss."

Therein lay the problem; Monty never seriously regarded Eisenhower as his superior and, privately, both were highly critical of each other's approach to the war. Ike once said, "Montgomery's the only man in either army I can't get along with." He understood full well that Monty was very popular with the British public, and with the Army he commanded, so for the duration Ike walked a diplomatic tightrope, attempting to appease while simultaneously exerting his authority. Even when the 1st Airborne Division was all but destroyed in Arnhem, Monty flatly refused to concede defeat.

As a direct result of Operation *Market Garden*, the 101st Airborne Division remained in this Dutch cul-de-sac until October 4, when it was transferred to de Betuwe, a place referred by paratroopers of the 101st as "the Island," just northwest of Nijmegen. The 82nd Airborne Division joined it in October. The 82nd had been taken out of the Netherlands 14 days earlier and sent to Suippes and Sissonne in France; the 101st went to Camp de Châlons. So, after 72 days of fighting in the Netherlands, and after having expended both men and weaponry, the 101st was eventually pulled off the front line for refitting. It wasn't until November 28 that the two divisions returned to Mourmelon-le-Grand, near Reims in France, for a well-earned rest (a site where Julius Caesar had billeted two divisions of infantry and several squadrons of light horse during the latter phases of one of his notorious gallic campaigns). Before the 101st arrived, Mourmelon-le-Grand had been occupied by German infantry who left it in a sorry state of repair.

Indicative of the action the divisions had seen before settling at their respective camps was that of Pfc. Joe Eugene Mann, Company H, 502nd Parachute Infantry Regiment, 101st Airborne Division. This is his Medal of Honor citation:

> He distinguished himself by conspicuous gallantry above and beyond the call of duty. On 18 September 1944, in the vicinity of Best, Holland, his platoon, attempting to seize the bridge across the Wilhelmina Canal, was surrounded and isolated by an enemy force greatly superior in personnel and firepower. Acting as lead scout, Pfc. Mann boldly crept to within rocket-launcher range of an enemy artillery position and, in the face of heavy enemy fire, destroyed an 88-mm gun and an ammunition dump. Completely disregarding the great danger involved, he remained in his exposed position, and, with his M1 rifle, killed the enemy one by one until he was wounded four times. Taken to a covered position, he insisted on returning to a forward position to stand guard during the night. On the following morning the enemy launched a concerted attack and advanced to within a few yards of the position, throwing hand grenades as they approached. One of these landed within a few feet of Pfc. Mann. Unable to raise his arms, which were bandaged to his body, he yelled "Grenade" and threw his body over the grenade, and as it exploded, died. His outstanding gallantry above and beyond the call of duty and his magnificent conduct were an everlasting inspiration to his comrades for whom he gave his life.

November 28, 1944, was a momentous day in the Allied calendar because that's when the first three supply ships reached Antwerp. The Canadian-built freighter SS *Fort Cataraqui* led the first convoy, and Antwerp opened for business again. More importantly, this crucial supply line could now provide much needed fuel and provisions for the ongoing Allied advance to liberate Europe. But there was still work to do. Despite the pervasive atmosphere of complacency at SHAEF, it wasn't over yet. For the months of September, October, and November, it has been estimated the Allies suffered more than 56,000 battle casualties.

It was while at Mourmelon that the men of the 101st and 82nd received replacement equipment and fresh clothes as they prepared for their next mission. The 101st was without most of its weapons and did not have entrenching tools or other equipment. By this time, the initial tidal wave of triumphalist euphoria that had transpired after the Normandy breakout had begun to dissipate during the subsequent savage fighting, as did confidence in Allied military acumen. Overriding this aspect there appeared to be a problem with available intelligence.

Many historians have referred somewhat disparagingly to "Allied intelligence" leading up to the Battle of the Bulge, as if it was a contradiction in terms, and, granted, there are few subjects that have the capacity to incite such a polarity of opinion among historians. But it's always interesting to reassess. Intelligence reports were disseminated prodigiously to all Allied intelligence departments for the duration, but not always closely analyzed. Specific and frequently highly reliable information provided by ULTRA code breaking would rarely, if ever, be included in SHAEF weekly summaries. This was accompanied by an inert complacency that would cause arguably one of the greatest intelligence fiascos of the whole war.

"One major fault on our side was that our intelligence community had come to rely far too heavily on ULTRA to the exclusion of other intelligence sources," said Gen. Omar N. Bradley, commander of the 12th Army Group, the largest American ground combat force ever created. He noted this detail in his autobiography. The intelligence ULTRA provided was often considered so sensitive that the data provided by Bletchley Park, the principal Allied code-breaking asset, was forbidden from inclusion in written intelligence reports or summaries. Despite its sensitivity, ULTRA had proven to be such an invaluable intelligence source that other sources such as reconnaissance, prisoner interrogations, and reports from civilians were often ignored if they contradicted the information provided by ULTRA.

Most of Belgium had been liberated during the first few weeks of September 1944, before the Allies reached the frontiers of the Third Reich. By the time they arrived, over eighty percent of the Belgian population was suffering from vitamin deficiency related conditions such as rickets and scurvy, although this was more prevalent in the north of the country than in the southern Ardennes region due to ingenious hoarding by the residents and the rich agricultural pastures there.

One veterinarian who lived in Bastogne during the battle was completely unaffected by German requisitions of forced labor, food, and livestock, and kept his whole family and innumerable relatives supplied with quality meat and vegetables for the duration of World War II.

From October 1944, the Allies began encountering disconcerting levels of German resistance as their armies began to advance deeper into the heart of the Reich. Allied intelligence services now came under scrutiny to produce the goods. By late fall, torrential rain that had inundated and beset the Allied armies in the Western Theater was beginning to turn to sleet and snow, causing temperatures to frequently dip below freezing along the whole Allied line.

Suspicions were aroused at Bletchley Park in early November, when ULTRA cryptanalysts succeeded in deciphering the Reichsbahn (German railway) codes, which clearly indicated that around eight hundred trains had been requisitioned by the German Army for the purpose of transporting men and equipment from the Eastern Theater to the west. This information was duly relayed to SHAEF and the European Theater of Operations (ETO), but at that time there were few officers there who believed the Germans had either the manpower or the means to seriously launch a major offensive in the west.

At the beginning of December, British Maj. Gen. Kenneth Strong, working as Eisenhower's personal G-2 (intelligence), had remarked that some German Panzer divisions were being removed from the front lines, and that there appeared to be more Volksgrenadier divisions congregating in the Eifel region than what was required to maintain a static front; surprisingly enough, Strong didn't regard this as a reason for consternation. What he didn't know was that, during the first week of December, no less than nine Panzer divisions had been removed from the Eastern Front and reallocated to the west. But, by this time, ULTRA had inadvertently been rendered ineffectual by a perplexing German radio silence. Generalmajor Heinz Kokott, commander of the 26th Volksgrenadier Division, positively exuded confidence when he mentioned the buildup in his memoirs:

The period of reorganization lasted five weeks. Delivery of weapons and equipment functioned smoothly. The personnel replacements were of good quality: they were fresh, healthy young men of great willingness, mostly former navy and air force personnel, but they lacked any combat experience and infantry type of training. The replacement COs were varied: the remaining COs with their combat experience in the East were now joined by some older ones from the air force, navy and army who had for some time been assigned to administrative positions in the interior, and also by a number of very youthful NCO trainees. Both categories had either very little or no experience at the front at all. The officer material was good. The regimental and battalion commanders as well as the company commanders were those officers who had proven themselves time and again during the Russian Campaign and who knew their stuff. The young officers who were then joining the division, all of them experienced in battle, brought, in addition to their ability, the best of spirits and willingness. The bringing up and arrival of new units in the rearward area, together with the strict order for cessation of reconnaissance activities for the first time, gave rise to conjecture.

The Volksgrenadier units the Germans planned to employ for this offensive were in many cases assembled from personnel previously considered unfit for duty for a variety of reasons. Some were considered too old or too young or were afflicted by a physical condition that otherwise prevented them from serving. There were also select groups, in jobs considered essential to the war effort, exempt from military service. Many who were exempt found themselves on the front line because a lack of raw materials, and incessant Allied bombing raids, were proving severely detrimental to maintaining productivity in some factories, particularly in the heavily industrialized Ruhr region. The Germans were also transferring recruits from other branches of the military into the infantry. The equipment of the Luftwaffe and Kriegsmarine (German naval arm) was all but wiped out or incapable of operation by this point in the war, so large numbers of these men became soldiers. The Wehrmacht (German Army) also began enrolling more conscripts from Nazi-occupied territories. During the ensuing combats, there were many cases of these men surrendering because they felt no obligation to risk their lives for Germany.

The result of all the changes in policy would have consequences. There were some German soldiers who fought in the Ardennes who had never previously held a rifle. They were usually cooks, bakers, clerks, etc., that hadn't experienced any formal combat training.

The lack of accurate and verifiable intelligence regarding the accumulation of these German forces in the west was becoming a problem. The pervasive consensus among the ranks on the Ardennes front was there was "something going down," but nobody knew precisely what. However, on December 14, Allied G-2 intelligence units' war maps still indicated only four German divisions opposite Gen. Troy Middleton's VIII Corps, with two Panzer divisions positioned to the rear of this area.

Despite Allied intelligence officers having received various warnings a German attack was looming, none of these reports were particularly specific. There was never any mention of numbers, commanders, or dispositions of German units. Even when the 28th Division, fresh out the devastating battle of the Hürtgen Forest, inadvertently captured two German prisoners down on the Luxembourg–Germany border, who had a lot of vital intelligence to impart, no one believed their claims of an impending massive German counter-offensive.

Heinz Kokott noted:

> During the evening hours of 15 December, the final troop movements took place. It was cold and dark. The narrow paths of the Eifel, some of which were covered with ice, were densely crowded with troops and vehicles which were moving forward to their positions of departure and their firing positions. In spite of efficient traffic control, traffic jams were unavoidable. Efforts were made to drown out the noise of the motors of the heavy prime movers by artillery harassing fire. After dark, the commanders informed the attack troops of the attack order. The troops accepted it with utmost seriousness. They were fully conscious of their decisive act. They were confident in their ability, their strength and the promise of strong air support as well as the effort by the war industries back home. Attitude and morale of the troops was good.

Hans Herbst was a soldier in the 116th Panzer Division, the "Windhund" (Greyhound) Division, that attacked with the 5th Panzer Army in the center:

> When we set off, I vividly remember seeing Hasso von Manteuffel [commander of the 5th Army] standing on a Panther [tank] shouting, "Schneller, schneller!" ["Faster, faster!"] as we passed toward the Belgian border. It was bitterly cold, and there was no heating in our halftrack [*sic*], so we did as best we could to keep warm. Shortly after crossing the border, we picked up supplies abandoned by the Amis [U.S. Army]. We had plenty to eat, and I had collected many cartons of "Lucky Strikes" in the halftrack.

"Wacht am Rhein"—often mistakenly translated as "Watch on the Rhine," but actually closer to "Rhine Guard"—was the German term for what is widely known as the Battle of the Bulge. It is a symbolic name taken from the title of a famous song from the time of the German Empire.

December 16, at 5:30 am, flares of red, green, amber, and white irradiated the predawn sky, followed in succession by ground-shuddering explosions and the continuous incessant blasts of German artillery. Out on the Schnee Eifel salient in Germany, Pfc. John Schaffner and another GI of the 106th Infantry Division stamped their feet to stave off gnawing cold that permeated every sinew. John spoke in hushed tones about home and complained about having to pull guard duty at that godforsaken hour.

In the distance they could hear the faint rumble of engines, but at that time they couldn't determine if they were German or Allied vehicles. John peered, snake-eyed, into the murky dense fog, shrugged his shoulders and blew into his cupped hands before saying, "Sounds like somebody is making tracks, buddy." The other GI inclined his head, asking "Is it ours or theirs?" John smiled, "Hard to say." Then, suddenly, a yellow flash illuminated the predawn gloom. A split second later a thunderous, guttural boom, followed by something that resembled a screaming banshee, pierced the mist. John dived onto the frozen earth and attempted to "crawl into my helmet." More *Nebelwerfer* rocket mortars, fired from five-barrel launchers and known as "screaming meemies," exploded nearby. The other GI took a direct hit and exploded into pieces of flesh and sinew that impacted the frozen ground like meat on a butcher's slab.

GIs of the 106th attempted to alert other units, but soon discovered that, owing to severed telephone cables, attempts to relay information were nigh on impossible; communications were further disrupted due to radio frequencies being jammed by the attacking Germans.

Along the whole Allied line, from just below Aachen to Luxembourg, mortars, artillery pieces, and tanks were unleashing their hellish cacophony on unsuspecting American positions.

That first day was one of incredible flux and chaos as the rage of Nazi Germany was unleashed against thinly dispersed American divisions, many of whom were untried and untested. Once the barrage had lifted in the 106th Infantry Division's sector, a chaotic tableau confronted forward observers, who reported gridlocks and extensive American convoys heading west with headlights glaring while flares and tracers zoomed overhead with alarming frequency. Some reports claimed the German patrols were effectively breaching the front line.

Hitler selected the Belgian Ardennes region because he had already ruled out Alsace–Lorraine as a potential target due to the presence of Gen. George Patton's Third Army there. His intelligence was quite reliable most of the time, at least when he chose to acknowledge it. He knew in advance that the Allied front in the Ardennes sector was thinly manned. He was convinced a blow there would inflict a sizable breach between the British and American sectors, which, in his estimation, would incite political, as well as military, dissonance between the Allies.

The other pressing item on Hitler's agenda was his fervent ambition to recapture the harbor city of Antwerp. He also estimated that the distance from the jump-off line to the strategic objective was completely feasible, and could be covered quickly, even if confronted by some resistance and inclement weather. The only serious natural obstacle was the wide River Meuse that runs roughly from north to south through the Ardennes.

He figured an all-out assault along the Ardennes front had the potential to completely isolate the British 21st Army Group in the north and allow for the encirclement and destruction of the British and Canadians piecemeal before American leadership (particularly political) could react cohesively. Hitler was prepared to gamble, which would culminate in the biggest battle in American military history.

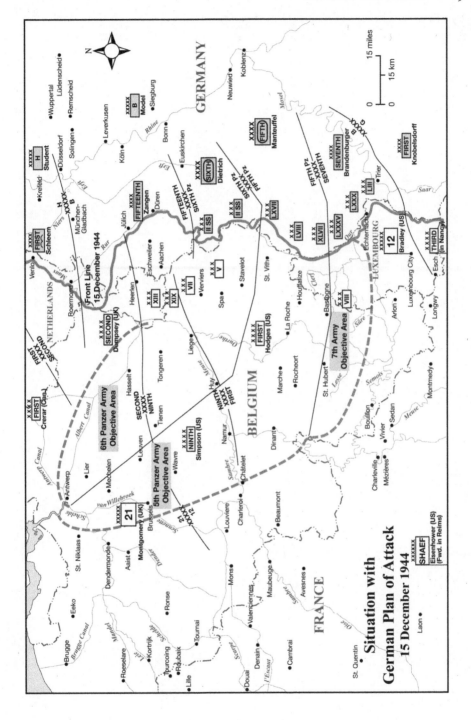

Situation with
German Plan of Attack
15 December 1944

CHAPTER TWO

We're Heading Where?

I was in Paris on a twenty-four-hour pass just after we returned from Holland, when a loudspeaker announced, "Report to your units immediately."

RALPH K. MANLEY, 501ST PARACHUTE INFANTRY REGIMENT,
101ST AIRBORNE DIVISION

For the Ardennes offensive planned for late 1944, Hitler designated three generals to command three armies. The 6th Panzer Army, selected to be the spearhead in the northern sector, was allocated to veteran Nazi, General Joseph "Sepp" Dietrich. His sycophantic behavior may have endeared him to the Fuhrer, but there were those who seriously doubted Dietrich's military and strategic abilities. By the end of 1944, time, trouble, and alcohol had taken a serious toll on his competence, and by leading the spearhead he was definitely punching above his weight. Some detractors said he couldn't even read military maps, a claim that didn't inspire his subordinates.

In the center was the most capable of all the German commanders in the field, Gen. Baron Hasso-Eccard von Manteuffel, who had been appointed commander of the under-provisioned 5th Army. He had served with Field Marshal Erwin Rommel and had studied under innovative tank genius Heinz Guderian. In 1968, Manteuffel lectured at West Point. He began his lecture with the following:

> What we are planning is a "grand slam" in an attempt to go all the way to Antwerp. I do not think we hold the cards. I would like to see the bid reduced to a little slam. After a penetration of the thin American lines in the Ardennes, the two panzer armies could wheel north. My own left flank would be protected by the Meuse in the west and we could cut off all of the First American Army north of the penetration. We could inflict tremendous damage.

Despite the general view that all heavily defended towns should be circumnavigated, Manteuffel wanted the capture of Sankt Vith—the first major Belgian town in the path of the 5th Panzer Army—to be a priority, because it still had working rail links to Germany and could be used as a base to block potential Allied reinforcements. He wasn't overly optimistic about the plan, he had reservations, and he wasn't overly enthusiastic about having Sepp Dietrich and the 6th Panzer Army with so many SS units on his northern flank, although there could have been other reasons apart from tactical ones for this. Manteuffel succinctly described Hitler's inadequacies by stating in a postwar interview:

> Hitler had a real flair for strategy and tactics, especially for surprise moves, but he lacked a sufficient foundation of technical knowledge to apply it properly. Moreover, he had a tendency to intoxicate himself with figures and quantities. When one was discussing a problem with Hitler, he would repeatedly pick up the telephone, ask to be put through to some departmental chief, and inquire, "How many so and so have we got?" Then he would turn to the man who was arguing with him, quote the number, and say, "There you are," as if that settled the problem. He was too ready to accept paper figures, without asking if the numbers stated were available in reality. It was always the same, whatever the subject might be, tanks, aircraft, rifles, shovels … Even if the numbers had actually been produced, a large part of them were still in the factories, and not with the troops.

Despite Manteuffel's opposition to and reservations about "Wacht am Rhein," it was superseded by his aristocratic Prussian sense of duty, honor, and loyalty, which would in turn mean he would do his utmost to carry out the plan to the best of his ability.

Placing a German army composed of regular soldiers alongside one made up of mainly SS units had, on occasion, proved problematic in the past. The relationship was indeed a complex one. The SS units were usually given priority regarding equipment and materiels and, such was the emphasis on hierarchical structures in the Third Reich, they tended to demean Wehrmacht units. Moreover, the propensity of certain SS units for committing atrocities against civilians and enemy combatants was also a source of disdain to many Wehrmacht officers. However, there remained a moral heterogeneity among the Wehrmacht, who maintained a grudging respect for the combat prowess of the Waffen SS, even if their tendency to divert from the plan wasn't always conducive to coordinating military operations.

Commanding the 7th Panzer Army in the south along the Luxembourg border was Gen. Erich Brandenberger. He had an impressive combat record and had been given the task of supporting von Manteuffel's flank and pushing through to the Meuse River. Once this had been established, his forces would anchor the southern German flank on the angle formed by the Semois and Meuse Rivers. He would also be expected to stop Gen. George S. Patton's Third Army in its tracks should it decide to head north to join the fray.

December 16, 4:00 am. From his forward command post, dressed in his full-length leather overcoat, von Manteuffel addressed his troops: "We are going to attack. Our fatherland is completely surrounded and our comrades at the front expect that everyone will do his duty. Forward march."

Along the Luxembourg–Germany frontier, approximately 25 miles east of Bastogne, the 28th Infantry Division's 110th Regiment was directly in the path of von Manteuffel's 5th Panzer Army. At zero hour, beneath low clouds and swirling mist, while the landscape was still dark, the attack began. The 26th Volksgrenadier Division (VGD) advanced on the left flank and the 2nd Panzer Division on the right; the notorious, but much depleted Panzer-Lehr Division (an armored training division formed in 1943) prepared to follow in their wake at 6:00 am.

The Panzer-Lehr was regarded as a particularly dangerous division by the Allies. It was assembled from instructors who taught the tank crews and demonstration teams. They were highly skilled and knew armored battle tactics and strategy like it was second nature. They were brought into service after it was realized keeping these highly trained individuals out of the fight was no longer an option. Besides, the construction of new tanks and the formation of new crews had almost ceased so it was no longer necessary to have tank training schools.

Colonel Hurley E. Fuller, commanding the 28th Infantry Division's 110th Regimental Combat Team (RCT), which consisted of the 110th Infantry Regiment and attached units, successfully repelled the first attacks. They came face to face with the first violent waves emanating from the two German divisions, collectively 31,000 men supported by armor, attacking across a six-mile front along the Luxembourg–Belgian border in the east. Vital hours were wasted by the 26th VGD as it became isolated between the Luxembourg villages of Holzthum and Consthum, which it had been ordered to capture. General Fritz Bayerlein, commander of the Panzer-Lehr Division, said:

> As the attack of 26th Volksgrenadier Division against Drauffelt did not succeed quickly and the American resistance in Hosingen and Rockholz on 16th December could not be crushed, units of Panzer Lehr Division, on orders from higher headquarters, were committed against Holtzhum and Consthum to win the Kautenbach bridgehead, and from there to push on to the west. The Panzer Reconnaissance Battalion was committed first and, later, 901 Panzer Grenadier Regiment also was committed. The Panzer Reconnaissance Battalion took Holtzhum, while 901 Panzer Grenadier Regiment attacked Consthum, which was doggedly defended.

At VIII Corps' headquarters in Bastogne, Maj. Gen. Troy H. Middleton was rudely awakened by the clamor of distant German artillery blasts. At 9:15 am, he said, "The troops may only abandon current positions if the situation becomes absolutely untenable." At 10:00 am, he called 12th Army Group commander Gen. Omar N. Bradley and informed him that the German attack, in his opinion, didn't appear to be a diversionary maneuver.

Not all the German 5th Army field commanders were convinced the audacious plan could work. General Bayerlein said during an interview:

> In the original plan, 26 Volksgrenadier Division was to take the crossings over the Our, then those over the Clerf, and establish bridgeheads. Only after this would parts of Panzer Lehr [sic] Division thrust west toward Bastogne over the Drauffelt bridgehead [south of Clerf]. As the attack of 26 Volks Gren Div against Drauffelt did not succeed quickly and the American resistance in Hosingen and Bockholz on 16 Dec 44 could not be crushed, units of Pa Lehr Div, on orders from higher headquarters, were committed against Holtzhum and Consthum to win the Kautenbach bridgehead, and from there to push on to the west. The Pz Reconnaissance Bn was committed first and, later, 901 Pz Gren Regt also was committed.

The Pz Reg Bn took Holtzhum, while 901 Pz Gren Regt attacked Consthum, which was doggedly defended. During this attack, 26 Volks Gren Div succeeded in capturing Drauffelt on 17 Dec 44. On orders from higher headquarters, the attack of 901 Pz Gren Regt was immediately discontinued, and the Regiment also moved through the Drauffelt bridgehead in order that a divisional attack could be launched against Bastogne. Consequently, the stubborn resistance in Consthum is not the first, but the second reason for giving up this plan. In general, the plan was to thrust forward where it could be done quickest and easiest, and to commit our troops at the first point we succeeded in establishing a bridgehead over the [River] Clerf.

Despite facing a veritable tsunami of German troops and armor, in the village of Weiler, Luxembourg, an infantry company of the 28th Division fought like cornered lions as it used mortars and antitank guns to successfully beat back two full battalions. The fighting became so intense the Germans requested a ceasefire to evacuate their wounded; then, at 2:30 pm, the first surrender notice during the Battle of the Bulge was offered to the GIs, who promptly refused and continued firing unabated until they inevitably ran out of ammunition. As dusk descended, they were compelled to pull back.

During that first day, five German divisions crossed the Our River heading west. According to a West Point manual, the normal division front in 1944 was about 5 miles (8 kilometers); the 28th's 110th Regiment alone was dangerously over extended, covering over 11 miles (18 kilometers) in the center of its division sector. It received the full brunt of the determined Nazi onslaught and, even though it was almost completely decimated in the process, those troops, who were originally from the Pennsylvania National Guard, made a truly heroic stand.

General von Manteuffel stated in no uncertain terms that he was disappointed with the first day's performance of his 5th Army. Well aware the delays caused by these tenacious American defenders had caused significant disruption to his strict timetable, he wrote:

By the night of 17 December our troops were in front of Sankt Vith, and on the evening of 18 December, I ordered the final attack on Sankt Vith, which was to begin at 1000 hours on 19 December. However, LXVI Inf. Corps was not composed of our best troops. 62nd Volksgrenadier Division was an especially poor unit and did not seem to be able to organize itself for the attack, because of a lack of leadership at all levels. My first order to 62nd Volksgrenadier Division was to move on Sankt Vith by the shortest route, but when it was apparent that the division was moving too slowly, I ordered it to hit just to the south of Sankt Vith. We wanted Sankt Vith very badly; in fact, it was vital to us in the first days of the attack. If St. Vith had fallen earlier, we would have been able to move on much more rapidly and very probably would have been able to aid Sixth [sic] Panzer Army, by preventing the American forces from forming a defense line along the Ambleve and Salm Rivers. St. Vith was much more important than Bastogne at that time, and those four days of waiting in front of Sankt Vith were of great disadvantage to Dietrich, on my right. My original plan was to move Panzer Lehr [sic] Division through Bastogne, if Bayerlein [Commander Panzer Lehr Division] could reach that town before the expected reinforcements arrived. However, when we discovered the 101st Airborne Division was there, I told Bayerlein to move south of Bastogne and not attempt to attack it, because we had OKW [Wehrmacht] reserves coming along behind.

The Panzer-Lehr Division was delayed quite significantly by roads that had become unnavigable and inundated by mud when it attempted to reach Bastogne. Moving west on its initially planned trajectory was nigh on impossible due to the poor conditions, which inevitably caused delays to the 5th Army timetable.

It had also been a terrible day for those American divisions that found themselves in the path of the German attack; every GI in the line must have prayed help would arrive soon. These delaying tactics and staunch defensive lines would buy time for the American forces to get troops and armor to Bastogne, but it was Middleton's quick thinking and remarkable grasp of the strategic situation that would eventually help protect the city the 28th Division was already acquainted with.

On December 17, Middleton continued making command decisions that would ultimately save Bastogne. He ordered 600 men of the 44th Engineers to merge with a desultory force consisting of some battered tanks, assault guns, artillery pieces, and divisional headquarters troops. When they were attacked by tanks and infantry, the engineers stayed low and held their fire, allowing the tanks to pass close by before opening up and inflicting havoc on the trailing German infantry. Weight of numbers eventually compelled the engineers to fall back to Wiltz, where Gen. Norman Cota of the 28th Infantry Division had established his headquarters. A mere 10 miles west of Bastogne, these resilient defenders slowed the German advance significantly and, more importantly, bought valuable time.

When brittle American defenses began to disintegrate in the west, Middleton acted again and instructed the 35th and 158th Engineer Combat Battalions to defend Bastogne until reinforcements could arrive.

Meanwhile, at the Hôtel Trianon Palace, in Versailles, France, SHAEF (Supreme Headquarters Allied Expeditionary Force) commander Gen. Dwight Eisenhower began the day reading yet another message from Field Marshal Montgomery. In this one, the field marshal reminded Eisenhower about a light-hearted wager the two had made on October 11, 1943. Montgomery predicted the war would not be over by Christmas 1944, whereas the American thought it would be. The message ended with the addendum that there was still nine days to go. The bet was still on, but the antipathy between the two commanders remained.

It was an auspicious day for the SHAEF commander, because that same morning he had also received word of his promotion to the five-star rank of General of the Army, which had been passed by Act of Congress two days before. This meant he effectively outranked Montgomery for the first time in World War II. Apart from the meeting, the only other appointment he was attending was a wedding in the palace's rococo-style royal chapel; his orderly, Sgt. Michael "Mickey" McKeogh, was getting married to WAC (Women's Army Corps) Pearlie Hargrave.

Just before midnight on the previous evening, Eisenhower had ordered the 7th and 10th Armored Divisions to assist Middleton's VIII Corps in the Ardennes. Around the same time, he ordered Gen. Jacob L. Devers (arguably one of the best tacticians in World War II) to halt all offensive operations in the south so he could help Bradley's 12th Army Group shorten its over extended lines.

On December 17, at 8:30 pm, Brig. Gen. Anthony C. McAuliffe—who was commander of the division's artillery and, in the absence of Maj. Gen. Maxwell D. Taylor, had been elevated to lead the entire division—received a phone call from Gen. Matthew B. Ridgway's XVIII Airborne Corps, which ordered him to prepare for immediate departure to join Middleton in the Ardennes, leaving December 19. At 9:00 pm, McAuliffe assembled the division staff and explained the breakthrough with only minor details. During the hours when Lt. Col. Ned Moore, acting chief of staff of the 101st Airborne Division, and temporary commander McAuliffe were explaining the situation, they received a phone call from XVIII Corps' Col. Ralph Eaton, chief of staff, confirming Ridgway's directive to leave as early as possible on December 18. Eaton told Moore that Werbomont, Belgium, was the destination for the 101st. Colonel Thomas L. Sherburne assumed the role of acting divisional artillery commander while McAuliffe led the 101st.

While SHAEF commanders debated the developing situation in the Ardennes, German troops were heading west, pouring into the Belgian Ardennes over the borders of Germany and Luxembourg. Gefreite (private) Jürgen Tegethoff, 3rd Company, Schwere Panzer-Abteilung 506 (Heavy Tank Battalion 506) was among them; he vividly recalled his service:

> I was the commander of a "Tiger," the largest German tank, which weighed almost 70 tons. I was drafted into the Wehrmacht in September 1941 at the age of 17 along with 20 of my fellow high school graduates at the Siebengebirgsgymnasium in Bad Honnef, but only eight of us returned from the war. After officer training, I became a lieutenant in December 1942 and saw my first action in Russia, where I was badly injured and hospitalized for almost a year. Then we went to the Ardennes, which was a hopeless battle for the Wehrmacht in my opinion.
>
> I had fought against the Allies in Normandy and had even witnessed the landings there. I wasn't bothered about the cold, after all I had served on the Russian front, but during the battle for Bastogne my tank was hit by artillery eight times, and eventually caught fire. Me and my four comrades from the tank crew were able to save ourselves. We were better off than many other soldiers.

Late on the morning of December 17, General Middleton took the necessary measures that would occupy all access roads to Bastogne. Three combat battalions of the 1128th Engineer Group, supplemented by all available men, combatants and non-combatants, were deployed in a semicircle around Foy, three-and-a-half miles north, around Neffe, just over a mile from Bastogne. While the fighting in Clervaux was still raging, Middleton decided to have the CCR (Combat Command Reserve) of the 9th Armored Division sent to Troisvierges to further block the route to Bastogne. This CCR, commanded by Col. Joseph H. Gilbreth, consisted of the 52nd Armored Infantry Battalion, the 2nd Tank Battalion, and the 73rd Armored Field Artillery Battalion.

Two hastily assembled barricades were set up where the roads from Clervaux and Troisvierges converged. Task Force Rose, commanded by Capt. Lyle K. Rose, manned the one at Antoniushaff. His CCR consisted of a company of Sherman tanks, a company of armored infantry, and a section of armored engineers. The second barricade was at Fetsch, at the junction where the westbound roads from Clervaux and Wiltz converge. Task Force Harper, commanded by Lt. Col. Ralph S. Harper, was assigned to deal with this vital intersection. His CCR was composed of the 2nd Tank Battalion and two companies of the 52nd Armored Infantry Battalion.

Good friends Pfc. William F. Greenplate and Pfc. Joel W. Rauls were both attached to the 9th Armored Division; they had experienced some hard fighting as they attempted to repel the Germans at Troisvierges. As the situation there disintegrated, the two friends decided it was time to make a run for it. William never talked about his experiences at Bastogne, until one day he told his daughter Virginia Kruta:

> I survived the war, it was being married that almost killed me. While retreating into Bastogne, I accidentally caught my wedding ring on a barbed-wire fence. The radio man was right behind me and cut me loose, but he forgot to hold the tension in the wire, so it snapped back on me and nearly took my damned finger clean off.

Virginia added that it was crooked for the rest of his life. Greenplate and Rauls were authorized to wear the Presidential Unit Citation for their service in Bastogne. Their fight didn't end out on the Luxembourg border because both men were sequestered into the SNAFU reserve as soon as they got within the city limits of Bastogne.

Around midday, Gen. Baron Heinrich Freiherr von Lüttwitz inspected the front lines, where his Panzer troops were advancing west. Corporal Ludwig Lindemann, of the 26th VGD, said:

> During the Ardennes Offensive our battle commander was Hauptmann Josef Raab, who had been awarded the Iron Cross on the Eastern Front for his bravery. With our sixty-five-man combat group under his command he had prevented Russian troops from breaking through. With him in command of our company we felt confident.
>
> The 77th Regiment and the 39th Fusilier Regiment of the 26th Volksgrenadier Division had taken the Americans by surprise and opened up the route to the west. After heavy resistance by the enemy in the town of Hosingen our division succeeded in surrounding the whole town. We in the 2nd Battalion had to fight for every cellar and every garden wall.

In Luxembourg, Gen. Omar Bradley had been hearing piecemeal reports of enemy activity in the Belgian Ardennes from General Middleton, among others, but this didn't deter him from getting in his staff car and heading to Versailles for a planned conference with his longtime friend Eisenhower. The relationship between the two was strong, but familiarity did have the tendency to inspire contempt and Bradley had, on occasion, the capacity to be rather condescending towards Eisenhower. He detested how the commander of SHAEF had been manipulated by Montgomery. This had caused so much consternation that, at one point, along with General Patton, who concurred wholeheartedly with Bradley's sentiments, he threatened to resign his commission. However, this was not the time to resolve personal matters, despite how distracting they had been.

In attendance at the meeting were Air Chief Marshal Sir Arthur Tedder (Eisenhower's British deputy), and Generals Walter B. "Beetle" Smith (SHAEF chief of staff), Harold R. Bull (his chief G-3, operations) and Kenneth Strong (the British chief G-2, intelligence). When Bradley left Luxembourg, he was completely oblivious to the fact that just 15-and-a-half miles to the east the Germans were attacking in force. The meeting was proceeding as planned when suddenly American deputy G-2, Col. Thomas J. Betts, entered the conference room and delivered a message to British Maj. Gen. Ken Strong, who digested the information, nodded, and then furrowed his brow. Montgomery had often referred to Strong disparagingly as a "Chinless wonder," and resented this thoroughbred Englishman for being a loyal and fervent admirer of Eisenhower.

Strong walked into the meeting, audibly cleared his throat (reminiscent of a best man at a wedding), and in slow measured tones imparted the following, "Gentleman, your attention please." All present directed their eyes to him as he solemnly read, "This morning the enemy counter-attacked at five separate points across the 1st Army sector." At first the statement was received with hushed exchanges as the officers digested the news, then Strong continued, "The enemy have attacked Middleton's VIII Corps boundary." No signs of alarm or concern registered on Bradley's expression, just a traditional, supercilious, half smile spread across his thin lips as he shook his head while insisting it was just a spoiling attack intended to draw Patton's troops out of the Saar region, where they had been attacking enemy positions around the fortress city of Metz.

Eisenhower wasn't convinced by Bradley's somewhat flippant appraisal and it became evident to all present he was taking on this information with significantly more gravity than Bradley had. He politely interrupted Bradley's ongoing diatribe with a look that changed from mild superciliousness to profound consternation as he imparted, "This is no spoiling attack, Brad." Chief of Staff "Beetle" Smith then stood up, walked around the large conference table to Bradley, placed a reassuring hand on his shoulder, and reminded the general he had been hoping for a German counterattack. Bradley appeared to momentarily change tack when he reciprocated that he had indeed been waiting for a counterattack, but added, almost laughingly, "I'll be damned if I wanted one this big."

Eisenhower's first knee-jerk reaction was to issue orders dispatching the 10th and 7th Armored Divisions to the Belgian Ardennes. The 10th Armored had already been moved to an assembly area just south of Luxembourg the previous day. It was an indubitably seminal moment in the story of the Battle of the Bulge that highlighted the opacity of previous intelligence reports regarding the condition and position of the German forces.

Eisenhower's resolute appraisal of the general strategic situation, and his realization of the significance of the German attack, proved crucial in his rapid response to the assault. This is what determined his rigorous response, despite what his good friend

Bradley insisted. During the Battle of the Bulge, he exhorted his battle leadership in a calm, optimistic, and methodical manner, which got the troops to where they were needed most and endeared him to his commanders in the field. His insight and perception of the emerging situation regarding the German offensive would prove a mitigating factor in the evolution of this crucial battle.

General Patton, commander of the Third Army, didn't attend that meeting in Versailles, but he was furious the 10th Armored Division had been extracted from his command. Visibly agitated, he shouted at anyone nearby, "But damn, that attack is probably just a diversion to thwart my army!" In the early afternoon, while the very determined German attack against the 28th Division was ongoing, the citizens of Bastogne were becoming decidedly uneasy. By 3:00 pm, the ancient town of Clervaux in Luxembourg was practically surrounded. The command post of the 110th Infantry Regiment had relocated to the Claravellis Hotel; at that moment the town's only defense was half a section of infantry and a single antitank gun. The situation deteriorated when German grenadiers, tanks, and self-propelled antitankers attacked in force. By 6:00 pm, after a bitter fight, the town had fallen.

Meanwhile, throughout most of the meeting in Versailles, Bradley remained intrinsically in denial concerning the nature and purpose of the German attack, despite the fact the First Army's G-2 was already in possession of a captured copy of Rundstedt's "Order of the Day" that had been transmitted to SHAEF from the First Army sometime around 11:00 that morning. The report clearly illustrated the German objectives. Despite open resistance from some of his subordinate commanders, including Bradley, the following day Eisenhower committed his strategic reserve, XVIII Airborne Corps, which incorporated the 82nd and 101st Airborne Divisions. The prospect of facing off against the 101st Airborne certainly incited consternation from the commander of the German 47th Panzer Corps. General von Lüttwitz wrote:

> On 17 December we had intercepted a radio message to the effect that the 101st Airborne Division was ordered to Bastogne in a fast, motorized march. I personally heard this message and was trying to get into Bastogne before the 101st Airborne Division got there.

At 8:00 pm, the 101st departed from the headquarters of Ridgway's XVIII Airborne Corps at Mourmelon-le-Grand, near Reims in France. A dozen regimental officers and staff officers met at the headquarters of the 101st. Brigadier General McAuliffe told his officers, "I only know that there is a breakthrough somewhere and we have to go there."

Lieutenant General James M. Gavin, who had temporary command of XVIII Airborne Corps, received notification that the 82nd and 101st Airborne Divisions had been alerted to move into action at daylight the following day, and to head, without delay, toward a place called Bastogne, which no one had even heard of. "We're going where?" asked Sgt. Ralph K. Manley, 501st Parachute Infantry Regiment,

101st Airborne Division. None of the troops stationed in Mourmelon had ever heard of this Belgian city. Sergeant Manley said:

> I was in Paris on a twenty-four-hour pass just after we returned from Holland, when a loudspeaker announced, "Report to your units immediately." So, we returned then from Paris back to our unit and immediately got on what clothes we had. I still had on my class A, of course, for being in Paris, and we loaded onto port battalion trucks, these semi trucks that had four-foot sidewalls on them and open tops, loaded onto those without overcoats and without overshoes and headed toward the Bulge, and it was very cold.
>
> We did not know actually what was going on. As we got back to our unit in Mourmelon, France, then we got our equipment and our guns and what have you, and were on trucks in minutes, headed off to Bastogne. We didn't know the situation, we just knew it was cold, and we had to go as we were without overshoes or overcoats. Again, with zero degrees, you can imagine, in open air trucks, going there, put in like cattle you might say, on trucks that weren't covered. They were actually port battalion trucks that were used to haul merchandise from the ships out to the warehousing areas, so that's what we rode to Bastogne on. Once we got there, of course, it was just dismount and head up the road to the city, on foot. We just missed others as they were coming out both wounded and disabled, were hobbling and going out in trucks coming out hauling bodies that had been killed and so on. That's what we met as we were going into Bastogne. We had our rifles, our hand grenades, our anti-tank mines, and things of that nature, and our explosives, composition C—twenty-five pounds of it, as a matter of fact, with each demolitionist.

Gavin left for Spa, Belgium, to conduct a meeting with First Army commander Lt. Gen. Courtney H. Hodges. On arrival, Gavin received additional information and was ordered to attach the 82nd Airborne to V Corps to bolster the defenses in the area of a place called Werbomont, a small village roughly 32 miles northwest of Sankt Vith, at the westernmost edge of the Ambleve valley. Their specific objective was to support existing units in the area and block the advance of the 6th Panzer Army, which consisted mainly of battle-hardened SS units such as the notorious Kampfgruppe Peiper. Captain Vincent B. Vicari, on the 101st Airborne Division's Artillery Headquarters Staff, said:

> We were just out of Holland, 10 days, when I got a phone call to tell General Mac [McAuliffe] to report to division headquarters right away. I went in and woke the general up and told him to go to division headquarters immediately, and I woke our sergeant up, his driver and told him to get the vehicle we gotta go to division headquarters. General Mac got dressed, I got dressed and I started to leave the building when he said, "Vicari stay by the phone and don't leave it." I went back because the phone was always in my room not in his. I stayed in the room and about two hours later the phone rang and I was told, "Vicari, notify all the battalions to pack everything up they'll be moving out." I said, "How can we move out we don't have any trucks" cos [sic] airborne doesn't have any trucks, we don't have any vehicles except the jeeps that we use in our glider battalions. I notified all the battalions and they asked me the same question and I told them the same as I was told, there were vehicles coming on a way down, and the vehicles came down.
>
> They had everything … [They] had cattle cars, trailers, two and half ton trucks, every conceivable type of vehicle that you can imagine, and I instructed them, don't leave anything behind because when this call came through we hadn't had a chance to refurbish ourselves. We hadn't had a chance to get new clothing, new jump boots, new shoes, and no galoshes.

We hadn't had a chance to replenish our ammunition. The only ammunition we had is what we had left over from Holland. Everybody did what they were told ... [We] didn't leave anything behind and none of us knew where we were going. I asked Colonel Kinnard and I said, "Where we going?" He said, "I don't know." We would drive with our lights on, lights off, lights on, lights off and no rest stop to relieve yourself or something, you did the best you could. Finally we were about five miles out of Bastogne when all these different convoys stopped. I asked Colonel Kinnard and he said that there was a town up above and we're probably going into town. It happened to be Bastogne and we pulled into Bastogne. The infantry stayed in their trucks up to a point on both sides of Bastogne, then they got out of their trucks and started walking to make contact with the Germans to establish some semblance of a line. When they made contact that became the line. We had 8 divisions plus a full artillery corps.

The Headquarters, 101st Airborne Division, narrative for December 1944 reads:

The early part of December found the 101st Airborne Division engaged in re-equipping and re-organizing after combat operations in Holland and executing a training program at Camp Mourmelon near Reims, France. These activities combined with improvements being made to the camp itself were being carried on until a telephone call at 2030 on 17 December 1944, from the Chief of Staff, XVIII Corps [Airborne] to Brigadier General Anthony McAuliffe, Acting Division Commander, alerted the division for immediate action in Belgium. A later message directed movement to begin at 1400, 18 December. All units of the Division were immediately alerted for movement, and OISE [Overseas Invasion Service Expedition] Section, Communication Zone were contacted for transportation. As much equipment, and supplies as could be gathered in the few hours before the Division was to leave were secured. The transportation furnished by OISE Section consisted of mainly ten-ton open truck and trailer vehicles with some two-and-a-half ton trucks. At 1215 on 18 December advance party consisting of Company "B" 326th Airborne Engineer Battalion, 101st Reconnaissance Platoon, and a detachment of Division Headquarters left Camp Mourmelon for WERBOMONT [P539000], Belgium. This town was 137 miles from MOURMELON and contact with XVIII Corps [Airborne] advance was to be made there. At 1225 General McAuliffe departed for WERBOMONT, and at 1400 the division proper began motor march with units in the following order:
    501st Parachute Infantry
    Attached: 907 Glider Field Artillery Battalion
    Battery B, 81st Airborne AA Battalion
    81st Airborne AA Battalion
    101st Airborne Signal Company, Division Headquarters
    and Headquarters Company; Division Artillery Headquarters and Headquarters Battery,
    506th Parachute Infantry
    Attached: 321st Glider Field Artillery Battalion
    326th Airborne Engineer Battalion [less Company B]
    502nd Parachute Infantry Attached: 401st Glider Infantry [less one Battalion], 463rd Parachute Field Artillery Battalion
    326th Airborne Medical Company
    801st Airborne Ordnance Company
    426th Airborne Quartermaster Company
    Strength committed at this time was 805 officers and 11035 enlisted men. At NEUFCHATEAU General McAuliffe was informed by VIII Corps that the Division was attached to VIII Corps with the mission of stemming the German offensive in the vicinity of BASTOGNE [P555580]. By means of officer guides, the march objective was changed from WERBOMONT, and the Division de-trucked in assembly areas in the vicinity of MANDE ST. ETIENNE [9500595], By 0900 of the next morning, 19 December the Division had closed in the assembly area.

The trip of about 107 miles had been made largely during the hours-of darkness and hampered to a certain extent by some rain and snow squalls.

At this time little was known of the enemy situation and confusion was rampant among friendly units in the area. It was realized however, by the Corps and Division Commanders that the enemy vitally needed the communications center of BASTOGNE. With this in mind, the 501st Combat Team was ordered to attack east and secure BASTOGNE. The 501st Combat Team jumped off at 0500, moved through the city and encountered enemy infantry and armor on the east perimeter. Contact was made with elements of Combat Command B 10th Armored Division, Combat Command R, 9th Armored Division, and small elements and stragglers of the 28th Infantry Division. In the meantime, 506th Combat Team was ordered to attack on the left of 501st Combat Team, in the direction of NOVILLE (3569641). After stubborn enemy resistance NOVILLE was occupied by the 506th Combat Team, although enemy continued armor-infantry attacks on the town, Indications of attacks on all sides appeared and combat teams were promptly employed in a perimeter defense of BASTOGNE. The western defense consisted of patrols furnished by 327th and 502nd Combat Teams, and the eastern defense consisted of positions held by 506th and 501st Combat Teams, and 326th Abn [Airborne] Engineer Battalion, Teams Cherry, O'Hara, and Desobry, of 10th Armored Division supported the Division in the east alms with Companies "D" and "C", 705th T. D. [Tank Destroyer] Battalion. In the meantime Division Headquarters had moved from MANDE ST. ETIENNE to Belgium barracks in BASTOGNE. The Division service area remained in the vicinity of MANDE ST. ETIENNE.

At 2200 on the 19th, an enemy attack out of the Division service area at which time the majority of the 326th Airborne Medical Company was captured, The 601st Ordnance Company and the 426th Quartermaster Company escaped capture with only slight losses. At this time the supply situation was indefinite and inadequate, and in an attempt to secure supplies for the Division, organic two ton trucks had been dispatched to the Division rear base and rear army installations to pick up ammunition …

When troops of the 101st Airborne Division, under McAuliffe, got the news, they hurriedly ran to grab what equipment they could lay their hands on. The men went into combat wearing what they had on at the time they were notified to move out. Those on passes were loaded into open-top trucks in their dress uniforms still smelling of booze. There were no seats in the trucks, so they had to stand or sit on the floor for the entire journey. The whole trip was utterly miserable. It was foggy, freezing cold, and it snowed occasionally; the paratroopers were so crowded in the trucks that only half of them could attempt to sleep on the floor while the remainder stood and endured it. A small number had woolen overcoats but, as they had all departed with haste, most were still wearing their regular jump uniforms and boots. This type of uniform would offer scant protection against the harsh winter conditions they were about to encounter. Their "Corcoran" jump boots were no protection against the cold either. The Airborne men would soon discover it was nigh on impossible to keep them dry. Some wrapped their boots in burlap and soaked them in water so they would freeze. They felt this approach kept their feet warmer. The race to Bastogne was on.

CHAPTER THREE

First into Bastogne

After the 101st had been to Holland they had so many casualties that they went to the rear echelons like army or railroad battalions or signal corps or whatever it might be, and asked for replacement volunteers to fill those vacancies in the combat units.

JAMES EDWARD MONROE, 502ND PARACHUTE INFANTRY REGIMENT

Most of the airborne units in France that rushed to heed the call to arms did so in 380 3.5-ton trucks, which were requisitioned to convey them to the Ardennes. The 3.5-ton truck was the most available transport vehicle at the time. They were known to be reliable on asphalt, gravel, and muddy roads, making them perfect for the task at hand. The only problem was that it was going to be, in some cases, a 13-and-a-half-hour drive, and there was no covering or seating on these vehicles. Neither division had any idea precisely where they were heading at that point.

The Ardennes had been a battlefield since time immemorial. It's the home of vertiginous forests of firs and broadleaf trees that extend along hills and valleys regularly bisected by fast-flowing rivers and streams. The Romans referred to the area as *Arduenna Silva* and Julius Caesar was one of the first writers to describe the Ardennes, in the book *Commentarii de Bello Gallico*, also known as *Bellum Gallicum*, his firsthand account of the Gallic Wars; written as a third-person narrative, he describes the Ardennes as "a frightful place, full of terrors."

It's an area that covers more than 4,250 square miles. The shape of the Ardennes region resembles an isosceles triangle, with a base of approximately 62 miles at the frontiers where Belgium and Luxembourg meet Germany. The quaint storybook villages of the Ardennes are still replete with winding cobblestone streets and alleys, half-timbered gables, and tile-roofed buildings with ornate shutters. Rippling brooks and serpentine streams run between the rolling hills and fields in the verdant countryside. Castles, monasteries, and ruins dating back to the era of Charlemagne can still be found there. It encompasses an area that reaches both Luxembourg and northern France in the south and southeast, and Germany in the north. On its western border is the Meuse (also known as Maas) River, and just over the German border to the east is the Schnee Eifel area, just below the infamous Hürtgen Forest.

In the south, the Belgian Ardennes joins the French Ardennes and the Semois River; to the east it has the Our and Sauer Rivers, both running through Luxembourg. The Meuse is a major river, which flows some 575 miles from its origins in France, north through Belgium, and then through the Netherlands where it empties into the North Sea.

Sergeant Albert Tarbell, of the Mohawk Nation, became a scout for Company H, 504th Parachute Infantry Regiment (PIR), 82nd Airborne Division. He recalled:

> I was on chute patrol duty with the MPs [military policemen] in the city of Reims. The 82nd was staying in Camp Sissone near Sissone, France. Our job was to intervene on behalf of the troopers should they get too rowdy or drunk and get arrested by regular Army MPs. We were usually able to reason with them and bring them back to the truck pickup point and avoid more serious charges. We were to go to the shooting range on the 18th, but when I arrived back at camp late that evening or early morning, there was a lot of activity going on. There were replacements all over the place. I remember hearing one of the replacements telling Sergeant Kogul that he had never fired an M1 before, and the Sergeant replied to him, "That's okay, son, you will learn soon enough." I still thought we were headed for the firing range. When I arrived back to my quarters Sergeant Fuller was waiting up for me. I asked him if we were ready and packed for the firing range. He said we surely were ready for the range, and it was then that I first found out about a German counterattack somewhere in Belgium. We did not get much sleep the rest of that night.

Sometimes, to the consternation of other members of H Company, before Albert went deep into the boreal forests of the northern Ardennes, he used to perform a little ceremony where he would commune with the trees. He was a magnificent scout and earned the respect of his highly decorated company commander James "Maggie" Megallas, who recalled:

> Albert would go off on his own and then return to our OP [observation post] with information such as, "There was two SS down there by the river, another three at the bridge and a couple on the edge of the forest, sir" to which I replied, "Jeez, Albert, will you leave some for us?"

While some German troops penetrated deep into the Allied line, others remained static waiting for roads to clear. Some GIs panicked while others dug in deeper and held on with all the courage and fortitude they could muster. That experience in the Ardennes was one that remained with most of the incumbents for the rest of their natural lives. Some of those who survived would attempt to dispel that torturous combat experience from their memories, but no one who was there and lived to tell the tale would forget. When recounting their experiences, they would run the whole gamut of emotions from abject terror to almost divine relief. On the Allied side, the attack was received with shock and disbelief, with responses that ranged from "Why didn't we see this one coming?" to "What the hell is going on?" James Edward Monroe, a technical sergeant with the 502nd PIR, said:

> After the 101st had been to Holland they had so many casualties that they went to the rear echelons like army or railroad battalions or signal corps or whatever it might be, and asked for

replacement volunteers to fill those vacancies in the combat units. So I volunteered for that service, for the 101st Airborne Division and they sent me to France, and from there the 101st Airborne Division invaded Bastogne. We were sent in by truck. They put one platoon on one side of the road and me and my platoon on the other side that was an entrance into Bastogne with heavy machine guns. We were protecting that road from any other combat units from the German Army that might want to come in there, into Bastogne.

OKW (Oberkommando der Wehrmacht, German supreme command) had identified control of the vital crossroads through Bastogne to be an absolute imperative to maintain supply and communication lines. The other town of particular note to the Germans was Sankt Vith, which at the time still had operational rail links running into Germany. But by December 18, it was clear to Field Marshal Walter Model, overseeing the offensive, that the 6th Panzer Army attack in the north was floundering, so he looked at the situation and decided to transfer some 6th Army units to the 5th Army. However, General Hasso von Manteuffel, commander of the 5th Army, wasn't having it all his own way and it was difficult to extract these units in the north and send them south. The abject failure of LXVI Corps to capture Sankt Vith by December 18 meant the town's significant road and rail network, which could have played an important role in bringing reserves up to the front, was not viable.

The specific instructions to the 5th Army and 47th Panzer Corps would be to attack directly through the Bastogne sector, cross the Our River on a wide front, bypass the Clerf sector, take Bastogne, and move to and cross the Meuse River south of Namur. General Heinrich von Lüttwitz, Panzer Corps commander, had stated in no uncertain terms:

> Bastogne must be captured, if necessary from the rear. Otherwise it will be an abscess in the route of advance and tie up too many forces. Bastogne is to be mopped up first, then the bulk of the corps can continue its advance. The northern bridgeheads across the Clerf and the Our rivers had been built by 2 Panzer Division. These were the bridgeheads, which controlled the movement of infantry on to the Longvilly road. The two lower bridgeheads, built by the 26th Volksgrenadier Division engineers over the same streams, made possible the sweep against the lines of communication south of Bastogne and the attack against the town from that direction. The dividing line between 2 Panzer Division and Panzer Lehr [sic] Division for the attack against Bastogne was on an east to west line about halfway between Noville and Bastogne. The objective of 2 Panzer Division was the road junction at Herbaimont northwest of Bastogne near Tenneville. The mission of Panzer Lehr Division was to take Bastogne from the south. This was the initial plan contained in the original order for the Ardennes attack.

While SHAEF (Supreme Headquarters Allied Expeditionary Force) commanders, led by Gen. Dwight Eisenhower, were still meeting to discuss how best to combat the emerging situation in the Ardennes, Adolf Hitler had convened a meeting at his infamous Bavarian retreat in Berchtesgaden known as the Eagle's Nest. The purpose was to discuss and assess how things were progressing with Operation *Wacht am Rhein*. The prognosis wasn't favorable. Despite the fact inclement weather had prevented German columns from being strafed and bombed by Allied aircraft, as they had been in Normandy, it was safe to assume, even at this early stage of the battle, that things weren't going according to plan.

The situation on the northern sector where the 6th Army had attacked was particularly unfavorable. As Kampfgruppe Peiper surged through the jumping-off point at the Losheim gap, a few tanks were disabled by German field mines, and they were having to contend with a stymieing 12-mile-long tailback. At that time, Field Marshal Model, one of the few leading German officers who dared to speak openly to his rather volatile Führer, suggested a single thrust with all three armies from above Aachen, as opposed to dividing them along the 90-mile front, would be a better approach—a battering ram as opposed to a trident. This proposal didn't inspire Hitler, who had the temerity to accuse the decorated Eastern Front veteran of cowardice.

The leading elements of the 6th Army had barely advanced five miles, and even Model's most successful panzer thrusts had only covered half the distance to the River Meuse. Several armored formations were already beginning to stall and complain about fuel and ammunition shortages. Most of the congested roads heading west were barely navigable due to snow, hoar frost, and the all-pervasive mud. Most importantly, the Americans still held the two key towns of Sankt Vith and Bastogne, which should have fallen by the evening of December 17, as both the northern and southern flanks of the attack had stalled, leaving the Germans with only a narrow corridor to break through.

After sardonically ordering his commanders to make sure their tanks kept up with the infantry, Gen. Gerd von Rundstedt said to Hitler, "We should abandon the offensive and prepare to defend the area we have gained." Hitler wouldn't tolerate any defeatist talk from his subordinates. Model was, however, slightly more optimistic; he insisted the offensive should proceed on the condition the main thrust be diverted to von Manteuffel's 5th Panzer Army in the center, where the most encouraging gains had been achieved. However, even these were falling short of their primary objectives.

Ludwig Lindemann, of the 26th VGD, said:

> At midday, 18 December 1944, [in Luxembourg] the Americans surrendered and we took sixteen Officers and three hundred and sixty-five men prisoner. Seven tanks were destroyed and a lot of war materiel was captured. This action opened the route to Bastogne. But what started as a military success would end in streams of blood. Today the cemeteries of that region speak loud and clear of what awaited our troops.

The Battle of the Bulge is often quite wrongly referred to as "The von Rundstedt offensive," mainly because this appropriation was broadcast to the world by the Allied press in December 1944; Gerd von Rundstedt had very little to do with either its planning or execution. Generalfeldmarschall Wilhelm Keitel, chief of OKW, and his deputy, Generaloberst Alfred Jodl, chief of the operations staff of OKW, were the main players when it came to preparations for the Ardennes counteroffensive.

Initially, von Rundstedt, who was Commander in Chief West, was not even informed of the impending counteroffensive. He spent his career with the Third Reich getting both promoted and sacked with alarming regularity.

By the evening of the 18th, Gen. Fritz Bayerlein's feared Panzer-Lehr, arguably one of von Manteuffel's best units, was continuing its advance to Bastogne, despite the fact its strength was a mere 40 percent of its tanks, 60 percent of its guns, and 60 percent of its authorized manpower. The terrible truth was that not one of the German divisions striking out towards Bastogne was at full strength, and some were considerably depleted. The 26th VGD was lacking an entire regiment. The 2nd Panzer Division was at 80-percent strength, but one of its regiments of grenadiers was on bicycles and therefore considered unsuitable for offensive operations. That particular regiment was used only for replacements. Units that later reinforced the 47th Panzer Corps ranged in strength from 50 to 70 percent.

By December 19, at 2:00 am, the Germans were within two miles of the city. It was at this point that Bayerlein made a critical tactical error of judgment. He reacted speciously to a persistent rumor an American division was preparing to surround him and his division; on the strength of this information, he decided to stop to regroup. This absorbed a few vital hours, which in effect allowed the American Airborne units to consolidate and reinforce the existing 10th Armored positions. Bayerlein resumed his attack at 5:30 am but, when his lead tank hit a mine, which killed the crew, he decided to call another halt and wait until daybreak before moving forward again. Time was of the essence on both sides during those first few nail-biting days of combat.

It's worth noting that, while attacking German troops were suitably attired for the cold weather conditions, most GIs stationed along the Ardennes front had not been properly provisioned with winter clothing. The decision not to issue cold-weather attire lay unequivocally at the feet of the Allied quartermasters, who had made the decision in August, which in turn left the men ill prepared for inclement weather. The quartermasters opted to ship only fuel and ammunition to this front because no one expected any significant action or the harsh winter that was about to hit the area, which necessitated warm clothing even without impending combat.

In time-honored fashion, the Americans stationed along the 90-mile front did what they always did best—they improvised. They learned what homeless people had known for years. They started packing newspapers between their skin and clothes. They were frequently seen wearing woolen blankets over their fatigues and pillowcases over their helmets. Some learned that if they held hands and pushed up against trees and rotated around the tree to create friction, it would help to keep them warm; this spectacle would have entertained the locals. If their foxholes were big enough, they would sleep three to each one. They would rotate sleeping positions so each man would have time in the middle, thus taking advantage of the body heat of the other two to stay warm.

These young Americans were in many ways the antithesis of the German Army. For all their capacity for technical innovation, the Wehrmacht was often restricted by its incapacity to operate without orders at anything below regimental level. Most Allied troops could operate autonomously down to squad level when the situation demanded. The Allies' ability to work with the terrain and use topographical features to their advantage when required would prove a significant advantage during the battle.

The Germans may have had better tanks, such as the Tiger II, but they needed terrain that was conducive to maneuvering the 69-ton behemoths. The Ardennes wasn't suitable, even though German armies had infiltrated the area before on no fewer than three previous occasions. In fact, both sides, despite the weaponry, tanks, and military vehicles available, and in some cases because of the weaponry, tanks, and military vehicles available, had to find ways to deal with the weather conditions and the challenging landscape of the Ardennes.

This was the place the Airborne divisions were heading towards. In early December, some GIs of the 28th Infantry Division were still in and around Bastogne. The locals had already really taken a shine to these fresh-faced young Americans, and many lifelong friendships had been established. One resident of Bastogne remarked, "We shared everything with the Americans, but some of the things they gave us in return were really not edible, and a Hershey bar was definitely not Belgian chocolate."

Private First Class Benjamin Elisberg was with the 3rd Battalion, 110th Infantry Regiment, 28th Infantry Division, when the first waves of Germans began to arrive in the Ardennes. He said:

> We had an observation post and I remember seeing a lot of enemy activity, vehicles moving around, and this was reported over the radio that we were observing a lot of German activity. At that time I remember somebody saying, "Well, don't worry about it, we'll keep it monitored or something and see what happens." And I remember during that time they gave me a three-day pass to go into some town to have fun. And that's where the Germans counter-attacked [sic] and I was trapped in a building. I remember this guy saying a tank was coming up the street and I opened up the back door and bullets came flying in as somebody opened up an automatic weapon. I closed the door, and then I remember running upstairs looking out a window and a couple of Germans out there throwing grenades. I tried I guess to get them in the window. I fired my rifle. That's it. Then they stopped moving. And we were running downstairs again and getting a grenade from the lieutenant, throwing the thing out as far as I could and firing stopped. I said, "let's get outta here."

A few miles south of Bastogne, the 101st Airborne Division was allocated the task of stemming the German advance. Its strength at the time was 805 officers and 11,035 enlisted men. Included in its ranks were four infantry regiments and all supporting arms, but they did lack some personnel and equipment. Sergeant Lee Weaver, G and Headquarters Company, 502nd PIR, said during an interview:

> Some highways came in and some roads came in and we had already, the Allies had already captured the Bastogne and the Germans had been pushed out. When the Germans started the

Bulge, the way I read and what I've heard, is that Hitler said that had to be taken. Bastogne had to be taken at all costs.

We got up to Bastogne before the Germans quite got there. The 101st Airborne Division and the units that were attached to it were sent out by General McAuliffe at that time. General McAuliffe, his aide was in charge of the division and he set up headquarters in Bastogne proper and all the divisions were set out all around Bastogne to hold it at all costs. The Germans were to take Bastogne at all costs. After a few days and a lot of fighting, we were about out of ammunition. We were about out of supplies of all kinds. The Germans had captured one of our medical outfits so we were in lack of medical supplies of some kind. It was snowing and it was cold. We didn't have any air cover because the weather was bad. This was like the 20th or 21st of December. My job was a little bit harder this time also because it was harder for me to get around, and to get around all the companies to get the morning reports, and get them back to battalion headquarters. Then I was to see that they got back to division headquarters, which was set up right close to downtown Bastogne.

XVIII Airborne Corps commander, Maj. Gen. Matthew B. Ridgway, was in England at his rear headquarters. The 101st Airborne's commander, Maj. Gen. Maxwell D. Taylor, was in the U.S., but, as soon as he heard his division had been sent into battle, he immediately organized a flight to Europe. His deputy, Brig. Gen. Gerald J. Higgins, was in England with 5 senior and 16 junior officers. As previously mentioned, due to these absences, West Point graduate Brig. Gen. Anthony McAuliffe, the division's artillery commander, was put in charge of operations around Bastogne. He would play a pivotal role in the defense of the town, but that wasn't the original plan. On the morning of December 18, after a short flight from England, General Ridgway arrived in Mourmelon-le-Grand, France. Lieutenant Colonel Ned Moore, acting Chief of Staff (G-1) of the 101st, briefed him on the developing situation in Taylor's vacant office. It was there he discovered the division was destined for Bastogne and the 82nd Airborne had been dispatched to Werbomont on the northern shoulder, directly in the path of the SS.

While the 101st was still on the road, heading north through Belgium, they had been originally earmarked for Werbomont, a good twenty-five miles north of Bastogne; McAuliffe had initially been ordered to report there. No one had taken the trouble to inform the 101st it was now attached to VIII Corps. The advance party that reached Werbomont on December 18 discovered it was in the wrong place; it was meant to report to Gen. Troy Middleton at his headquarters in Bastogne. It didn't make a great deal of difference to the two airborne units that were deploying. They just wanted to get there and get on with the job. Pfc. Bill Hannigen was with H Company, 82nd Airborne, and said:

My brother was with the 101st down in Bastogne. We were very competitive, as close brothers usually are. I took great pleasure in reminding him that we saved his scrawny ass. When we were both home we used to argue about who had done the most jumps. When he'd say "four," I'd say I'd done five just to rile him. I think we both had a hard fight. I didn't talk about my experiences for 65 years.

General McAuliffe's incidental visit during the late afternoon that same day proved to be quite fortuitous; it was then that he received orders from Middleton to defend Bastogne. On the strength of this, McAuliffe made immediate preparations to reroute his division. At that time, Middleton had yet to inform McAuliffe that three teams from the 10th Armored Division had already been dispatched to three locations around Bastogne. However, XVIII Airborne Corps wouldn't become fully operational until the morning of December 19.

During that same morning, under cover of darkness, German tanks attacked an engineer roadblock just a few miles to the west of Bastogne. Unsure of his target in the gloom, Pvt. Bernard Michin waited until a German tank was only 10 yards away before firing his bazooka. The ensuing explosion, which disabled the tank, blinded him. As he rolled into a ditch with blood streaming from his eyes and forehead, he heard machine-gun fire close by. He threw a grenade at the sound, which suddenly stopped, and then somehow managed to struggle back to his platoon. Michin, who regained his sight several hours later, received the Distinguished Service Cross for his courage under fire. The fight to defend Bastogne was gradually taking shape.

CHAPTER FOUR

Dig In and Get Ready

All the newspaper and radio talk was about the paratroopers. Actually the 10th Armored Division was in there a day before we were and had some very hard fighting before we ever got into it, and I sincerely believe that we would never have been able to get into Bastogne if it had not been for the defensive fighting of the three elements of the 10th Armored Division who were first into Bastogne and protected the town from invasion by the Germans.

ANTHONY MCAULIFFE, ACTING COMMANDER, 101ST AIRBORNE DIVISION

General McAuliffe was exaggerating slightly. It wasn't a whole day before the 101st arrived, more like a few hours, but these were hours integral to the defense of Bastogne. Going back to that first day of the Battle of the Bulge, December 16, while some members of the 101st were enjoying a short sojourn in Paris, five German divisions crossed the Our River almost unimpeded. That river courses through Belgium, Luxembourg, and Germany. When the attacking forces reached the diminutive lines of the 28th Infantry Division, some GIs proclaimed in no uncertain terms that attempting to stop the waves of German armor, artillery, and infantry was like trying to carry water in a colander.

It's difficult to articulate the sheer, unadulterated terror these young Americans must have experienced when they witnessed the massed waves of Germans arriving during those first vital hours. The 28th's 110th Infantry Regiment was smack bang in the center of the division sector when it received the full fury of Gen. Hasso von Manteuffel's 5th Panzer Army. "The smell of shit and cordite is what I remember," said one GI of the 110th. "We fired so hard that our fingers were freezing to the triggers, giving us blisters, but the thing I remember most is the smell. I reckon that a lot of our guys didn't wait for the order to evacuate." The delaying actions of the 110th led to its inevitable annihilation, but in the process it purchased valuable time required to organize and reinforce the defenses at Bastogne. It was a desperately fearsome situation.

By the close of that first day, the Germans had pitted a force of roughly two hundred thousand men against 83,000 Americans; the Germans had at least a 6-to-1 advantage in infantry and a 4-to-1 advantage in superior armor. All along the Allied line, the tide of resistance ebbed and flowed as German attacks were temporarily repulsed in some places and defenses disintegrated in others.

Major General Troy Middleton convened an urgent meeting with his old friend, the feisty Maj. Gen. William H. H. Morris Jr., the 10th Armored Division's commander, at VIII Corps' headquarters in Bastogne. So far Middleton had gauged the situation perfectly, which had allowed him to calmly and competently organize the defense of Bastogne before reinforcements arrived. His clear thinking and remarkable tactical skill helped to stall the German advance, but he is rarely credited with this vital contribution. He had no problem delegating either while constantly searching for further solutions to tactical problems; he placed a lot of confidence in his subordinate commanders.

Middleton had originally intended to use a part of the 10th Armored in direct support of the 28th Division but, as things transpired, and as the situation evolved, he instructed Morris to send one combat command (CCB) to the Bastogne area and commit the other command (CCA) to assist the 4th Infantry Division down in Luxembourg. When the 10th heard about the problems up north, it was near the town of Reméling, France, still undergoing some restoration work after the damage incurred fighting with Gen. George Patton's Third Army during the punishing battle for Metz.

Owing to its excellent capacity for rapid deployment, the 10th Armored was the first division to arrive in Bastogne after the German counterattack, and the first to establish defenses at preassigned locations. Its CCB had been divided into three teams, each named after its respective commander: Team Cherry was commanded by Lt. Col. Henry T. Cherry Jr.; Team O'Hara was led by Lt. Col. James "Smilin' Jim" O'Hara; and Team Desobry was headed by the young, gangly Maj. William Desobry (commanding officer of the 20th Armored Infantry Battalion, 10th Armored Division). At the time it arrived in Bastogne, the 10th Armored Division consisted of 40 tanks, the 705th Tank Destroyer Battalion—which had arrived from Kohlscheid in Germany and Heerlen in the Netherlands, complete with 76-mm self-propelled guns—and two battalions of 155-mm artillery.

Lieutenant Carl W. Moot Jr. was serving with the 420th Armored Field Artillery Battalion, which would play a key role during the siege of Bastogne. He was a forward observer who served as front-line eyes for artillery firing missions. Moot would discover to his chagrin when his unit arrived in Bastogne that the German Army was not the spent force they had been told about. He wrote:

> I returned to the 420th Bn. HQ shortly after dawn. Battalion Commander Colonel Browne, most of the Bn. Staff and a number of other officers were there. Col. Browne said that the 420th was to move out as soon as possible, the division was moving to the vicinity of Luxembourg. There had apparently been a German breakthrough northeast of Luxembourg and the Division was to help stop it as soon as possible. There was a flurry of activity preparing to move out and

as I recall the Battalion rolled out onto the road within an hour or two. We proceeded towards Luxembourg, I think we traveled 70 or 80 miles and ended up in a small town in Luxembourg about dark. I was assigned as Bn. Duty Officer and spent the night sorting maps and making up sets of maps for each Observer, Battery CO, etc.

Using his calm, methodical approach to organizing defenses, General Middleton accurately determined von Manteuffel's 5th Panzer Army was advancing in the direction of Bastogne from the north, northeast, and east on the main approaches to the city. The purpose of the 10th Armored's CCB was to establish defensive blocking positions in the hope of preventing the advancing enemy forces from capturing this key city.

Middleton got straight down to business. He immediately indicated on a map where he wanted Col. William L. Roberts, the CCB commander, to send his three teams. Team Cherry was at the head of the approaching 10th Armored column. It was ordered to head northeast to cover the approach to the village of Longvilly. Team O'Hara was assigned a sector along the precarious Bastogne–Wiltz road in expectation of an assault from the east. Team Desobry was sent to Noville, roughly five-and-a-half miles northeast of Bastogne. This team consisted of 15 medium tanks, five light tanks, a company of infantry transported in M3 half-tracks, a platoon of five M10 tank destroyers, a unit of mechanized cavalry in three armored cars, and six Willys jeeps.

Team Cherry, which had been the first of the reinforcements to arrive in Bastogne, was divided into two teams under the respective commands of 1st Lieutenant Hyduke and Captain Ryerson. Roberts accepted these orders unquestioningly at the time, but privately thought his teams had been dispersed too thinly to offer any concerted resistance against the onslaught. Middleton was oblivious to protests and repetitively insistent the allocated positions should be held at all costs.

Roberts trusted his old friend implicitly; he had served with him in World War I and been his classmate at the U.S. Army's Leavenworth military college. At VIII Corps' headquarters in Bastogne, they studiously reviewed the developing situation and decided where to allocate the three teams. "Sir, there will inevitably be stragglers," Roberts said. "I want your permission to use these men." The corps commander immediately acquiesced. Roberts managed to round up 250 men, some of whom were from CCR (reserve), 9th Armored Division, with most hailing from the 28th Division. Over the next few days, the ranks of this ad hoc unit increased to around six hundred GIs. The purpose of what became Team SNAFU was to be used mainly as a reservoir for the defending force. It became a temporary home for stragglers; other units were given permission to draw from the proverbial well as the need arose. It would be used to check the houses in Bastogne and the surrounding area for Germans, among other things.

As the evening descended early on that gentle rolling landscape on December 18, Roberts convened with the vanguard of his column a mile south of Bastogne. As each team filed past, Roberts diligently issued Middleton's instructions.

Team Desobry's advance guard arrived in Noville at around 10:00 pm on December 18. It had one intelligence and reconnaissance platoon, 20th Armored Infantry Battalion, a section of 1st Platoon, Troop D, and the 90th Cavalry Recon squadron. They reported there wasn't any immediate significant enemy activity apart from the occasional stray vehicle that drifted in from areas already overrun by the Germans. Lacking comprehensive knowledge of the nature of the enemy forces, or the direction from which they would arrive, Major Desobry decided to establish three outposts on the low ridges situated roughly three-quarters of a mile to the north and northeast of the center of Noville. A section of medium tanks and a platoon of armored infantry manned each outpost.

When they disembarked at Noville and took up position, they had absolutely no idea the entire 2nd Panzer Division, commanded by Col. Meinrad von Lauchert, was heading in their direction. The division had been one of the units that had almost annihilated the 28th Division's 110th Infantry Regiment, and pitilessly hammered task forces of the 9th Armored Division's CCR. According to the German assault plan, von Lauchert's panzers were arranging a rendezvous with Gen. Fritz Bayerlein's feared Panzer-Lehr and Gen. Heinz Kokott's 26th Volksgrenadier Division approaching Bastogne from the east. The reputation the Panzer-Lehr had earned, however, exceeded its ability by that point of the war. The three diminutive American teams had little concept of the sheer magnitude of the task they had been given.

As members disembarked from their vehicles, one "tankie" from Team Desobry emerged from the turret of his M4 Sherman with a deeply disgruntled look on his face. He complained about having spent 14 uncomfortable hours in his tank and when he saw his friend Jerry Goolkasian, B Company, 3rd Tank Battalion, both men griped about the journey. Jerry noted,

> We'd all eaten something bad down in France and we're all griping about having the shits. Problem was that we were on the move and couldn't stop to get out and take a dump. The smell inside the cab was indescribable, but once the krauts started hitting us we quickly forgot. Worst fucking time of my life I can tell you.

What Jerry didn't mention was that it would have been quite a cold journey too because most M4 Shermans in Europe weren't equipped with heating.

The team didn't have to wait too long to see combat. At 4:30 am, the seemingly interminable flow of stragglers homing in from the east stopped abruptly. The atmosphere in Noville was tense with anticipation of the first German attack, which came just an hour later. A group of German half-tracks rumbled along the Bourcy road just east of Noville but, due to the thick fog, the GIs at the roadblock couldn't determine whether the approaching vehicles were German or American. That particular road hadn't yet been mined, and Desobry's tanks were a few hundred yards to the rear of the position, so there was no armored deterrent nearby. The front sentry yelled "Halt!" four times in quick succession to no avail.

Then the GIs heard someone in one of the vehicles say something in German. That was their cue to shower the half-tracks with grenades, many of which exploded inside the vehicles. Screams of agony pierced the coal-black night as the surviving Germans leapt from the half-tracks and took up positions in ditches beside the road. A ferocious firefight followed that lasted around 20 minutes until Sgt. Leon D. Gantt, realizing he was up against a numerically superior force, gave the order to withdraw a hundred yards so his men would be out of range of the "potato-masher" grenades the Germans were hurling from the ditches. Then one of the Germans turned a half-track around and, as his comrades scrambled aboard, retreated into the mist. It later transpired they were a reconnaissance element and had completed their mission.

Lead elements of the 101st Airborne Division had reached Bastogne late on December 18, and the timing of their arrival couldn't have been more serendipitous. During the night of December 18/19, the German advance had coursed down the Wiltz–Bastogne road to within two miles of the city. As the travel-weary paratroopers trudged up to their designated locations, they witnessed many desperate and terrified stragglers heading to Bastogne. Many of the paratroopers flagrantly accosted these men and attempted to relieve them of any weapons they were carrying. Technician Fifth Grade Phil Burge, C Company, 55th Armored Engineer Battalion, said, "We saw paratroopers from the 101st Airborne Division marching into Bastogne. They had come in by truck, since it was impossible to drop them in by air. Eventually the whole division of the 101st Airborne was in Bastogne. But we were there first, by a matter of hours." Sergeant Paul Bebout, 1st Battalion, 501st Parachute Infantry Regiment (PIR), 101st Airborne Division, said:

> When I arrived in Bastogne I was in pretty good shape. I didn't need any medical attention right away. The fog was so thick you could hardly see in front of you. At first it rained but then it started snowing, and I think we had about three to four inches. The only place to go was the foxhole. I had my foxhole dug up at the OP [observation post] where I had my phone so I could communicate with my mortar crews. We had nothing with us, no warm winter clothing, not enough weapons so we had no choice back then, we had to bum these things off the guys that were falling back.

A little earlier in the day, at around 4:00 pm, General McAuliffe's party and Colonel Roberts convened at VIII Corps' headquarters in the former Belgian Army barracks known as the Heintz Barracks. During the occupation, it had been used as a recruiting station and maintenance garage by the German Army.

With McAuliffe now firmly in command, Col. T. L. Sherburne had temporarily filled his vacated position as commander of the 101st Airborne Division's artillery. He arrived with his assistant, Capt. Cecil T. Wilson, at around 8:00 pm on December 18, at a crossroads in Bertogne, northwest of Bastogne where the road forks. Sherburne asked a military policeman (MP) directing traffic whether any 101st units had passed that way. The MP shrugged his shoulders and couldn't provide a definitive answer, referring Sherburne to his sergeant, who reliably informed the colonel that General McAuliffe and his officers had been there a few hours previous but had then left for Bastogne.

The after-action report of Company C, 609th Tank Destroyer Battalion, demonstrates how willing and able the unit was to go straight to the hemorrhage and attempt to deal with the situation as it evolved.

> The Company arrived in Bastogne 2130 18 December 1944. At 1030. Dec 19 the 3rd platoon was attached to Team Desobry and proceeded to join that unit at Noville. During the day this platoon destroyed two Mk V tanks, 1 Artillery gun and dispersed gathering infantry with 76mm. The 2nd platoon and Rcn [recon] platoon supported the 2nd Bn 327th Regiment 101st Airborne Div by MG [machine gun] and 76mm heavy HE [high explosive] fire on the attack on Bizory and Margeret. One Rcn man was wounded. In the afternoon the 2nd platoon was moved to form a roadblock on the approach from Marvie. Rcn was given a mission to locate the enemy firing across the Arlon road south of Remifosse; the mission was executed but the MG had been withdrawn.

The tank destroyer was either the M10, often called a "Wolverine" by American forces, or the M18 Hellcat. The British adopted and adapted the M10 tank destroyer for their own purposes and gave it the name "Achilles." The standard M10 gun was replaced by a more powerful British antitank quick-firing 17-pounder. American tank destroyers were usually held in reserve, until dispatched to wherever enemy armor was massing, or hidden in defensive positions where enemy armor was expected. The M10 Wolverines and M18 Hellcats of the 705th Tank Destroyer Battalion played an integral role in the fight for Bastogne. The M36 version would arrive sometime later.

The 3-inch gun on the M10 was originally developed as an antiaircraft weapon but had the capacity to employ a variety of ammunition, such as armor-piercing and high-explosive shells. It had a .50-caliber heavy machine gun mounted at the rear of the open-top turret, which a crew member, or whoever drew the short straw, would have to stand behind on the tank's hull to operate. Whoever had the job of working the machine gun was terribly exposed, and it wouldn't have been an endearing prospect during the winter of 1944–45. Another downside was the open-top turret, which made it vulnerable to grenades and artillery tree-top bursts.

Team Desobry and the 1st Battalion, 506th PIR, had four Hellcats from the 705th Battalion at their disposal. This "Tank buster" had one of the highest kill rates of any World War II tank and reputedly helped to disable 30 German tanks at Noville, including some Tigers.

A company of paratroopers from the 1st Battalion, 506th, commanded by Lt. Col. James L. LaPrade, was ordered up to Noville to provide support for Team Desobry. When LaPrade arrived at the 20th Armored Infantry Battalion's command post at 11:30 am, December 19, a slight but vociferous altercation ensued between him and Major Desobry concerning who would be in overall command. The one thing Desobry and LaPrade agreed on was that this ship didn't need more than one captain so, with LaPrade being senior, he assumed the assignment. This detail would shortly become superfluous.

The village of Noville lies about a half-mile in a shallow valley that is prone to mist emanating from the trees and the ridges at most times of the year, but especially in late fall and winter. It's behind two high ridges that extend to the northeast and northwest. Behind the village are a few logging forests that reach almost to the perimeter of Bastogne.

The defenders at Noville now had 30 tanks, six M10s, and around a thousand troops, augmented by the four M18 Hellcats, but it wasn't enough to fight a pitched battle against the Germans' seven thousand troops, 80 superior tanks and a whole gamut of artillery, which included 88-mm guns. Most Allied soldiers at the time had the propensity to refer to any incoming German shells as being fired by 88s, when this was frequently not the case.

Colonel Robert Sink, commander of the 506th PIR, often referred to as "Five-Oh-Sink" in honor of its long-term leader, wasn't the kind of person to wait in the office for news from the front, so he went up to Noville to make a personal reconnaissance. He was held in high regard by the men of his regiment. After the Brécourt Manor assault in Normandy, Sink recommended 1Lt. Richard Winters for the Medal of Honor, but it was never awarded. While other E Company men earned Bronze and Silver Stars, Winters received the Distinguished Service Cross. The caliber of those airborne men cannot be understated. Of the 5,800 men who volunteered to become paratroopers in the 506th, only 1,948 succeeded in completing the training.

Sink talked to LaPrade about the orders for the combined defense of the town. The plan in its entirety was for B Company to defend to the northwest, while A Company held the northeast. C Company was given the task of covering the southern half of the perimeter. Team Desobry remained in the center of Noville in preparation to strike out in any direction as the situation demanded.

A company of the 506th had arrived in Noville with most of the regiment's equipment still back on the roads. At 2:30 pm, they attacked with ammunition procured from the 10th Armored, and from units falling back west, some men even wearing helmets hastily snatched from casualties. When the order to attack came, the 506th advanced in three columns. This beggars the question whether Desobry and LaPrade would have given the order to attack if they had known the full strength of the German divisions nearby. Probably not. As the attack got underway, both flanks advanced relatively unimpeded, but the center column was stopped in its tracks by 10 Mark IV tanks that were moving south on the Houffalize road.

At this juncture, while the company on the right flank promptly withdrew to avoid being isolated, the left flank became embroiled in a fierce firefight beside a small wood. It eventually managed to disengage and struggle back to Noville. General Freiherr von Lüttwitz, 47th Panzer Corps, said:

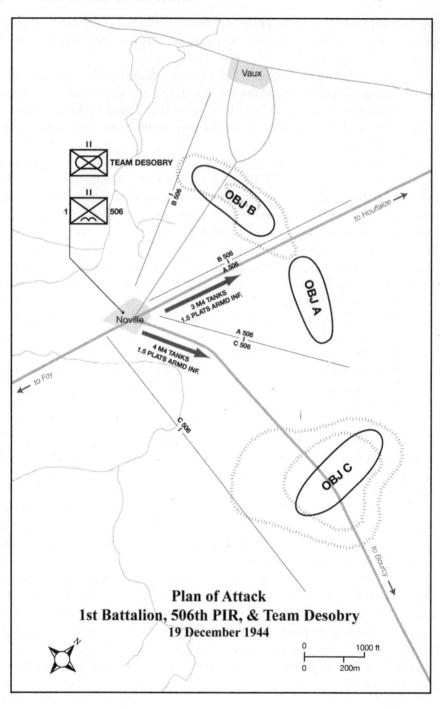

Vaux

TEAM DESOBRY

1   506

B 506

OBJ B

to Houffalize →

B 506
A 506

3 M4 TANKS
1.5 PLATS ARMD INF.

OBJ A

Noville

A 506
C 506

4 M4 TANKS
1.5 PLATS ARMD INF.

← to Foy

C 506

OBJ C

to Bourcy →

**Plan of Attack
1st Battalion, 506th PIR, & Team Desobry**
19 December 1944

0   1000 ft

0   200m

The 2nd Panzer Division was moving fast, It had met heavy resistance in Clervaux from elements of the 28th Infantry Division, but without further contact with the enemy it moved along rapidly to a point on the Longvilly road. At the road crossing immediately east of Allerborn there was a panzer fight lasting about one hour with heavy losses to American armor.

At that time, Team Desobry was already attempting to stave off concerted German attacks from three different directions. During the afternoon of December 19, the 3rd Battalion from the 506th was brought into the line, from Recogne to the Halt station, and ordered to defend the village of Foy while the 2nd Battalion was held in reserve. This meant most of the 101st Airborne's 506th Regiment was now committed to defending Bastogne's northern approach roads. By the morning of December 20, all four of the 101st's infantry regiments had arrived and taken up positions, joining 11 artillery battalions, elements of two armored divisions, and a tank destroyer battalion.

Second Lieutenant Harry L. Begle, Jr., H Company, 506th PIR, was wounded on December 20, for which he was awarded the Purple Heart and Bronze Star. He was the assistant platoon leader of 2nd Platoon:

> About 0800hrs I was about 500 yards east of Foy in the H co line. We heard the infantry and the tanks coming from behind the dirt road in front of us and I couldn't see squat it was so damn foggy. We heard gun and artillery fire and saw some dim figures in front advancing to our positions. All of a sudden I was WIA by small arms fire and artillery shell. A bullet went through the right hand and a shell fragment through the helmet that ended up in the left side of my neck. I was sent to England to the 162nd General Hospital for one week and was subsequently transferred to the 184th Hospital.

While in England, he met his future wife, 1Lt. Virginia Howland, Army Nurse Corps. They were married on June 19, 1945. Lieutenant Begle was promoted to first lieutenant on July 1, 1945. In December 2017, Begle recounted his experiences during that period in more detail to his daughter, who recorded them:

> December 19, 1944
> In a small town called Foy. Soldiers had a map that showed foxholes—2 soldiers each. They were told to tie-in with the 501. It was getting dark and they had no passwords. They got to the edge of the woods looking for railroad tracks. They turned back through the woods and found a haystack where they bedded down. They had no blankets—it was so very cold.

> December 20, 1944
> They woke up to machine gun and mortar fire in the haystack and the Germans set it on fire. They got behind a potato pile, covered with manure. Bullets were firing. A Sergeant had been hit in the haystack. Clark and Harry head back to the field and could hear the Germans put in the mortar. It was very foggy—they could not see but could hear the German tanks. They radioed for artillery fire on the tanks. Clark and Harry got back to the injured Sergeant [he was hit in the knee] at the potato pile and Clark took him and told Harry to stay as long as he could hold out. He stayed as long as he could and then said to a dozen soldiers to pull out. Soldiers would fire over their heads so they could get out and run back through the woods.

Harry was then looking for the rest of the platoon. He had to run through the field. As he was running, he got shot in his right hand, and the rifle dropped out of his hand. He saw a ditch and jumped into it [on the side of the road]. He was wearing a leather glove and thought his hand had been shot off.

While in the ditch, a tree burst [steel] hits tree and explodes. Harry passed out for a few seconds. Pieces of shell fragment went through his helmet into his neck. The other soldiers in the ditch were killed. Harry then got out of the ditch and ran to Command Post and asked for the aid station. Soldiers carried morphine with them but Harry did not want to take it. When he reached the aid station, he was told to get in the jeep. A lieutenant, Roger Tensley, was on the hood of the jeep—he was dead. The jeep headed to Bastogne.

All the bones in Harry's fingers [ring finger and little finger], were fractured. The doctors wanted to cut off his fingers and Harry said emphatically, "NO." Because Harry was an officer, the doctors did not amputate them. If Harry had been an enlisted man, the doctors would have amputated the fingers. Harry was wearing his military school class ring. The doctors sent him to a dentist who used equipment to cut off the ring from his finger. The ring finger was extremely swollen.

Lieutenant Wayne E. Tennant, 705th Tank Destroyer Battalion, was also in action near Foy:

> The 705th TD Bn arrived in the Bastogne area on the 18 December 1944, with orders to report to the 101st Airborne Division. I was a Company Commander of Company C and my orders were to report to and support a 101st Airborne Infantry unit in a grove of trees [on the road to Foy] about three miles north of Bastogne. I left my Headquarters platoon and one platoon of tank destroyers in Bastogne and took two platoons of tank destroyers [eight TDs] with me. I found the grove of trees in the dark, near midnight, kept one platoon there with me and sent the other platoon on into Foy. The next morning just as it was nearing daylight we started receiving heavy fire. We also started receiving casualties, and I was one of them.

Meanwhile, Sherburne had returned to the crossroads and told the MP, in no uncertain terms, that he was to instruct any 101st units that came by to head directly to Bastogne with all haste. At that time, the 101st artillery had an additional unit in their ranks. The 463rd Parachute Field Artillery Battalion was initially part of the 17th Airborne Division, but when the emergency call to arms occurred, the recently promoted commander Lt. Col. John T. Cooper approached McAuliffe to offer his services. McAuliffe politely mentioned the 463rd wasn't part of his division, but suggested he should make the same offer to Col. Joseph H. Harper, commanding the 327th Glider Infantry Regiment. Harper gratefully accepted Cooper's offer and the die was cast. The 327th immediately took up positions south of Bastogne and prepared for battle. Private First Class Joe Pisano, F Company, 327th, said:

> I was with the mortars, I had a rifle. We didn't think nothing about getting surrounded, we was always surrounded. We were surrounded when we was in Holland, that's what airborne was. We were at the town of Marvie, it was a suburb, outside Bastogne. We weren't in Bastogne itself, if you look at a map it's like four o' clock. We defended that part. Eventually we defended the whole southern perimeter, the 327th Glider infantry, we did. They [the Germans] were attacking every day, our guys were marvelous. They can't make a movie as good as that was. Every day we fought them off. I had a whole rifle belt and two bandoliers, and hand grenades.

After the airdrop into the south of France as part of the Allied invasion known as Operation *Dragoon* or, somewhat derisively, the "Champagne Campaign," the 463rd had been provided with twelve 2 1/2-ton trucks, twenty-six 1/4-ton trucks, and an ample supply of 75-mm ammunition, which included over two hundred antitank rounds. In contrast to most American units heading to Bastogne, the 463rd had a ready supply of wool overcoats and "mud-pack" overshoes it had received before arriving at the Airborne camp in Mourmelon-le-Grand on December 12. The unit's presence would eventually prove integral to the defense of Bastogne.

CHAPTER FIVE

Lights Out

There was a truck with bodies on it, and as one rounded the corner, some of the pieces of bodies fell off the truck.

RALPH K. MANLEY, 501ST PARACHUTE INFANTRY REGIMENT,

101ST AIRBORNE DIVISION

Private First Class Ralph Frank Youngmann, 9th Armored Division, described those first petrifying encounters with Gen. Hasso von Manteuffel's forces:

> Well, we repelled the first group that came up. And, I don't know, we fought them for maybe 15 minutes or 20 minutes. It wasn't a very long fight. But because they were coming up a very steep hill, up to where we were at the top of the hill, we were in a perfect position. And then after about another half hour or so we were pretty quiet. We could hear them whistling and bugles blowing and horns going off. And lights were shining through the fog. You could see the lights from the other side of the river. Finally, they started to hit us from the right I think this time, trying to get up. There was a draw running down along our right flank. And we were spread out so thin we couldn't even see the outfit on our right or the outfit on our left. And a couple of our guys got hit. One squad was completely surrounded and they were captured. The first, I think, the first or second charge that came up, they were taken. It was our machine gun squad. So they were our first real casualties of the Battle of the Bulge that I knew of. We had a couple of other firefights, which weren't very organized. They were just a few riflemen shooting at us from different angles and so forth. But it was very frightening, especially for the kids that had never seen this much.

The 327th Glider Infantry Regiment (GIR) combat team had been informed and alerted during the early hours of December 18, with the instruction to be ready to ship out by noon, or as near as possible. Throughout the ensuing hours, equipment and ammunition was issued but, owing to availability, transport wasn't ready until 4:00 pm; hence, as the convoy lethargically rumbled into life and left Mourmelon-le-Grand for Bastogne, daylight was fading fast. At one point during the white-knuckle drive, the combined column of the 101st Airborne Division extended 95 miles, all the way from Bouillon in Belgium to Reims in France. Surprisingly enough, there wasn't too much congestion on the road at the start, but that changed as they neared Bastogne and long delays began to hamper progress. It was a desperate race against time to get everyone in position before the Germans reached the perimeter of Bastogne. Before midnight on the 18th, all four regiments from the 101st Airborne had disembarked from their trucks and, much to the relief of the 10th Armored teams, were beginning to be deployed in and around Bastogne.

> After Action Report 327th Glider Infantry Regiment:
>
> On 18 December, 1944, the 327th Glider Infantry and attached First Battalion, 401st Glider Infantry [referred to in reports and herein as Third Battalion], with the 463rd Field Artillery Battalion attached, left Camp Mourmelon, France, in truck convoys at 1955 hours headed toward Belgium. Notice for the movement had been precipitate due to the critical situation in the Ardennes sector where large German Forces had broken through American lines and were advancing toward the Meuse River through southeastern Belgium. The convoys continued enroute until 1000 hours, 19 December, until they reached Flamizoulle [*sic*], Belgium, at coordinates 491 614. No enemy interference was encountered by the convoys nor were any enemy observed on the route taken, but at 1630 hours enemy activity was reported in the vicinity of coordinate 4764, and the reconnaissance patrol reported large numbers of evacuees from Luxembourg moving along roads southwest of Bastogne, Belgium (555580). Also elements of all types from units which had been in the sector toward which the regiment was going were withdrawing in the opposite direction.

Team Desobry had established a roadblock and placed a thin screen of infantry around the perimeter of Noville. The initial intention to lay minefields to the north and northeast was abandoned due to the ominous flow of American soldiers from other units falling back from the east on the approach roads through the village, which must have been unnerving to say the least for the 10th Armored soldiers. Despite the terrible attack they had just endured, one particular platoon of the 9th Armored Division's CCR (Combat Command Reserve) showed exceptional fortitude, and was duly integrated into Team Desobry for the duration of their heroic stand. They reliably informed Major Desobry of the magnitude of enemy forces currently moving toward Noville from the east. One GI from the 9th Armored didn't necessarily inspire confidence among Team Desobry's men when he made it his mission to inform as many of them as possible that "The whole fucking German army is heading your way."

Technician Fourth Grade Leon A. Jedziniak, a medic with A Company, 501st Parachute Infantry Regiment (PIR), 101st Airborne Division, remembered:

> We had just gotten back from the Netherlands, and we were still getting new equipment when we were told to get on the trucks to go up to Bastogne. I walked through the city when we arrived and they told us to go to Neffe, and we ran into the Germans pretty soon after we left Bastogne. The first night I was with ten guys and we were with the 705 Tank Destroyers. That was the only time I was warm during my time in Bastogne. They took me out and I was with a different unit for two days, but I do not remember the number. Most of the time we did not have enough men for a full platoon, especially once guys were getting wounded or frozen feet.

Private First Class Ben A. Molinaro, C Company, 327th GIR, 101st Airborne Division, traveled to Bastogne still wearing his dress uniform. On the way there, he saw GIs going in the other direction, so he tenuously asked his sergeant, "Why is everyone going this way and we're going forward?" He didn't recall the reply, but it was probably something he didn't want to hear. When they got to Bastogne, they were told to dig in. "We dug-in and everybody thought it was going to be a quiet position." Ben ended up at an aid station due to severe frostbite, but his concern for his buddies at the front appeared to override any medical problems he was enduring. "When I went there were hundreds of guys that was there with their bellies almost shot off, I felt so bad I said, 'Get me out of here, I want to go back.'" This wasn't spontaneous bravado on his behalf. There was an amazing esprit de corps among the different units that made up the 101st.

Private First Class John Fletcher, 54th Armored Infantry Battalion, 10th Armored Division, remembered joining the 327th:

> Being greatly outnumbered, we were forced back into Bastogne and then the 101st Airborne joined us. We first hit the Germans outside of Wiltz. After very heavy fighting, my unit was forced back into the small town of Marvie, which is on the perimeter of Bastogne. We were attached to the 327th Glider Infantry. Marvie is in a depressed area, which helped us because the German artillery was going over our heads.

The after-action report for the 327th read:

> At 1500 hours, 19 December, the Regimental Command Post was established at Mande St. Etienne, Belgium (500596). The First Battalion immediately was moved to the vicinity of Bastogne where it was attached to the 501st Parachute Infantry. The Second Battalion that night contacted the 502nd Parachute Infantry with foot patrols. At 2245 hours at the crossroad at 446650 a convoy of negro troops were attacked by about 100 Germans dressed in civilian clothes, led by officers in uniform. During the fight which took place the enemy captured several U.S. vehicles. Later, shortly after midnight, after enemy small arms fire and the firing of a captured American gun were reported near 446630 [vicinity of the areas occupied by the Division Ordnance Company and the Division Medical Company] the Third Battalion was sent out to clear the area of Germans.

Before it was sent forward to Longvilly from Bastogne, Team Cherry had been divided into two sections. First Lieutenant Edward P. Hyduke commanded one section and the other was led by Capt. William F. Ryerson. As soon as they got to Longvilly, they discovered an extremely precarious situation developing in front of the village. They had taken up position earlier that evening, sometime around 7:30, when Hyduke, commanding A Company, 3rd Tank Battalion, had halted the lead elements of his force just west of Longvilly, which nestles in a dip between several low hills. There weren't many roads in that area at the time and, due to the undulating nature of the terrain and heavy fog, it was difficult to see more than a few yards ahead.

They soon discovered to their chagrin that all roads heading west were virtually gridlocked with vehicles of CCR, 9th Armored Division. So, accompanied by his S-3 (operations), Lt. Col. Henry T. Cherry Jr. drove out to the forward positions of his team to reconnoiter the situation for himself, in an attempt to ascertain the proximity of the German advance. He discovered that, with only one battalion of infantry, two batteries of artillery, and supporting tanks, CCR had established roadblocks to the east and north of the village. Throughout the previous few hours, they had been the targets of repeated German attacks. Setting up the roadblocks had been a spontaneous and courageous decision by CCR, because they hadn't received any specific orders as such. Consequently, they weren't entirely sure if they should stay put in Longvilly or pull out.

A similar situation was unfolding in front of Captain Ryerson, who was directed to dispatch a patrol westward from Longvilly to reopen the road to the village of Neffe using two squads of armored infantry and an M18 Hellcat tank destroyer, which had been requisitioned from the 9th Armored Division for the duration.

Once Colonel Cherry had the information he required, he returned to Bastogne to report to the CCB commander, Col. William L. Roberts, who had established his command post a few yards from the center of the city at Hotel LeBrun on Rue du Marche. Cherry realized the 9th Armored's CCR was falling back when the crisp night air along the narrow road west became thick with choking exhaust fumes from many vehicles, accompanied by the throaty, indolent grumble of wheels and tank tracks that reduced centuries-old cobbled roads to gravel. On a few occasions, they forced the colonel off the road. The serious implications of this retreat meant the attacking German forces had the potential to completely isolate Team Cherry's position. Something had to be done and done quickly.

Thankfully, Colonel Julian J. Ewell, commanding the 501st PIR, 101st Airborne Division, had personally conducted reconnaissance to the east of Bastogne while on leave there several weeks prior. At 6:00 am, his platoon was attacked by German tanks and infantry that were at that moment zeroing Team Cherry's reconnaissance platoon at the Neffe road junction. They managed to disable one tank with a bazooka, but it didn't help stem the momentum of the German advance, which eventually caused the American line to fracture and fall back. For this and other actions, Ewell was awarded the Distinguished Service Cross:

> The President of the United States of America, authorized by Act of Congress, July 9, 1918, takes pleasure in presenting the Distinguished Service Cross to Lieutenant Colonel [Infantry] Julian Johnson Ewell (ASN: 0-21791), United States Army, for extraordinary heroism in connection with military operations against an armed enemy while serving as Commanding Officer, 501st Parachute Infantry Regiment, 101st Airborne Division, in action against enemy forces on the night of 18–19 December 1944, at Bastogne, Belgium. In the darkness of 18–19 December 1944, Colonel Ewell's regiment was the first unit of the 101st Airborne Division to reach the vicinity of Bastogne, Belgium, then under attack by strong enemy forces. While his regiment assembled, Lieutenant Colonel Ewell went forward alone to Bastogne to obtain firsthand enemy information. During the night of 18–19 December 1944, Lieutenant Colonel Ewell made a personal reconnaissance amid intermingled friendly and hostile troops and on 19 December, by his heroic and fearless leadership of his troops, contributed materially to the defeat of enemy efforts to prostrate Bastogne.

At around 7:00 am that same morning, in an effort to get through to Bastogne, Gen. Fritz Bayerlein had launched his Panzer-Lehr Division in an all-out attack against

Team Cherry. This action forced the decision to abandon the outpost at Neffe and get back to Bastogne to avoid incurring more casualties. As they fell back, the fear the Germans would get behind Team Cherry's position and isolate both them and Lieutenant Colonel Ewell's platoon grew by the minute.

While traversing the road west to Bastogne, the outpost team met the 1st Battalion, 501st PIR, going in the opposite direction. One of them shouted at a paratrooper, "Where are you going?"

"We're going to meet the Germans," replied the airborne man.

"There are thousands of them, and they have tanks," retorted the GI. Allegedly unfazed at this information, the exchange continued briefly.

"We have these secret can openers," said another paratrooper, "We'll just jump on the tanks, open them up, and take the Germans out." It's relatively safe to assume the retreating soldiers were not amused. But this was typical of the braggadocio attitude the Airborne soldiers had, and it had sustained them already through two major campaigns; the only major difference here was the weather.

A few of Ewell's men managed to reach Lt. Col. Henry Cherry who had established his command post at the solidly built Château Vanderesken, 300 yards south of Neffe, which was coming under sustained attack from two platoons of German infantry, supported by two Panther tanks. Later that same morning, Ewell sent in his 2nd Battalion which almost immediately spotted four German tanks, an armored car, and around one hundred infantry arriving at Neffe from the direction of Mageret in the east. It was around 10:00 am that two German platoons, supported by two tanks, attempted to take Château Vanderesken. They were greeted by a withering fusillade that took them completely by surprise. Three soldiers from Team Cherry, in position near the chapel, managed somehow to reach the château where the alarm was raised. The building and adjacent outhouses were transformed into ad hoc bunkers complete with automatic weapons, procured from vehicles, strategically placed around the château. It came under attack from three sides simultaneously but, undeterred, the defenders repulsed each attack and inflicted heavy losses on the enemy. Not one of them made it inside the château, which isn't all that surprising with the 501st PIR nearby. Pfc. Edward Hallo had enlisted on December 7, 1942, at age 22 after hearing about a new training program for paratroopers. In December 1944 he was runner for Capt. Stanfield Stach, A Company, 501st PIR, remembered scrounging for food and taking whatever he could find, included procuring rations from dead soldiers, and ended up contracting hepatitis from the unhygienic conditions. He recounted his experiences during the Battle of the Bulge:

> … on our left flank was the 506th. So we got roped in with the 506th. But the 501st was the ones that had first contact. When the officer sent back the coordinates where we were, he sent back the coordinates where the officers were, not where we were. There was just a few fellas left in the third platoon. Some of the platoon sergeants, shouldn't have been platoon sergeants, just dumb. Like when we had to help out C Company one time. We didn't know where the

Germans were in a patch of woods, but we had to know what to do about them, and the company commander said to the platoon sergeant, "Take two men out there and start digging a foxhole." I said to our officer, is he nuts? Out in the open? and you wanna dig a foxhole? you gotta be crazy, [the officer said] "Hal, we told him but he wouldn't listen to us." I took two men, before we went, I looked for the lowest part of the ground. I said, "I'll go first, you dive for that and don't move." The platoon sergeant took one of our original men out there. You could hear the shovel hit the ground twice and he was killed. That was that. After that we captured 19 Germans, took them back to C Company and let them have them. I was never scared, but I think my scout got a little antsy.

With each hour that passed, the 501st consolidated its position. The main approach road was being stalked by American artillery, which convinced the attacking Germans that reaching Bastogne from that direction would be extremely difficult. The alternative route was through Mont but access to this road was prevented by the defenders of the château. A German summary of the action stated that, during the first hour of combat, 84 of their soldiers were either killed or wounded.

B Battery, 907th Airborne Battalion Field Artillery, commanded by Capt. Gerald J. McGlone, was positioned 500 yards behind the 501st PIR with the purpose of disrupting the German attack towards Neffe. The result was quite remarkable. They prompted Bayerlein to begin to think he was facing a considerably more powerful enemy than he had initially assumed. On the strength of his suspicions, he decided to take cover in the cellar of a house near Neffe train station. More importantly, the heterogeneous group defending the château had caused the Germans to stall their attack for four crucial hours. There's little doubt this was prompted by the arrival of Airborne troops.

Meanwhile, Château Vanderesken gradually became reminiscent of The Alamo, as Cherry's headquarters team moved rapidly from one side of the building to the other to fire at oncoming Germans. They did this to convince the Germans they were attacking a bigger force than the one that was actually in the château. However, a few Germans managed to get close enough to throw incendiary grenades through the windows. Eventually, the roof caught fire, and within minutes it had become a blazing inferno.

On the evening of December 19, a section of Lt. Col. Julian Ewell's 3rd Battalion, 501st PIR, reached Team Cherry's command post at the château with their welcome reinforcements. The château roof was already well ablaze, but despite this, Team Cherry held out until the situation was irreparable and the German attacks had begun to dissipate. Lieutenant Colonel Henry Cherry contacted Gen. Anthony McAuliffe with the message, "We are not being driven out, but we are being burnt out. We are not retreating, we are moving." Cherry, it should be noted, was a fervent admirer of General Patton, and at the time there were those who said that to some extent he even attempted to emulate his hero. The remainder of Team Cherry retreated to Mont, but Ewell and Cherry never let their guard down against the incessant, probing attacks orchestrated by General Bayerlein's troops and, consequently, thanks to this concerted and stubborn defense, the Germans didn't make it beyond Neffe that day.

Nevertheless, advancing German panzer columns in other sectors, enervated by their initial successes, were becoming increasingly determined to take Bastogne. As they moved forward, armored units progressed in a zigzag pattern, often referred to as the "ricochet tactic," veering from left to right towards the center of resistance as they moved forwards. Unbeknown to the Germans, this tactic worked to the benefit of the defending American forces, giving them the time and capacity to move and deploy as the situation evolved. Therein lay the strength of all Allied armored units. Meanwhile, the 101st was getting into the fray and the plan to defend Bastogne was gathering momentum.

Sergeant Ralph K. Manley, 501st PIR, 101st Airborne Division, said:

> It was very cold. We met troops that were coming out, wounded [this, that, and the other], walking as we crossed paths, us going in, and them coming out—those who were disenchanted, having been overrun by the Germans and so on—a truck with maybe a series of bodies on it, and as one rounded the corner, some of the pieces of bodies fell off the truck. At that time they had grouped together clerks, anybody who was a soldier, to go to the front, and some of those not having seen that just keeled over in their tracks because they had not seen that type of wartime before. We did not know actually what was going on.

The prevailing weather conditions during that first week or so in the Ardennes were referred to as "Hitler weather" by German meteorologists, who had predicted it before the attack. In hindsight, it was a relatively safe prediction for that time of year, bearing in mind that rivers, streams, and forests dissect the Belgian Ardennes region and dense mist is a common occurrence there in the winter. That winter of 1944–45 was the coldest on record according to the "Weather report for south Belgium," issued by the Meteorological Office, London, on Wednesday, December 20; it forecasted persistent fog and heavy snow showers expected on the high ground. It would also be cloudy, overcast, with a mild northeasterly wind. Temperature: −15°C.

No matter how unique and effective the American capacity for improvisation was, there was little that could stave off the life-draining, freezing temperatures experienced on the front lines and in the foxholes. Fortunately, the citizens who remained in Bastogne for the duration were more than willing to share their homes, their food, and their cellars with the American soldiers, even though electricity and water had been cut off. Living by candlelight under constant fear of bombardment inevitably established strong and enduring ties with the locals, which in some cases have endured up until the present day.

Second Lieutenant Everett "Red" Andrews of the 377th Parachute Field Artillery Battalion said:

> I hold the record for the shortest time spent as a forward observer ever, I peeked my head above the fox hole to see if we hit the targets, and next thing I knew I was clutching the blood from my mouth in my hands and trying to put it back. I thought I was going to die. I was twenty-two

years old, I didn't know. I guess besides my bright red hair at the time, that was another reason folks call me "Red." I have the utmost respect and admiration for the infantry Soldiers, who have experienced the most severe conditions imaginable.

Andrews, who rose to the rank of colonel during a 20-year military career, continued:

> They had very miserable experiences. Compared to them, I had it easy. They were in foxholes in the bitter cold, I lived in a house in the village. The Belgian people showed us tremendous warmth and gratitude for being there with them. I stayed with one of the few families in the area that did not evacuate when the Germans arrived. They didn't speak English and I spoke pidgin French, but we were able to form a very deep bond. They looked on us as protection from the Germans.

The Leroy family included Arthur Leroy, his wife Madeline, and four small children named Elise, Madeline, Irene, and Gilbert. Their home was half living quarters and half cow stables. For warmth, the family slept with the cows at night, leaving Andrews and his soldiers to sleep in the house in sleeping bags. They would spend free time sharing stories about the war and listening to the family's radio, powered by the troops' generator, to keep abreast of the latest news.

All three CCB teams were beginning to show signs of faltering in their efforts to prevent the Germans from reaching Bastogne. Some were sustaining the attack better than others, but although the addition of 101st Airborne soldiers helped stifle the momentum of the German attack in some locations, it wasn't enough.

Pfc. Edward Hallo, A Company, 501st, recounted his experiences while heading out in the direction of Team Cherry:

> B Company was on the right of A Co and they were in the lead going toward Neffe on the morning of Dec. 19th. Our job was to act as feelers to find the enemy, A Co was sent up along a railroad track. There were groves of trees then clearings and other groups of trees. The railroad track was built up on & higher level of ground. There were clearings all along between the groves of trees. The 3rd platoon was on the left side of the railroad track and the company was on their right and had started marching up, and just as we got past the second grove of trees we could hear voices and it was late in the afternoon. We knew dusk was settling in, we could hear voices in the foreground. We decided to stay near this grove of trees and everybody grabbed a tree and waited to see what would happen. The voices began to get louder, Sgt. Chamberlain, who was our 1st Sgt at the time, ran over the railroad where we only had one squad that was on the left hand side of the tracks and Chamberlain ran over to the other side and announced, "Don't fire until we give the signal" and then he ran back. The rest of the co was on the right hand side of the tracks. This one squad we were in was on the left side of the tracks. Laying down on the ground you couldn't see over the railroad track and you didn't know what was on the other side. Behe was with me, I always considered him the mascot of the company, a little guy. He had a grenade on the end of his carbine. Behe says "What is the signal?" I said, "He didn't say what the signal was. Just pass the word down the line and we'll play it by ear."
>
> It was getting dark fast, you could hear the voices getting louder and louder, then we spotted the Germans coming across this wide open field towards us, they were taking their sweet time in spread formation. I'd say the Germans on our side were about 7 to 10 yards in front of us and Behe says "I'm not going to wait any longer" and he fired this grenade at this German and

all hell broke loose. The Company fired too. I had the 2nd tree. Lt. Meyer and he were behind the first tree and he turned and said, "Hallo, have the MG section aim down and cover the railroad tracks." Behe was left of me and we had a tree between us and the enemy. Behe must have blown the German apart with the rifle grenade, We all had a target. We just kept firing for a period of time. We just laid there waiting to see what would happen.

By this time it was getting pretty doggone dark and Monk Meyer came up and announced, "We're going to pull back to the group of trees behind us. Hallo, you stay here with the MG section and stay as long as you can while the rest of the company pulls back." I said "Okay." The company had moved back and there was a lull. Then all of a sudden there was a lot of noise and it was coming from down along our left flank. I said to the guys, "We'd better try to get out of here. I think the Krauts are going to move down on our left flank and set up a machine gun and we're going to catch it sure as hell." It was so dark that we held hands with the free hand and I looked up to see the sky between the rows of trees. We ran through the woods just as fast as we could. Carrying a machine gun you really can't run very fast. We got beyond the clearing and got in contact with the company behind us.

We stayed there that night and the next day we got the orders to move up again to see what the situation was. The whole company was on the right side of the railroad. I don't think the company realized the Germans were closer to us, the 3rd platoon on the left, than they were on the right side of the tracks. We moved up to the area we were in the night before and we were all on the right side of the railroad tracks. The scouts were out. They were more or less to the right. I stayed ahead of Capt. Stach, and we were moving up and I was closer to the railroad track. As we moved up, the very tree behind which our MG had been the night before, there was a German there. I raised my rifle in the air in the "enemy in sight" signal and everybody got down. I don't think the scouts on the right hand side knew we were moving up and this German started to take aim from behind that tree so I quickly took aim and fired and saw this German lunge forward. I don't know if I killed him or not. The same time I crawled forward and took out a grenade and threw it as hard as I could over the railroad track and crawled back.

The firing started on the side of the railroad track. I don't know what was going on over there. We fought for quite a while. We finally secured the position.

When queried about the later action when his platoon was sent to support the 327th north of Marvie, Ed said, "We had to take a position on a slight slope and I don't know where that was, I think that was when we had gotten the word that the Germans were coming through the line or the day after and we were to hold at all costs." Asked if he could see any houses below the slope, Ed couldn't recall: "There was only one house I can remember, one airplane came over and dropped some bombs and made some big holes, there was a bunch of 88s that came through the woods at us and all we could do was drop down and seek shelter. Those 88s they fired at us were really tremendous." Asked about the embankment, Ed said, "That was in the B Co[mpany] area and they really got slaughtered, and they met more enemy fire than we did. Word got around that B Co had really got into it."

Up in Noville, the situation on the 19th was becoming desperate. The axiom of war states that attackers only need a 3-to-1 advantage to have a realistic chance of achieving their objectives. The Germans definitely had the upper hand numerically, but they were beset by the same problems. Thanks to the vagaries of the ever-shifting fog, neither side at any location was ever entirely sure how strong the other was. To some extent, this worked to the defenders' advantage. When the fog occasionally lifted, it appeared to Team Desobry that the Germans were fielding a whole panzer division.

Team Desobry and 1st Battalion, 506th PIR, had definitely battered the attacking 115th Panzergrenadier Regiment, but it was far from over. This was probably because the Germans had an inaccurate picture of the developing battle and had acted over cautiously to some extent. By the time the 47th Panzer Corps prepared to storm Bastogne, they believed they were facing a much stronger American force; this was in all likelihood due to the concerted delaying actions of the three roadblocks. Preceding these initial holding actions, General Bayerlein even considered the premise he was the one being enveloped by American armor. This caused a significant delay to his plans and it has even been speculated that, if he had headed straight to Bastogne during those first 48 hours, he would have taken the city intact. But this wasn't the purpose General von Manteuffel had designated his 5th Army for. "My original plan was to move Panzer Lehr [sic] Division through Bastogne, if Bayerlein could reach that town before expected reinforcements arrived. However, when we discovered the 101st Airborne Division was there, I told Bayerlein to move south of Bastogne and not attempt to attack it, because we had … reserves coming along behind."

Desobry's GIs at the front line witnessed the ominous faded orange flashes illuminating the dense mist, followed a split second later by a shell fired from a tank or artillery piece that would go whizzing past, if they were lucky. Many weren't. Beside the temporary 20th Armored Infantry Brigade's aid station, located inside a café on Noville's main street, there was a sizable ammunition dump that had the potential to be struck at any moment. Due to excessive incoming fire, Team Desobry soldiers abandoned their foxholes and fell back to Noville; however, it was obvious to all but the mortally incapacitated that the position in Noville was becoming increasingly untenable.

It was estimated at the time that the Germans were landing between 20 and 30 shells every 10 minutes on the defensive positions at Noville. The roofs and interiors of several houses were ablaze, and a few vehicles had also caught fire. Unaware of the magnitude of the force bearing down on Noville, Desobry and Laprade decided to put their differences aside for a while and launch a counterattack. During the early afternoon December 19, an assault by A Company, 506th, was repulsed by heavy tank fire and forced to return to Noville.

Out on their flanks, B and C Companies managed to reach the lower slopes of the ridges in front of Noville both east and west. The fog cleared momentarily and it was then, at that very moment, that they noticed the ominous sight of an approaching company of enemy tanks supported by infantry. This induced most of the men from the two companies to seek cover. They continued to maintain small-arms fire at the attackers until the fog descended again. The combination of fog and smoke restricted visibility to around five yards. At around 6:20 pm, Colonel Sink called the division command post to inform it the situation in Noville was becoming exceedingly precarious. He recommended pulling back his forward battalion to a point north of the small farming village of Foy. Sink's report set in motion a chain of calls that would culminate in Gen. Anthony McAuliffe calling Gen. Troy Middleton to relay the information regarding the current situation. Middleton remained intransigent and uttered an unequivocal, "No. If we are to hold on to Bastogne, you cannot keep falling back."

Private First Class William J. Stone, Battery B, 321st Glider Field Artillery Battalion, 101st Airborne Division, said:

> On the morning of the 19th we moved out with the 1st Battalion, 506th PIR to Noville which we were to defend along with Team Desobry, CCB, 10th Armored Division, which had been defending the village since the previous evening. During the march we met soldiers of the 28th Infantry Division who were moving to the rear toward Bastogne. They told us that the Germans had fired at them using tanks captured from the 9th Armored Division. We began to understand just how serious the German attack was. None-the-less we maintained the esprit and confidence typical of soldiers of the 101st.
>
> Noville is seven kilometers [just over four miles] northeast of Bastogne. ... [About one-and-a-half miles] southwest of Noville is the hamlet of Foy. Noville lies in a saucer-like depression with high ground all around it except in the west. This made it difficult to defend against the German attack from the east as we did not have the high ground. Between Noville and Foy the ground sloped from east to west with the high ground on the east. Noville was critical because it contained the junction of roads important to the German movement westward. It was also important to the Germans because, if they chose, they could drive on Bastogne from the north along the axis of the Noville–Bastogne road. Our defense of Noville also gave the remainder of the 506th time to occupy and improve positions behind us to the south and to tie into the 501st Parachute Infantry Regiment on the right flank of the 506th. While talking with the officers of the company with which we were working, Canham learned that they had no ammunition for their carbines. As artillerymen we were armed with carbines and had enough ammunition to share with them, which we did. In addition, the riflemen did not have sufficient ammunition for their rifles and there was a shortage of hand grenades and rocket launcher projectiles. This was remedied somewhat just as we were entering Noville.
>
> The S4 [*sic*, logistics] of the 1st Battalion came riding up with a jeep trailer full of ammunition, which he passed out to the riflemen as they entered the village late in the morning. [Second Lieutenant George C. Rice, the] S4 of Team Desobry also managed to obtain ammunition, which he distributed. We stayed in Noville for a few hours but that afternoon we left and spent the night with another battalion of the 506th near Foy. To this day I do not understand why we were ordered to leave the 1st Battalion. Shortly after we left, it attacked out of Noville along with Team Desobry in an attempt to gain the high ground to the east. This attack was supported by the fires of the 420th Armored Field Artillery Battalion, which was in direct support of the team. Regardless, the fires of the 321st would certainly have enhanced the possibility of success for the attack, which did not achieve its objective.

CHAPTER SIX

Disintegration and Destruction

> If we are to hold on to Bastogne, you cannot keep falling back.
> TROY MIDDLETON, VIII CORPS

The situation in Noville had devolved to an attritional slugging match, whereupon German tanks literally got to within yards of Team Desobry's positions. Under these deadlocked conditions, the opposing forces continued to fight it out almost face-to-face while the fog descended again and closed in so thickly this time the soldiers could barely discern the muzzle flashes of their own guns. This didn't prevent the GIs from maintaining a withering rate of fire. For every desperate hour that passed, the teams held their ground against relentless German attacks, even though their casualty rates were rising quite dramatically.

At one juncture, Maj. William Desobry had contacted Col. William Roberts, commanding the CCB (Combat Command B) in Bastogne, to request permission to withdraw his forces, but the colonel refused the request point blank and told Desobry to stay put, on the premise reinforcements from the 506th Parachute Infantry Regiment (PIR) had been dispatched to assist the armored team in Noville.

Holding most of the roadblock positions under heavy German fire was becoming unsustainable, and the suggestion of making tactical withdrawals evolved from a mere suggestion to an imperative in a very short time. It's often referred to as "Murphy's law," i.e., anything that can go wrong will go wrong; it's usually the case that even when the situation seems like it can't deteriorate any further, it does, and it did.

The 1st Battalion, 506th PIR, had been rushed north through Foy to Noville in support of Team Desobry, which was already fiercely engaging their Shermans and tank destroyers from the 705th Tank Destroyer Battalion against a number of attacking panzer groups. They successfully repelled several concerted attacks at the Noville crossroads, including a coordinated tank/infantry charge. Even though Desobry and his tankers destroyed 15 German tanks, they also incurred terrible losses. There were occasions when tankers fought almost point blank against Tigers, Mark IVs, and Panthers ominously emerging from the fog, all the while sustaining a seemingly constant incoming artillery barrage.

Team Desobry was flanked a number of times but, together with the 506th PIR, it held the town for almost two full days, which provided time for the other defenders of Bastogne to dig in and fortify their positions around the city. Then disaster struck when a German shell landed in the street just outside the command post in Noville. The explosion killed Colonel Laprade outright; Major Desobry, who was nearby, was peppered with fragments of white-hot shrapnel. Despite the severity of his wounds, and with one of his eyes resting on his bloodied cheek, Desobry was taken to Roberts's headquarters in Bastogne to report on the situation in Noville. Roberts was shocked at the appearance of his young major's blood-covered visage and wasted no time ordering him to report immediately to the 101st Airborne Division's medical facility northwest of Bastogne at Barrière-Hinck. It was the westernmost position of the 101st. Lieutenant Colonel David Gold, division surgeon, and Lt. Col. Carl W. Kohls, the division's supply officer, had personally chosen the location. Desobry tells some of his story:

> When they hit the building they really took it down. And they killed LaPrade, I guess probably 10 to 12 guys, and I was badly wounded, hit in the face, head and the eyes. The guys took me down into the cellar and when I came to they told me I was badly wounded and the doctor said that I had to go back to the hospital. So I said, "Well, I want to go back and talk to Colonel Roberts," the Combat Commander, because I was convinced that we couldn't stay in Noville, and we had to get back on that ridgeline at Foy where we could do a much better job. But I wanted to go back and tell him. He hadn't come up to see us. The only ones that would come up to see us during the day were General [Gerald J.] Higgins from the 101st and Colonel [Robert F.] Sink, the [506th PIR] regimental commander, nobody from the 10th Armored. They knew what the situation was and they had agreed with us that we ought to go back to Foy. They didn't have the authority to say that though. So I wanted to go back and see Roberts and so I asked that they get my jeep and take me back there and so the jeep driver went out to get the jeep and he never came back.

Thankfully, more 101st Airborne units were still arriving, but a serious problem was emerging at the division clearing station at Barrière-Hinck, a place most GIs couldn't pronounce and where Desobry had been taken for treatment. Captain Jacob Pearl, 326th Airborne Medical Company, wrote:

> At approximately 2230, 19 December 1944, an enemy force estimated at six armored vehicles consisting of half-tracks and tanks, supported by one hundred infantry soldiers proceeding southwest from the direction of Houffalize, Belgium on route N 26 and attacked the Division Clearing Station of the 326th Airborne Medical Company. The Division Clearing Station was sprayed by machine-gun from the half-tracks for a period of approximately fifteen minutes. The tents in which medical treatment was being carried out was [sic] struck by machine-gun fire. Six division trucks were set afire and lighted the area so that the red crosses on the Division Clearing Station tents were visible to the enemy. Machine-gun fire continued after the trucks were burning and after the nature of the installation was visible to the enemy. Following cessation of machine-gun fire an enemy officer approached the station and questioned Lt Colonel David Gold, Division Surgeon, the senior officer present. After a discussion with the enemy officer, the Colonel surrendered the 326th Airborne Medical Company to the enemy. The enemy allowed the organization thirty minutes to load the equipment and personnel on the vehicles and then carried them back to the German lines.

The German officer in charge at the time was tank commander Eberhardt Stefan of the 116th Panzer Division. Private Carmen Gisi, 401st Glider Infantry Regiment (GIR), was one of the first soldiers to find the decimated 326th Airborne Medical Company tents. "There were paratroopers with their throats slit still lying on cots with IVs in their arms. A German patrol came passing by and we ambushed them. We must have shot 13 of them."

With Desobry incapacitated and Laprade dead, Maj. Robert F. Harwick, LaPrade's executive, who had arrived in Noville just at the close of the afternoon's fighting, took command of the combined force. The armor passed into the hands of Maj. Charles L. Hustead, rendering the name change to "Team Hustead" for the duration. This all occurred while Desobry was being treated. He later praised the 101st medical services warmly for treating his wounds, and claimed they saved his life because the Army medical facility administered sulfa powder, performed a blood transfusion, and gave him medication to deal with any subsequent infections. After being captured, a German doctor tended him; Desobry recalled this was a desultory and painful experience. When he became a prisoner of war, and after being hospitalized at Ibbenburen, Desobry spent the remainder of the war incarcerated at a *Stalag* at Falingbostel, in Germany, a branch of the infamous Bergen-Belsen concentration camp near Brunswick.

Sulfa, or rather, sulfanilamide, helped to significantly decrease the mortality rate for wounded during World War II. American soldiers were taught to immediately sprinkle sulfa powder on any open wound to prevent infection. Every soldier, both infantry and paratroopers, was issued a first-aid pouch that was to be attached to his waist belt. This pouch contained a package of sulfa powder and a bandage to dress the wound. Some of the main components carried by combat medics during World War II were sulfa powder and sulfa tablets.

While the 506th PIR's 1st Battalion remained in Noville, the 3rd Battalion was dispatched to Foy to establish a defensive line between Bastogne and Noville. It was deployed on the left and right of Foy on the 19th. The 2nd Battalion was dispatched on the 20th; it was placed in reserve in the nearby village of Luzery. By late evening, Gen. Anthony McAuliffe had sent all platoons of C Company of the 705th Tank Destroyer Battalion to join the 506th. His second in command, General Higgins, had been promoted to brigadier general in August 1944 at age 34, making him in effect the youngest general officer in the Army. When he got back to the 101st headquarters, he said to McAuliffe, "I think we're way out on a limb. There's too much distance between LaPrade in Noville and [Lt. Col. Robert L.] Strayer [commander of the 2nd Battalion of the 506th PIR] in Foy. It is my judgment that the Noville force had better get out."

Colonel Robert F. Sink, commander of the 506th PIR, had also arrived at the same conclusion. He had informed McAuliffe the situation in Noville was becoming increasingly precarious and he pressed home that, in his opinion, the 1st Battalion should be withdrawn to a point north of Foy. On the strength of this, McAuliffe called General Middleton and conveyed Higgins's and Sink's assessments of the situation, adding his personal recommendation the force be withdrawn. Middleton rejected this suggestion unequivocally. The information was then relayed to Sink, whose response wasn't recorded, but it's pretty safe to assume he didn't burst into a festive song.

The regimental diary for 506th PIR noted:

> 20 December 1944 At 0930 hours there was a Company Commanders' meeting at the Battalion Command Post. At 1015 hour a strong combat patrol consisting of "A" and "C" Companies and the 3-2 section plus attachments from Headquarters Company was sent out to clear the woods near the railroad. It was reported that a Company of Germans had infiltrated through the lines between our White Battalion [Dog, Easy, Fox Company 506th] and a unit of Klondike [501st Regiment call sign] and had dug in behind the lines. With two companies abreast our unit attacked the German position at 1105 hour and cleared out the first section of the woods. Then our unit attacked the remaining group and cleared out the rest of the woods, captured over 100 prisoners and killed approximately 60 Germans. About 18 prisoners were turned over to Klondike. Other Germans were flushed out of the area into the hands of other units. Sixteen more of these were taken prisoner by units of our Battalion on outpost at Luzury, making a total of about 134 prisoners taken by this unit plus others who were wounded and evacuated through medical channels.
>
> Our combat unit returned at 1530 hours. Our losses were 43 enlisted men and 2 Officers, including Capt. Leeson, Commander of "A" Company, who was SWA by small arms fire below the heart. At 1530 hours we received word from Kidnap [506th Regiment call sign] to conserve ammunition. That night Capt. Kessler was assigned to and joined the Battalion taking over command of "A" Company.

General Freiherr von Lüttwitz, commander of the 47th Panzer Corps, wrote:

> The 2nd Panzer Division, after attacking and taking Noville without resistance about 1500, on 20 December moved its reconnaissance elements on westward as far as Salle, north of Flamierge. They then drew fire from the roadblock directly to the west. These reconnaissance forces then turned northwest of the roadblock. At 2400 hours the reconnaissance team reached the bridge by Ortheuville. We then proceeded to build up the bridgehead in front of Tenneville. We had assumed from the beginning that 101st Airborne Division would remain in Bastogne and fight. Having been given their zones, we assumed that both divisions could proceed in good style and could keep together without too much difficulty When we found that 2nd Panzer Division could not continue with its advance westward past Tenneville, I proposed to the Army Commander [Manteuffel] that we change the plan and concentrate all our effort against Bastogne, using all our forces to take the town. This was disapproved; instead, we were ordered to continue in the general line of advance given the first order, with Panzer Lehr [sic] Division advancing south of Bastogne and Panzer Division advancing north of Bastogne. As they advanced, 26th Volksgrenadier Division was to close in behind, invest the town from the east, and subsequently take Bastogne when the occasion became favorable. I knew that VIII Corp [U.S.] had no reserve and therefore, for the first time, I was not afraid of being hit in the flank. Further, Seventh [sic] Army was supposed to be on my southern flank, and I was assuming that with their right flank they would take Libramont. At this time, 116th Panzer Division was reaching Nadrin on my right flank.

General Fritz Bayerlein, then leading the Panzer-Lehr Division, wrote:

> On 20 December, the Infantry Regiment 78 of the 26th Volksgrenadier Division was
> subordinated to Panzer Lehr [*sic*] to carry out an attack on Luzery, via Bizory. Eight anti-tanks
> were subordinated to the regiment for this purpose. But the attack of Inf Regt 78 came to a halt
> before Bizory. The attack of Panzer Grenadier [*sic*] 902 on the road via Neffe towards Bastogne
> in the evening of 20 December was repelled with heavy casualties.
>
> Pz Gren Regiment 901, commanded by Oberst Paul Freiherr von Hauser, reinforced by one
> Panzer Company and one Artillery Battalion was employed to attack Marvie via Bras. Artillery
> was by order of the Corps withdrawn from Wardin on the night 20/21 December, to thrust,
> together with the Engineer Battalion south of Bastogne, towards Saint-Hubert. This task force
> advanced in the night via Lutremange–Hompre–Sibret into the area Gerimont–Tillet.

Once the 327th GIR had disembarked from their vehicles at the village of Flamisoul, west of Bastogne, and while Col. Joseph H. Harper, commanding the 327th, was establishing his command post at the village of Mande-Saint-Étienne, the inevitable request for urgent assistance came in from Marvie, east of Bastogne. The 1st Battalion was sent out immediately to support the right flank of the 501st PIR there, which was experiencing some incursions into its defensive line. At 4:00 am on the 20th, the 327th command post, along with the 2nd Battalion, was relocated to Bastogne. The 3rd Battalion remained out west in the village of Flamierge (about 2,000 yards east of Flamisoul) and established contact with the 502nd PIR in Longchamps a couple of miles to the northeast. This meant all three battalions of the 327th had been committed to the fight.

Lieutenant Colonel Ray C. Allen, commander of the 1st Battalion, 401st GIR, ordered his companies to take up positions astride the Marche road, and prepare to hold the ground not far from Mande-Saint-Étienne, roughly two miles west of Bastogne. Lacking precise knowledge of the proximity of German forces, his specific instruction to his men was: "Spread the men out in simulated glider loads for a simulated landing."

Meanwhile, the 1st Battalion, 327th GIR, was positioned in proximity to the 10th Armored Division's Team O'Hara in Marvie. Just south of the little village of Wardin, roughly three miles southeast of Bastogne, Team O'Hara had established a roadblock on some high ground astride the main Bastogne–Wiltz highway, even though the position didn't provide any real advantages at the time due to the all-enveloping thick fog that bedecked the rolling landscape. The following is a rather eloquent description of Marvie and the surrounding area from the annals of the 327th Glider men:

> A small stream divided the town, and the streets to the north and south rose rather sharply
> from the creek bottom. The southern end of the street was almost on the top of a hill which
> afforded observation down the valley which turned to the east and along which ran the road
> to Wilt. This hill also afforded good observation across the valley to the South for about 500
> yards to the high ground, which was thickly wooded. Team O'Hara's position was on equally

high ground east of Marvie. The ground to the west was high and after rising sharply from the stream on the south leveled along a flat ridge running north to Bastogne. The south end of the ridge was thickly wooded to the east of the Arlon Highway. F Company was given the mission of protecting the west flank of the battalion, this Wide ridge and the Arlon Highway. One platoon of I Company to defend the hill in the center, which for convenience we will call. Hill 500, also the south - of. Maras. 3 Company to defend Marvie from the fields to the southeast and also to make coordination with Team O'Hara. The reconnaissance of all company officers was hastily made and the battalion began to dig its fox holes and make more concrete plans for the defense.

The fog prevented any Allied air support for the duration, which in effect deprived the American units on the ground of all the tactical advantages they had enjoyed up until that point, with the exception of the recent fiercely contested Battle of the Hürtgen Forest. Both the 28th Infantry Division (Pennsylvania National Guard) and the 4th Infantry Division had participated in that battle, and both were in dire need of refitting when the German attack commenced on December 16. In the case of the 28th, it had lost up to 80 percent of its strength, and the 4th wasn't much better off. Meanwhile, the units in Bastogne were repelling the attacking German forces with every weapon they had at their disposal. It would take courage, coordination, and timing. One particular Airborne soldier was just as interested in acquiring souvenirs as he was in defeating the Nazis. James Edward Monroe, technical sergeant, 502nd PIR, said:

> Lo and behold there was a recon unit with 4 officers and 1 noncom that come down the road there heading into Bastogne. The mortar squad who were there fired a shell and blew that vehicle they were in to pieces. We were closer than they were to the road so we went down there and checked it out and of course everybody was dead, there was a big mass of mess and whatever. There were some parts and pieces that we gathered up, which is known as the spoils of war I guess. That's how I came across those two pistols this German officer had two pistols so we gathered up what we could you know, anything that was any good we divided it up among all of us and we brought them home as souvenirs.

Out east near Wardin, in proximity to Team O'Hara, Lt. Theodore R. Hamer ascended a small hill in his tank, but before he could reconnoiter the situation the tank took a direct hit, wounding the crew and killing one unfortunate member who was tragically burned alive. Then another medium tank got hit, injuring the driver. The four remaining tanks pulled back behind a ridge to avoid further losses. Then German artillery began dropping on American positions. At that moment, some Germans were brought forward in a Kübelwagen to do some mine clearance. As soon as they came into view, five half-tracks and five medium tanks opened fire. The vehicle and its occupants had a lucky escape. Minutes later, another group of Germans was spotted northeast of Wardin.

Just as O'Hara dispatched light tanks to deal with the situation, infantrymen emerged from the woods behind his positions and approached his team shouting, "We are from the 501st Regiment!" The rest of their company remained close by

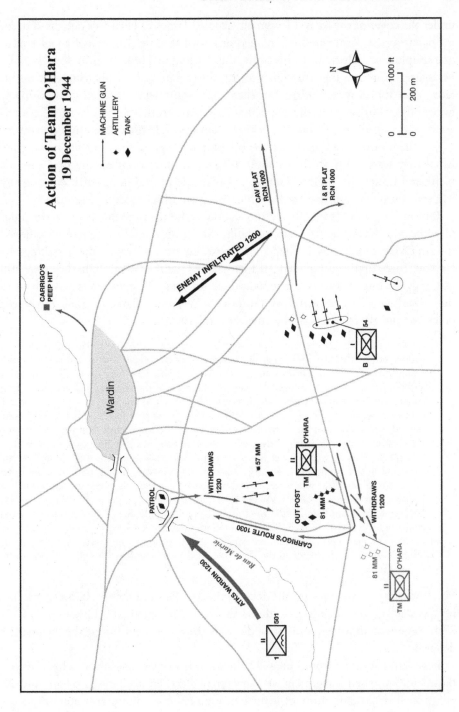

Action of Team O'Hara
19 December 1944

MACHINE GUN
ARTILLERY
TANK

under the cover of the trees. Lieutenant Colonel James O'Hara was delighted to see the paratroopers. Renowned as a tremendous combat leader, his men often referred to one simple physical attribute, his smile; they nicknamed him "Smilin' Jim," because no matter how dire the situation was, he always sported a reassuring grin on his face. Most found it reassuring, but there were some who regarded it as positively unsettling. Shortly after the appearance of men from the 501st, the Germans attempted to infiltrate O'Hara's position from multiple directions simultaneously.

On the morning of December 19, B Company was on the right of A Company when they were ready to follow their orders and moved out on the road towards Neffe and Longvilly. Their job was to act as feelers to find the enemy. A Company was sent up to the railroad tracks, which were on a higher level of ground.

Out in Longvilly, Team Cherry and all attached units were finally given the order to withdraw. When the first tank on point duty with the retreating column moved towards Mageret, it was immediately destroyed by a German shell, stalling the convoy. Three divisions targeted 1st Lieutenant Hyduke's men while they were still in Longvilly, but they wouldn't remain there for long. An eyewitness account from the 482nd Anti-Aircraft Artillery (Automatic Weapons) Battalion (Self-Propelled) described the effectiveness of the enemy's artillery:

> As we waited for an opening into Bastogne, it became very evident that the enemy was gaining fast in his drive, for their artillery began to fall closer and closer to our column, until finally it was hitting in our immediate area. Vehicles and men were hit by flying shrapnel and the screams for medics were drowned by the crack of the bursting artillery shells. Split second decisions had to be made and it was decided to take as much of our equipment across country as we could. Tec 5 [Technician fifth grade] E Humphrey and Tec 5 Frank Walsh were injured before we could move, by flames from a gasoline truck which had been set afire by the bursting artillery. Meantime, the crew of an M-16 halftrack [sic] distinguished themselves by winning a battle with a Tiger Royal tank. Tec 5 Davidson was the only gunner on the track and he was wounded in the leg. When he saw the approaching tank he asked to be lifted into the machine gun turret. Davidson opened fire with his four guns but not before his two cannoneers had been wounded by the machine guns on the tank. PVT Stewts was hit on the hand and Reinhardt in the leg. As the tank met the fire of the machine guns, the commander evidently thought he'd found the whole American army for the tank could not run fast enough to get away from the continuous rain of slugs. The M-16 had been put out of action in the engagement so the three wounded men abandoned it and made their way to an aid station.

Von Lüttwitz was furious with the delay of the 2nd Panzer Division in Noville; while he was ranting and raving, he ordered the 26th Volksgrenadier Division's (VGD) 77th Regiment to attack and assist the 2nd Panzer in eradicating this belligerent defensive line.

Less than two miles from Longvilly, the commander of the Panzer-Lehr Division, Bayerlein, launched a regiment of panzergrenadiers, an artillery battalion, and 20 self-propelled antitank guns in a further attempt to eradicate any opposition. At roughly the same time, Col. Meinrad von Lauchert's 2nd Panzer Division was attacked by CCR (Combat Command Reserve) from the 9th Armored Division. He responded by sending in six 88-mm self-propelled guns, reinforced by 15 tank destroyers to silence the upstart Americans, who in contrast to what most German generals had prematurely assumed, were defending with unexpected tenacity and courage.

Von Lüttwitz said:

> During the night, Panzer Lehr [sic] Division got on a country road to Mageret. The point of the Division got to Neffe early in the morning and reduced the roadblock. When Panzer Lehr Division came to a halt in front of the Chateau Neffe, a regiment was ordered to go immediately from Bizory to Bastogne. It thus was deployed in a manner, which put its line directly against the deployed American infantry lines. When this combat team was stopped in the north, another combat team from Panzer Lehr Division was sent southward against Wardin and Marvie with the mission of getting to Bastogne. This combat team was brought to a stop about one-half kilometers southeast of Marvie. From this time on we were stopped on this line.

By this stage, the defenders and attackers were numerically about the same strength. CCB had initially arrived with only two thousand seven hundred men, but once the 101st Airborne Division and other units had augmented their positions, the total defense force numbered almost twenty-three thousand. American command, control, and communications problems, as well as general supply shortages, occasionally may have detracted from the effectiveness of the defense, but these deficiencies were never insurmountable. One of the biggest problems experienced by most fighting units was lack of ammunition. As combat intensity increased, and overland supply lines were gradually severed, shortages eventually reached critical proportions and the conservation of ammunition became imperative.

Fuel deficiencies for the attacking German divisions were also reaching a precariously low level. Their hungry tanks devoured gasoline at a prodigious rate as they maneuvered in low gear along the winding roads of the Ardennes, or as they idled sitting in self-inflicted gridlocks. Their rate of consumption was five times higher than Operation *Wacht am Rhein*'s planners had originally estimated. The fuel situation deteriorated even further as the panzers moved west, and swiftly outdistanced the supply columns, which had become hopelessly bogged down. Consequently, much of the gasoline so painstakingly amassed for the offensive never even left Germany.

At VIII Corps' headquarters in Bastogne, Col. William Roberts had suggested to Gen. Troy Middleton that, due to the interminable flow of American stragglers from the 9th Armored Division's CCR, and men from the 28th Infantry Division falling back west to escape the advancing Germans, he could probably use the men to form a defensive reserve. The suggestion was received favorably and had culminated in the breach birth of Team SNAFU. Middleton later confirmed his approval in writing.

Within a week of Roberts making the request, SNAFU's numbers had risen to around 600. Although they were initially designated as a reserve, they would eventually play a key role in plugging gaps around the Bastogne perimeter. On Gen. Anthony McAuliffe's orders, a retreating column falling back from the east, equipped with 155-mm guns, also known as "Long Toms," was requisitioned for the duration. This provided timely support for the artillery southeast of Bastogne, in proximity to the Panzer-Lehr. Unfortunately, this column was captured. Despite this, the artillery continued to deploy, as the situation evolved, by placing a battery of the 907th Field Artillery Battalion, equipped with 105-mm howitzers, about a mile northeast of Bastogne and a further battery three-quarters of a mile east of the town, next to the command post of the 81st Artillery Battalion.

Staff Sergeant Paul W. Slevey, B Company, 327th GIR, wrote to his friend George Kosimaki:

> On Dec. 20 we came across the bridge into Bastogne, passed the Hotel LeBrun and on to the town square, then down the main street. Just past St. Peters Church we went through the town gate to the next crossroad, we went to the left and up the hill, this is on the road to Neffe. Near the top of the hill a lane led off to the right, we went up a short distance and dug in. I dug a foxhole along with Sgt. Robert Balchuck, we finished just before it started to get dark. The CO wanted Sgt. Balchuck to take a message to one of the platoons, he wasn't sure where they were so I said I'd help him find them. On the road we went up to the fence row that would have led us to the platoon but at that time artillery started coming in so we each took to the ditches, after the third round we got up and ran until we heard more coming. This time when we stopped looked over and saw a religious shrine at the WS side of the road. I laid there and said a little prayer, and when the next round came in I cussed out the Germans. Sgt. Balchuck said he was hit, would make it back to our hole. In the hole he laid on his stomach and I lifted up his overcoat and with my zippo looked to see if he was bleeding. He went to the aid station and came back next morning. That night Pvt. Luke Anderson was KIA. Pvts. Frank Petco, John Iski Jackson were SWA [seriously wounded in action], Pvt. John Pavol was in a foxhole a little down the hill from where we were, and in the morning when he stood up he could reach over and touch a dud that landed by his hole.

These first few days had severely tested all the American forces, but on the whole they were giving as good as they got, and that indigenous esprit de corps among the paratroopers remained solid. Their number was decreasing, but so was the Germans', hence this detail never distracted them from the job they had been allocated. This, among other things, is what made them unique. Nevertheless, constant fighting took an unprecedented psychological toll on all the Allied soldiers involved and some would never speak of their experiences, or even care to recall them for the rest of their natural lives, but the battle for Bastogne continued unabated, and the situation was approaching its nadir.

CHAPTER SEVEN

Hand to Hand, Face to Face

People don't know what cold is. Nobody could get to us, or they didn't even try because it was so cold. I was able to pack some extra socks, but not everybody had them, so a lot of guys had their feet ruined. Miserable.

PAUL ROGERS, E COMPANY, 506TH PARACHUTE INFANTRY REGIMENT,
101ST AIRBORNE DIVISION

Most of the 101st Airborne troops had been actively engaged around the perimeter of Bastogne for a few days. They had sustained and repulsed numerous attacks, but they had also discovered that fighting a determined enemy wasn't the only adversarial matter that required full attention. Even the simple perfunctory action of relieving oneself while in a foxhole became a precarious endeavor, particularly when temperatures were dipping even further to the point where −20°C had been registered. Water froze in the men's canteens, depriving them of the most basic necessity to hydrate; one paratrooper introduced a bit of black humor when he quipped, "It was so cold that even birds were walking." Many shook so violently from the enveloping cold at night that sleep and rest became a nigh-on-impossible aspiration. Under these atrocious conditions, the human body can only sustain so much; cold and deprivation would take its toll. Consequently, while attempting to generate heat, the body consumes more calories than those that were available with the meager rations. The inevitable result only served to compound the utter misery and life-draining fatigue the soldiers had to contend with.

Frostbite was prevalent. This occurs when skin and body tissues are exposed to cold temperatures over a prolonged period of time. Extremities such as hands, feet, nose, and ears usually show the first signs through symptoms often described as a "pins and needles" sensation, followed by numbness. Frostbitten skin turns hard, pale, cold, and becomes desensitized. With cases of early frostbite, after the skin is thawed, it becomes red and extremely painful. In more severe cases, the skin may appear white and numb, which indicates the tissue has started to freeze. Very severe frostbite may cause blisters, gangrene (blackened, dead tissue), and damage to deep structures such as tendons, muscles, nerves, and bone.

Sergeant Paul "Hayseed" Rogers, E Company, 506th Parachute Infantry Regiment (PIR), 101st Airborne Division, never returned to Bastogne in the winter. He remembered the cold with great clarity:

> It was the worst place you could be. It snowed, and it got cold. And I mean cold. People don't know what cold is. Nobody could get to us, or they didn't even try because it was so cold. I was able to pack some extra socks, but not everybody had them, so a lot of guys had their feet ruined. Miserable. We lit fires during the day. My first foxhole was a slit trench. But frost got in that right away. The next foxhole was more spacious, with a roof of tree limbs and dirt to protect against "tree bursts," the rain of iron and wood that fell when artillery rounds detonated in heavy timber overhead. Below-zero temperatures are especially difficult if you have no clothes. It was not only 29 days on the ground, but also 29 days in the ground, with no structure whatsoever. None. Zero.

Another problem was hypothermia. There are essentially three types of hypothermia. Acute hypothermia (often called immersion hypothermia) is caused by sudden exposure to cold such as immersion in cold water or being caught in a snow avalanche. Exhaustion hypothermia is caused by exposure to cold in association with lack of food and exhaustion such that heat can no longer be generated. Chronic hypothermia is a slow build that comes on over days or weeks. Early symptoms of hypothermia include slurred speech, trembling, exhaustion, stumbling, and impaired judgment. Left unchecked, these symptoms can induce mental confusion, unconsciousness, and eventually death. Imagine having to contend with all that and still be expected to fight? There were many cases of hypothermia along the whole front during the Battle of the Bulge.

Most American soldiers that had fought through the fall had already experienced a condition known as "Trench Foot," a ubiquitous medical condition in World War II caused by prolonged exposure of the feet to damp, unsanitary, and cold conditions. It had already been acknowledged in World War I, hence the name. As resourceful as ever, those Americans confined to foxholes often slept with their wet socks in their armpits and crotches, in the hope of drying them overnight, if they didn't freeze to death.

As casualties mounted, dead bodies were often abandoned and left to freeze in the snow. The skin of the dead assumed a deep claret color because blood in the capillaries beneath the skin froze so quickly. The site of so many dead became so commonplace that men would even use them as temporary seating while they consumed their rations. Infantry constituted roughly ten percent of the U.S. Army but accounted for over ninety percent of the casualties incurred during the Battle of the Bulge.

Now that the 326th Airborne Medical Company's facility at Barrière-Hinck had been compromised and forcibly dismantled, the 501st PIR established an aid station on the east side of Bastogne in the Petit Seminaire chapel. They had to tear out the pews to make room for the numerous litters that arrived almost constantly;

they even emptied the sacristy to fashion an ad hoc operating theater. This place became the collecting station for the entire 101st Airborne Division. Casualties inevitably mounted to the point that wounded men were packed together like sardines in rows along the floor of the church, leaving hardly enough space for the medics to navigate between them. Two battalion surgeons worked ceaselessly in front of an altar in an alcove, under the watchful compassionate stare of the Blessed Virgin. One young volunteer nurse, Augusta Chiwy, with the 10th Armored Division and 101st Airborne, was denied access to one of the communal cellars:

> I had an armband around my arm. This was because if you were a doctor or medical person you had to wear an armband. I showed them my armband, and then they told me that at the seminary they could probably use people with armbands. So I went to the seminary. And what did I see? A long hall, with someone standing at the very end. The person asked me what I wanted. So I responded, "They told me that everyone had been evacuated, but maybe there would still be someone here at the seminary." This person told me that everyone at the seminary had been evacuated as well. So, I said I would go back home. He asked me where I lived and I said I lived at the end of the town. So, he told me to come and look at something. I approached him and he told me to look at the Germans that were right outside. The town had just been fired at and we were going to fire back. I went toward the door and waited and suddenly, "Bang!" Gunfire on Bastogne. Everything started to tremble. I saw these cellar steps, and saw people I knew. I followed them just to be with them. Then a nun who saw me said, "Hail Mary, full of grace," and told me I could not stay there. There was no room for me. So, I left.

She would eventually volunteer to work under the expert guidance of 20th Armored Infantry Battalion, 10th Armored Division, surgeon Dr. John "Jack" Prior who was at that time gathering his wounded men in preparation for evacuation from Noville.

Since December 16, soldiers from the 9th Armored and 28th Infantry Divisions had been putting up a monumental fight against overwhelming numbers. By the time they arrived in Bastogne from surrounding areas, they were in a pitiful state. While some required immediate medical attention, others less afflicted were assembled across from the Hotel LeBrun (10th Armored's command post) on Rue du Marche just yards from the main square, which was known somewhat unimaginatively as "Le Carrefour" ("the square"). Today it's called "Place McAuliffe" and there's an excellent bust of the general in the far corner beside a tank from the 11th Armored Division. Back in the winter of 1944, there was little respite for the 9th and the 28th as they were ordered to augment the SNAFU reserve.

Meanwhile the defenders had to contend with mounting casualties that afflicted both sides during this momentous battle, and conditions at the outposts were reportedly continuing to deteriorate. Team O'Hara maintained a tenuous grip on the situation, but it was time to make decisions. They had been attacked during the early afternoon and had successfully managed to disable two tanks supported by infantry, but the position was soon overrun by a further combined attack of panzers and grenadiers. The survivors suffered so much concentrated fire, and losses incurred as a direct result, that there were hardly enough men left to assemble a platoon.

At 3:00 pm, Team O'Hara was ordered to retreat, under cover of a huge barrage provided by the 420th Armored Field Artillery Battalion. At roughly the same time, General Fritz Bayerlein's Panzer-Lehr Division claimed it was being attacked from all sides. The general decided he had to eliminate American forces along his flanks before his troops could resume the offensive.

Captain Vincent B. Vicari, on the 101st Airborne Division Artillery Headquarters Staff, said:

> The 101st Airborne established some sort of a line, and when they made contact that became the line, within a couple of days, people don't know we had eight divisions plus a full artillery corps against the 101st Airborne Division. They just kept pushing us back, and pushing us back and they finally encircled us. One of the fellas that went to OCS [officer candidate school], he was an FO [forward observer] assigned to one of the infantry regiments, and they needed time to establish some semblance of a line. Junior, I called him junior. He said, "I'll stay here and direct artillery fire against them until you can establish some sort of a line." Colonel sent someone up and told them to fall back. He went back and I looked at him and I said, this was just recently, "Hey junior did they put you in for a medal?" He said, "Yeah when I got back he tapped me on the shoulder and said, 'Nice job', because that was the furthest thing from my mind." Nobody was looking for medals. Throughout World War Two we had two MOH [Medal of Honor] recipients. None of us were concerned about getting medals. We got two unit citations from the United States government, one from France, two from Belgium and one from Holland. We got the medals but they forgot the lanyards. The farthest thing from my mind, coz [sic] now I think about it I would like to leave them to my grandchildren. I don't wear them. I've never worn any.

Bayerlein discovered American resistance to his attacks was considerably stronger than what he had been told to expect. He had personally witnessed his men getting a severe beating in Neffe, and on the strength of this he suggested to Gen. Heinrich von Lüttwitz that the entire 47th Panzer Corps was required to sustain the momentum of the 5th Army attack against Bastogne. General Heinz Kokott, the 26th Volksgrenadier Division commander, was also becoming slightly disillusioned with the prevailing situation; he uttered dispassionately that the original plan was no longer feasible, and the three divisions needed to merge to combine their efforts if they wanted to continue pressing the stubborn defenders.

Private First Class Vincent Speranza, H Company, 3rd Battalion, 501st PIR, 101st Airborne Division, said:

> What does it take to take the life of another human being. To look into his eyes and know that your face is the last one he will ever see? When the fighting was hand to hand you didn't even think about it, you just did what you had to do, you or him. We were only doing what we knew how to do best, and we were the best.

Numerous veterans from Team Cherry, Team SNAFU and Ewell's 3rd Battalion reported a peculiar apparition that occurred just inside the village perimeter of Longvilly, where the road goes into a roughly 1-in-6 downhill gradient. On the righthand side, there's a beautiful little grotto hewn into the solid rock, dedicated to the Virgin Mary, where many American tanks and vehicles stopped briefly; some GIs got out to pray, some just got out to take cover. It's still there today. When bullets and bombs are flying, it isn't a bad time to discover religion, and that's precisely what happened to quite a few on that icy hillside in Longvilly. In one communal cellar in the city itself, a paratrooper was christened by Father Godelaine.

Almost directly opposite the grotto, some GIs claimed they had seen a vision of Jesus Christ, which occasionally emerged from the dense mist. They did see Jesus, but it wasn't an apparition. It's a white, life-sized, stone statue that's well over a hundred years old and is still there today. Any GI who had the occasion to look to his right when retreating would have seen it. Some realized what it was, but some didn't. It wasn't difficult when terrified and facing death to be impressed with this vision in the mist. Private First Class Joseph Sylek of the 9th Armored Division's Combat Command Reserve was in the convoy heading west when he came across the statue:

> Our outfit pulled into the Valley on a Monday night 18th December 1944. The ground was soft and we were not able to pull the vehicles off the road for fear they would sink in. All that night Germans laid in on us with artillery fire. Early Tuesday morning we were surrounded and they began to close in on us. As the day rolled on the enemy showered us with mortar, artillery and machine gun fire. No kidding we were scared, our tanks and tracks were the main target. We ran to the slopes that formed the wall of Death Valley. There were three things we could do, fight a hopeless battle to the last man, surrender or try an escape. My squad was disorganized, my company scattered. I took a narrow path on the slope that let into a pine grove. Ten or fifteen yards in I noticed a stone stairway covered with pine needles climbing and winding up a hill stepper and higher than Norfolk street. At the first bend was the first station of the cross. It was carved from white rock mounted on a marble block. I blessed myself and went on up and at each bend was another station. Just before I reached the top and yet not in full view of the head of the stairway was a full size of the statue of Mary, the mother of God. A few steps more revealed our lord on the cross. As I approached the crucifix a German Burp gun opened up on me. From that moment my path was shielded by Christ. I am sure of that because no man could have come out the way I did and still live to tell about it. I had shells landing close enough to throw me off my feet and its deadly shrapnel sing by. I prayed for the courage to endure all this. I pray now for more to carry me through.

By now the Bastogne perimeter was shrinking quite dramatically, and preparations were made to establish a new line of defense. The 10th Armored Division's tanks and vehicles would operate as a mobile defense to be placed where and when required.

Team Hustead (formerly Team Desobry) endured a rough night up in Noville. Both Col. Robert Sink, 506th PIR commander, and Brig. Gen. Gerald Higgins, deputy division commander, were also very much aware of the evolving predicament and together they decided, despite McAuliffe's strenuous objections to this move, they had no other option than to retreat. They had personally witnessed two tanks destroyed after they had attempted to enter Noville. During the night, while the 506th's 2nd Battalion took up position in Luzery, the 3rd Battalion established a line of defense in Foy, marginally south of Noville. This in effect created an east–west line of defense between Noville and Bastogne, which was intended as a viable escape route for Team Hustead and the 506th's 1st Battalion. On their right, using the northeast line of a railroad track, Ewell's 501st entered Bastogne from Bourcy. On the left was the 502nd.

The most important factor at that time was to establish a strong defense line closer to Bastogne. Major Homan, commanding the 2nd Battalion of the 501st PIR, received a section from the 705th Tank Destroyer Battalion's B Company, equipped with four guns. They had arrived in Bastogne from Laroche after being ambushed in Bertogne, and after being delayed by a destroyed bridge just to the north of the village.

> After Action Report 327th Glider Infantry Regiment:
> The Regimental Command post at 0400 hours, 20 December, moved on foot to Bastogne with the Second Battalion, and at 0500 hours the 326th Engineer Battalion was attached to the Regiment. The day was marked with three main skirmishes. At 0530 hours Company "A," Third Battalion, killed ten Germans, nine of which were in civilian clothes, at 448629. Later, from 0715 hours to 1015 hours, this company fought off a strong German attack which was supported with three tanks.
> The enemy withdrew to the northeast. At 1130 hours, at 560555, four German tanks, a number of half-tracks, and at least 100 infantrymen, supported by artillery fire, attacked the Second Battalion. At 1245 hours the enemy withdrew. They had lost two tanks and one half-track. This battalion then occupied Marvie, Belgium (575560). The rest of the day, Germans on the Second Battalion front appeared to be organizing and consolidating for attacks with armor and infantry. Only intermittent enemy artillery fire and small arms fire were encountered until morning, 21 December. Eighteen prisoners had been taken on 20 December by the Second Battalion. On 20 December all roads leading from Bastogne were cut by the Germans and American forces in the Bastogne area were completely surrounded.

That after-action report wasn't entirely accurate. The complete encirclement of Bastogne would actually occur a day later. For the citizens who had remained in Bastogne, and as perimeter defenses gradually contracted under the weight of the seemingly incessant German onslaughts, the situation appeared to be deteriorating by the hour. In a desperate attempt to escape the fighting, refugees from surrounding villages had made for Bastogne, in the hope of finding some protection and sustenance there. This meant the communal cellars in and around the city quickly filled to capacity as people sought shelter wherever they could find it. The refugees arrived in droves and steadily descended into whatever communal cellars were available, bringing with them stories of terrible devastation and destruction from the surrounding areas. Two resourceful Bastogne citizens, Louis Requin and Justin Gierens, organized a fully functioning bakery in one of the cellars, which was quite an accomplishment considering that, by this time, there was no electricity or running water inside the city.

The people of Bastogne are known as "Les Bastognards" and are a special breed. Tenacious, generous, pragmatic, and stoic, they were no strangers to conflict, but this time it was different. Father Vanderweyden, a priest from the village of Marvie, close to where Team O'Hara and the 327th were located, urged his flock to abandon their homes and seek refuge away from the fighting. Many of these people would never see their homes again. The priest ensured he was the last person to leave the village before he set out across the fields toward Bastogne. He took a circuitous route to the city's perimeter, finally arriving at the chapel of Notre-Dame-de-Bonne-Conduite. His progress was abruptly halted when a crew member of a Sherman tank aimed his grease gun and asked the priest where he was going. Vanderweyden replied in perfect English that his village was under attack, and he was seeking shelter in Bastogne. The soldier thought it dubious that this person had come into town from the east, where some of the heaviest fighting was occurring. The tanker suspected Father Vanderweyden was a Nazi infiltrator and decided to escort him to the cellar beneath the 20th Armored Infantry Battalion's command post at the Hôtel LeBrun where he was held captive until the following afternoon.

After he'd proven his identity, Vanderweyden was seen going from cellar to cellar offering absolution and attempting to bring some solace to the desperate civilians there. He eventually worked as a military chaplain and held an open-air mass to the east of Bastogne, at Mardasson Hill (the location of the largest American war memorial outside the U.S.). Throughout the mass, he was in full view of the enemy, who fired artillery shells that exploded near his temporary altar, but these didn't deter him from completing his service. It would take more than that to shake a Bastognard priest.

In Bastogne, the local administration had begun preparing the cellars as soon as they acknowledged that the Germans were heading west. Shortly after the first German bomb impacted close to Église Saint-Pierre on the main street, at 3:00 pm on December 18, the citizens and some GIs took to congregating in private and communal cellars. One of these cellars was beneath the Notre-Dame school about a hundred yards up the street from the church. It became home to more than six hundred civilians, and around fifty nuns.

They all crouched and flinched in terror every time bombs and ear-shattering explosions impacted near the cellar, causing clouds of asphyxiating dust to shake loose from the ancient rafters. This, combined with acrid, pungent tobacco smoke, rendered the air in the cellar almost unbreathable. This vast subterranean space was illuminated by sparse candles and narrow shafts of light that occasionally pervaded the murk. With water and electricity supplies disconnected, sanitation was provided by strategically placed buckets that quickly filled and overflowed, adding a nauseating stench as temperatures plummeted below zero. The atmosphere was imbibed with incessant, resonant screams of panicking children intermingled with the agonized, derisive wails and moans of the wounded and dying that provided an interminable calamitous drone that would have tested the resilience of even the sturdiest observers. Sergeant Ralph K. Manley, 501st PIR, 101st Airborne Division, remembered the situation only too well:

Of course we did not get a resupply of K rations, which were all we had in the paratroops. We didn't have the C or D rations … or the canned fruits from the local people who were scared to death. Many of the locals, of course, had gotten out, but others stayed there, and so they, too, were subjected to the bombing and shelling that we were. Many civilians were in their cellars, and a number of them had canned meat. This was before the days of freezers and that type of thing. They would cook meat and put it into jars and pour lard over it to preserve it. They shared this with us. Being a demolitionist, I was out on the edge, in a foxhole. In this case, the ground was frozen, but we were in a barn lot with all the feces and cattle stuff that was coming out, so it was easier to dig a foxhole there. You can imagine what I must have smelled like. We disabled some tanks that were coming through with the bazooka, but they got very close. Often times you maybe had two in a foxhole, but in this case it was just one because the ground was so hard to dig, at least on the surface with the snow. Also, you didn't want to reveal your position because of the black dirt on top of the white snow, so you had to get snow and cover over the soil that you had dug out of the foxhole.

When we were digging some of the foxholes around, some of our soldiers came across gardens that had some potatoes left and things like that, dark black potatoes that had been frozen. But it was something to eat, and one of us even killed a chicken that had about froze to death and ate the raw chicken in order to have something to eat.

Before daybreak on December 20, Colonel Roberts ordered Capt. William Ryerson and the remainder of 9th Armored Division's CCR to weave their way back through the 501st PIR's 2nd Battalion defensive line just outside of Bizory. The 327th Regiment's 2nd Battalion command post received orders to proceed from Flamizoulle to Bastogne, where it duly arrived at 6:00 pm. While the command post was being set up, the 2nd Battalion moved on to Marvie to reinforce the 326th Engineer Regiment. The 327th's 3rd Battalion remained behind in Flamizoulle, where it set up a command post in a nearby copse of trees.

Team O'Hara was still near Marvie, and still protecting the Wiltz–Bastogne road, when it began to receive intense fire from the Germans. Once again, due to dense mist, it was difficult to ascertain the strength and direction of the attacking force, but the defenders were sure German tanks were heading their way.

Three significant attacks occurred on December 20 in Lieutenant Colonel Ewell's sector, but on each occasion his infantry, armor, and tank destroyers fought them off. Enemy activity on the flanks of the 501st and 506th PIRs didn't really amount to much, but one of these firefights, during the clashes at Noville and Neffe, proved strategically more beneficial than the others.

Around the same time, Team Hustead up in Noville reported to McAuliffe that it was running desperately short of armor-piercing shells, which prompted the general to finally consider the possibility of abandoning that location. The time had finally arrived for American forces there to pull out and get back to Bastogne. The only problem was, when the 796th Anti-Aircraft Artillery Battalion received orders to try to break through to Noville, it discovered German forces had captured Foy, which is situated on the main road between Bastogne, Noville and Houffalize. Three German tanks were covering the road. The 796th captain reported the situation to the 3rd Battalion, 506th PIR's commander who was only too happy to add the unit to his ranks. The most pressing item on the agenda was to clear the road so the platoon was incorporated in his plan to retake Foy, which was, at the time, little more than a hamlet consisting of a few farmhouses (not much has changed). It had been taken from the 1st Battalion, 506th PIR, by the 2nd Panzer Division on December 20, which in effect severed the line of retreat to Bastogne for Team Hustead and other remaining paratrooper units. It was going to be a thorn in the side of the 101st Airborne on more than one occasion. Either way, there was no time to lose if Team Hustead, and other teams on the fringes, were going to make it back to Bastogne alive.

CHAPTER EIGHT

The Hole in the Doughnut

The German attack around the southern side of Noville was rapidly becoming more successful. Because of this, the Noville force was in danger of being cut off from the rest of the 506th and so there was little time to plan the withdrawal.

WILLIAM J. STONE, BATTERY B, 321ST GLIDER FIELD ARTILLERY BATTALION, 101ST AIRBORNE DIVISION

There's an incredible amount of conjecture and misinformation widely disseminated regarding the defense of Bastogne by the 101st Airborne. There's even a monument dedicated to E Company near Bois Jacques that states in no uncertain terms: "In the wood behind this monument, on 18 December 1944 'E' Company of the 506th P.I.R. 101st Airborne Division U.S. Army dug their foxholes in the Bois Jacques Woods as part of the defense perimeter of Bastogne." The problem is that E Company was not in those woods as indicated by the monument, and it's fair to state the actual foxholes on display are about as authentic as the Shroud of Turin, despite what some rather unreliable Bastogne tour guides insist.

Some books even claim the 101st arrived in Bastogne during a blizzard. This is simply untrue. The first flurry of snow arrived in the area on December 20, when competing weather systems from Russia and the Atlantic introduced an assortment of snow, blizzards, fog, and freezing rain. The 5th Panzer Army was reputedly hampered by fog and snow during its attempt to take Bastogne, which is entirely possible, but the initial attack only had to contend with freezing fog.

Eventually, inclement weather conditions became a detriment to both sides, but although freezing temperatures were consistent throughout, the bad weather wasn't as continuous as some authors state. All in all, the defenders had the advantage of well-organized interior lines. The Germans may have bluffed, because the truth of the matter is they never really had a strong enough force to attack Bastogne from different directions simultaneously.

The 101st Airborne and other units definitely had the advantage as they continually shifted strength to repel incoming attacks as and when they were launched. Although Bastogne was regarded as a key road junction on the southern flank of the attack, it was not the main axis of advance during the Battle of the Bulge. It didn't have to repel the spearhead, which occurred, albeit disastrously, in the northern sector.

General George S. Patton once said, "Nobody ever defended anything successfully, there is only attack and attack and attack some more." He may have been referring to static defense lines such as Eben-Emael, or the Maginot Line, or even the Siegfried Line, but the defense of Bastogne was anything but static. When considering Bastogne, it should be noted that in most siege situations, as previously mentioned, it's often better to defend than attack. Defenses are inherently easier to manage and coordinate. Attackers are usually disadvantaged by lack of cover, which in effect renders them exposed and vulnerable. To win, the attackers must be able to continually press forward and secure positions, hopefully without incurring too many casualties. Defenders then have the job of repelling attacks from entrenched positions. Even though this was definitely the case during the battle for Bastogne, the defenders still had a fight on their hands, and they had no intention of just defending. Initially, Gen. Anthony McAuliffe had said he wanted a static defense, but under the circumstances this simply wasn't feasible. Many veterans who fought at Bastogne mention they were moved around quite a lot as the situation evolved.

Sergeant Joseph P. "Shorty" Madona was serving with Motor Platoon, I Company, 3rd Battalion, 506th Parachute Infantry Regiment (PIR), when the first attack to retake Foy got underway. He did a great job of fighting hand to hand, and face to face. On December 20, he was the platoon sergeant of the 2nd Platoon. They were strategically placed between the 1st and the 2nd Platoons of H Company. In an attempt to relieve pressure on the 1st Battalion and 10th Armored Division troops while withdrawing from Noville, he was posthumously awarded the Silver Star for his incredible courage during this action:

> The President of the United States of America, authorized by Act of Congress July 9, 1918, takes pride in presenting the Silver Star [Posthumously] to Sergeant Joseph P. Madona United States Army, for gallantry in action while serving with the 506th Parachute Infantry Regiment, 101st Airborne Division. On December 20 1944, he was in command of his squad during an attack against the enemy in the vicinity of Foy, Belgium. His unit was attacking across open terrain exposed to intense enemy fire. Enemy infantry units, supported by artillery and tanks, were entrenched on the military crest of the commanding ground that had to be taken by our forces. Seeing that machine gun fire was hindering the advance of adjacent units, Sergeant Madona exposed himself to heavy enemy fire and moved forward toward the enemy positions. Observing this action, the remainder of his squad and platoon followed him in a swift and victorious attack. On one occasion during the engagement, Sergeant Madona's rifle jammed. Swinging his rifle over his head as a club, he led his squad into and through three enemy machine gun emplacements, and captured all three guns and crews intact without losing a single man. His courage, aggressiveness, and bold determination, inspired his platoon to a swift attack that ended in opening the main highway, and enabled an isolated friendly force to withdraw down the road with their vehicles and wounded personnel. His actions were in accordance with the military traditions of the United States.
>
> General Orders: Headquarters, 101st Airborne Division, General Orders No. 26 (March 18, 1945)

While the 501st PIR had established a new defensive position, Capt. William Ryerson and Team Cherry's C Company, 20th Armored Infantry Battalion, were holed up in three houses northwest of Mageret, diligently waiting for reinforcements all day; sadly, to their detriment, none arrived. The perimeter was shrinking, and establishing new defensive lines became an urgent imperative.

The first hesitant flush of dawn on December 20 hadn't brought any comfort for the GIs dug in on the perimeter around Bastogne. As they prepared to meet another grueling Nazi onslaught, the skies hadn't cleared and dense mist still blanketed the whole area. It had been yet another restless night with little or no sleep for the men huddled in their foxholes, communing with the frigid earth, while repressing the inevitable longing for the warmth and comfort of home, thousands of miles away.

Private First Class Carl Dalke, serving with the 101st Airborne Division's 506th PIR, recalled the fight to save Bastogne as being the toughest, with his unit surrounded and trapped in arctic-like conditions. When his best friend was killed, he said it was "gut wrenching, but at no time did we ever think that we would lose, even though we were outnumbered seven to one." The ratio may have been a bit of an exaggeration, but it shouldn't detract from the severity of the conditions he and many thousands of his comrades endured.

Those foxholes were home to many during the siege but digging through the frozen soil with a small trenching shovel was incredibly difficult. Some GIs recommended tossing a grenade to loosen up the soil before starting to dig; this worked for some. The only problem with a freshly dug foxhole, as Sgt. Ralph K. Manley said, was the black earth around it had to be covered otherwise it would have been too easily visible for the attacking Germans. Naturally, some found out the hard way. Some GIs utilized the bomb craters created by German artillery rounds as foxholes, and covered them with bracken, sheets of tarpaulin or any available canvas for insulation.

Some of them even placed tarps on the base of the foxhole so any residual warmth created by bodies in close proximity wouldn't drain into the frozen earth. An alternative way to stay warm was to leave the safety of the foxhole or bomb crater and go out on patrol. This may have kept the blood circulating, but it wasn't a particularly endearing prospect, therefore most preferred their foxholes, because while there they thought German snipers and artillery couldn't get to them. How wrong they were.

One of the biggest problems encountered by everyone out on the perimeter was dealing with wounds when confined to a foxhole or defensive position. Private First Class H. Neil Garson, B Company, 80th Armored Medical Battalion, recalled:

> I was a PFC then, and I was put up on the crossroads to wave the drivers with the ambulances to make a right turn to where the aid station was, outside of Bastogne. I was there when the 101st Paratroopers came marching down the highway toward Bastogne. We gave them stuff we had collected from our ambulance, and blankets. They weren't in their usual woolen uniforms, which were warm, and here it was very cold out. Here they came marching in; they dropped

off from the trucks about a half-mile from where we were. We tried to give them what we had left over from the wounded in the ambulances. Before we had time to set up, I was at the crossroads, and here comes a whole company or battery of 105 cannons; they were retreating. Suddenly a colonel in a jeep caught up with them, turned them around. They were also used to keep the Germans from capturing the town. As for our men, they were suffering trench foot. Later on I saw many men suffer so much from this that we had to cut off a limb. We had a vehicle, a truck, which was fitted out as a place where the doctors had everything necessary for removing limbs.

There's a bitter wind that blows through the high points in the Ardennes during winter known as the "Siberian draft," which would on occasion have made it feel considerably colder than it actually was. Winter clothing was a perpetual problem for the defenders of Bastogne, which would have been particularly demoralizing when they saw attacking German soldiers wearing their very comfortable looking, insulated, white camouflage uniforms. Patton's Third Army requested 50,000 yards of white muslin to fashion white tunics as winter camouflage. COMZ (Communications Zone) didn't have the material available but instead provided 5,000 mattress covers, which yielded 10,000 white snowsuits, but they wouldn't be available to the 101st who had to prove themselves to be masters of improvisation for the duration.

Second Lieutenant Robert Potach, Headquarters Company, 2nd Battalion, 502nd PIR, said:

> Our winter gear came the following March, when it's spring in Belgium. Our winter gear would have been very welcome, but I don't know where it was. We didn't have it. I'm deaf in this ear, because I'd drop [the mortar shell] with my right hand because I'm right-handed, so my ear was right next to the firing tube.

In the villages on the perimeter close to where the fighting was, Airborne battalion medical detachments were quick to establish ad hoc aid stations; these were often little more than timber and dirt-covered foxholes, which usually had a main section located in a farmhouse or any other convenient building nearby that still had a roof. Each Airborne regiment would have had between five to seven jeeps at their disposal, along with one or two ambulances to assist with collecting and evacuating casualties. The absence of trained litter bearers in Airborne units exacerbated the work of the medics who constantly struggled to extract casualties from woods that weren't accessible to jeeps.

Despite the adversity, morale among the Airborne troops was relatively high. It took a hell of a lot to suppress that braggadocio attitude and that profound sense of camaraderie that permeated every unit in the 101st. In the *506th Regimental Journal*, published between June 1944 and July 1945, the activities in and around Bastogne were reported thus:

> On Tuesday, Dec. 19, the Germans rolled up from the east and collided with the American tanks, which had gone out to meet them at neighboring villages. A shuddering, small-scale battle developed and the Americans lost many a tank. But the Germans halted momentarily.

Then the main weight of the enemy veered around the milling fight, probed at other entrances to Bastogne.

Wherever the Germans poked there were Americans. The Germans kept on wheeling around the town, by the next day had it surrounded, a little island fortress in a swirling sea of gunfire. Headquarters, hoping for a weather break for air attack, radioed Bastogne for its positions. Replied Bastogne: "We're the hole in the doughnut."

On the first night one of the worst things that could befall an island of besieged happened to Bastogne: the Germans captured its complete surgical unit. Bastogne's wounded would have to get along without amputations, without fracture splints, without skilled care at all.

Through Wednesday and Thursday Bastogne battled almost continuously on its perimeter, suffered tortures in the over-crowded town. Shells poured in from all sides. Some three thousand civilians huddled in cellars with the wounded. Food was running low—the Germans had also captured a quartermaster unit. Ammunition was dwindling—an ordnance unit had been taken too. Gasoline was down to tricklets, the Fire Brigade, to save fuel, did not keep engines running, clanked off to hot spots on cold motors.

By Friday Bastogne was a wrecked town, its outskirts littered with dead. There had been at least four fighting Germans to every American, the elements of eight enemy divisions. The dead were probably in the same ratio. Bastogne had already cost the Germans dearly, in time as well as troops. On one day alone the enemy had lost 55 tanks and hundreds of men who tried to infiltrate the lines against the G.I.'s Tommy Guns and mortars.

It was ascertained that, on December 20, owing to the rapidly deteriorating situation for American forces to the east of Bastogne and the number of casualties incurred there, the 101st Airborne Division's medics hadn't arrived equipped with the usual allocation of medical supplies, but they would have had extra blankets and litters available. One particular detachment from a medical depot company reached Bastogne carrying a few tons of medical supplies, which were augmented with the discovery of an abandoned First Army supply dump there. This was all well and good, but they hadn't anticipated the high number of casualties and the capture of the 326th Airborne Medical Company's facility at Barrière-Hinck. Consequently, medical provisions ran low after the first few days of combat. One particularly interesting detail emerged when GIs inspected the location of the attack on the 326th Medical Company. Eleven German corpses were found wearing civilian clothes, concealing their military dog tags.

Stories of Germans wearing American uniforms were widely disseminated among Allied soldiers. The group of impersonators were mostly on the northern shoulder and had been part of the abortive Operation *Greif*. OKW (Oberkommando der Wehrmacht, German supreme command) had sent orders to all headquarters on the Western Front asking for soldiers who possessed a working knowledge of English, particularly American English. What transpired was that only a handful of men were found who spoke English well enough to have a decent chance of passing as a native speaker. Most of them were regular soldiers that had to undergo a crash saboteur and commando course. These men were commanded by Col. Otto Skorzeny during the Battle of the Bulge. Eight were captured and executed at a place called Henri-Chappelle, the location of one of the largest American cemeteries in Belgium.

The remainder struggled back to their own lines. Skorzeny's name had the power to send Allied commanders into paroxysms of panic. His reputation was well deserved after his successful raid to rescue Italian leader Benito Mussolini in 1943. Soldiers on checkpoint duty came up with questions—like "Who won the World Series in 1934?" or "Who was Mickey Mouse's girlfriend?"—to try to weed out pretenders. Many American soldiers and even Allied generals were detained at checkpoints for giving the wrong answer. Truculent Field Marshal Bernard Montgomery had absolutely no idea what the answers to these impertinent questions were when he arrived in the Ardennes. In characteristic fashion, he flatly refused to prove his identification. The American sentry didn't recognize him and shot his tires out. The field marshal was then somewhat unceremoniously hauled off under guard into a nearby barn and had to be physically restrained, despite noisy protestations, until his identity could be confirmed.

The physical effect of the German infiltration may have been rather limited, but the psychological effect was quite profound because within a few short days of the news getting around, there weren't many GIs in the line who hadn't heard of those "Krauts wearing our uniforms." This naturally extended to the 101st Airborne in and around Bastogne; that's where Lt. Col. Paul A. Danahy, the division G-2 (intelligence) heard about it. After the battle at Crossroads X, the intersection which had been the focus of a desperate struggle, the 327th Glider Infantry Regiment reported that many of the Germans were wearing civilian clothes or American uniforms as a ruse. The ones Danahy referred to were careful to keep some items of German military clothing in case of capture. They wouldn't have been Skorzeny's men, though. There were also stories of Germans driving Shermans, which was corroborated by a number of GIs. Some of this equipment had been purloined from the 106th Infantry Division that had been almost decimated out on the Schnee Eifel in Germany.

When Skorzeny's soldiers were captured, they told their interrogators their mission was to reach Paris and assassinate the Allied supreme commander, Gen. Dwight D. Eisenhower. This was an intentional lie. They had been instructed to say this purely to propagate unrest among the higher echelons, and it worked very well. When Eisenhower, at the Trianon Hotel in Versailles, heard Skorzeny was leading this clandestine operation, his headquarters was transformed into a veritable bastion. Tanks and machine guns were placed around the perimeter and the palace, and a doppelgänger was brought in to lure out any potential Nazi assassins. Eisenhower was just hedging his bets.

The disguised Germans may well have infiltrated the 101st perimeter at Bastogne. Staff Sergeant George Mullins recalled:

> The time moves slowly as the tank continues to fire in the valley a short distance in front of us. A lieutenant appears from behind us. I don't remember seeing him before. I feel there's something not right about this man. He looks way too clean and rested for my comfort.

He approaches and says to me and my machine gun squad, "The Germans are very close, just a short distance over the hill in front of you. You can fight it out with them or surrender. Do as you wish." He disappears as fast as he showed up. A few minutes later a trooper comes by telling us that someone is passing a rumor through the troops that we are surrounded. If the person spreading the rumor is caught, it will be a court-martial for him. This is not a threat, it's a promise. I chuckle as he leaves. I'm an Airborne trooper, we're always surrounded. Now I really begin to think about the lieutenant that just left. I'm pretty certain he was a German wearing a GI uniform. I never saw this man again.

On December 20, at 1:30 pm, operational control of all units in the Ardennes passed to General George Patton and his Third Army.

Team Hustead loaded up its wounded and prepared to leave Noville for the time being and head south to Bastogne. The retreat proved problematic from the offset. A thick fog enveloped the whole area again, reducing visibility to between 5 and 10 yards. While the combat for the 506th PIR moved from Noville to Recogne, a desperately nervous situation ensued as remnants of Team Hustead, heading towards Foy, were nearly sandwiched between the 77th Panzergrenadier and 26th Volksgrenadier Regiments. This had the potential to subject the fragile convoy to yet another running battle as it attempted to reach the relative safety of Bastogne. It also meant the 10th Armored Division's Combat Command B, the 705th Tank Destroyer Battalion, the 755th Field Artillery Battalion, and the 333rd Field Artillery Battalion would all become part of the 101st Airborne Division for the duration.

The 333rd was one of the only all-black units to fight in Bastogne. In most cases, black artillery battalions fought as part of white artillery groups. However, several times in the war, white artillery battalions worked under the command of a black artillery group led by black officers. While this mixture of battalions occurred episodically in Europe, nowhere was this level of unit integration more necessary or the ability of both units to cooperate more critical than during the siege of Bastogne. The 333rd and 969th Artillery Battalion were composed entirely of black soldiers; the latter was equipped with M1 155-mm howitzers, one of the heaviest pieces of artillery available to American forces at the time.

This was in contrast to the 101st, which was in effect a light Airborne unit with only 75-mm and 105-mm howitzers at its immediate disposal. Artillery played a vital part in the defense of the city. Before December 20, General McAuliffe had anticipated the prospect of becoming surrounded by German forces when he positioned available artillery units around Bastogne, capable of firing to all points of the compass on command. The 969th took up positions southwest of Bastogne near Villeroux. The Germans were close enough that the 969th suffered casualties from mortar and small-arms fire; the battalion had to pull back to Senochamps. Most of the battalion withdrew again to the vicinity of Bastogne itself on the afternoon of Christmas Eve, losing several men when German aircraft bombed the

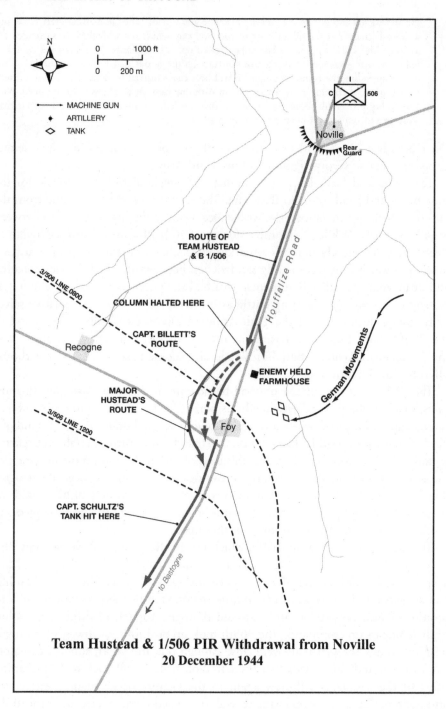

N

| 0 | 1000 ft |
| 0 | 200 m |

MACHINE GUN
ARTILLERY
TANK

ROUTE OF
TEAM HUSTEAD
& B 1/506

Houffalize Road

3/506 LINE 0800

COLUMN HALTED HERE

CAPT. BILLETT'S
ROUTE

Recogne

MAJOR
HUSTEAD'S
ROUTE

3/506 LINE 1200

Foy

CAPT. SCHULTZ'S
TANK HIT HERE

to Bastogne

Noville

Rear
Guard

ENEMY HELD
FARMHOUSE

German Movements

C   506

Team Hustead & 1/506 PIR Withdrawal from Noville
20 December 1944

town that night. The situation was changing by the hour as the following itinerary demonstrates. It also shows precisely how active this unit was:

> After Action Report [Extract DEC 1944–JAN 1945 redacted], 969th Field Artillery Battalion [155mm Towed]
> 20 December 1944, 0330 Call received from group re-enemy roadblock established to our rear. 0800 Call received from group stating that on receipt of our code word "Execute" bn would march through Bastogne to vicinity of St. Hubert. 0930. "Execute" received. Bn left its position for road march presumably to St. Hubert. Bn. pulled off road and went into position south of Bastogne. 1100 Bn was instructed to place unobserved fire on road North of Noville. "Execute" again received after enemy infantry approximately 10 had infiltrated into Battery area of 771st FA. 1440. Bn pulled off the road again into rendezvous area approximately 4 miles south of Bastogne.

Major General Troy Middleton and McAuliffe met in Neufchâteau, where the corps commander expressed his reservations regarding the prospect of being surrounded. It was the first time Middleton had voiced his trepidation on the subject. He told McAuliffe the German 116th Division was approaching from the north. This wasn't entirely accurate. The 116th was circumnavigating Bastogne, and never had the intention of striking out for it, but Middleton wouldn't have been aware of this. The German units in the north hadn't been redirected at the time; they had other issues to contend with and were more focused on getting to the River Meuse in the east. General Hasso von Manteuffel had no intention of attempting to capture Bastogne with the initial assault; he would eventually leave that task to the reserves in the second wave, but with some reservations, because at the time he was determined to reach his primary objective, which was also the Meuse.

During the meeting in Neufchâteau, Middleton expressed some reservations regarding the defense of Bastogne that he hadn't mentioned before. He said he wasn't entirely sure Bastogne could be held with the present units in place. Numerically, it probably could, but supplies were already running low. As the two generals parted company, Middleton said something to the effect of, "Don't get yourself surrounded, Tony," but apparently McAuliffe took the remark with some levity. Any jocularity would soon be dispelled. As soon as they parted company, the general told his driver to get back to Bastogne as fast as he could. The timing was incredibly fortuitous—just 30 minutes later, that same road to Neufchâteau was blocked by the Germans.

Even at that juncture, McAuliffe had suggested Middleton should take control of the 101st. The reasons for this aren't entirely clear, because the armor and infantry had worked quite well together, but McAuliffe felt there was a lack of cohesion between the two. It's fair to say there was often fierce competition between Allied armored and infantry divisions, but the differences would have become redundant when in combat.

Private Ralph King, a machine gunner with H Company, 506th PIR, recalled:

> On the 26th of September I was wounded in my wrist during the fights in the Netherlands and was taken to the hospital. I came back in time to the unit in Mourmelon before moving out to the Ardennes. On the 21st I was in the main line at Bois Champay where that morning the Germans were putting a hail of artillery fire on us with breaks in between.

During one of the barrages, King was wounded by shrapnel in his shoulder. "I was taken to route madam [sic] and put against a tree whilst sitting on the ground. Shortly after the medics arrived I was taken down to the military barracks at Bastogne. Opposite the rifle range was a makeshift hospital where they took me first and took care of my wounds." The 705th Tank Destroyer Battalion had set up an X-ray station and medics attached to the 81st AA were helping the wounded as well. After that he was taken to the rifle range which was used as a hospital for walking wounded. "It was bitterly cold in that place and the only thing that kept us from starving was bullion [sic] soup."

It transpired that neither command had a clear view of the situation. General Heinz Kokott, leading the 26th Volksgrenadier Division, wrote a rather premature assessment:

> The 2nd Panzer Division has taken Noville. The enemy is in flight-like retreat from Noville via Foy to the south. The Panzer Division is in pursuit. The fall of Foy, if not already taken place, is to be expected at any moment. After the capture of Foy, the 2nd Panzer Division, according to orders, turns to the west and drives into the open terra. The Panzer Lehr [sic] Division is still outside of Neffe, but has taken Wardin and is advancing quickly via Marvie. The enemy there was apparently weak and unprepared. Marvie possibly already taken by now?
>
> Impression of enemy: The enemy feels himself beaten, is retreating and is merely trying to cover his withdrawal through delaying resistance in the sector south of Foy–Bizory–Neffe. It is now the primary mission of the 26th Division with all its available elements to proceed via Wardin–Remoifosse for an encirclement of Bastogne from the south, then to penetrate Bastogne from the southwest or west. The Panzer Lehr Division, with main effort on the left near Marvie, will close in on Bastogne from the southeast. According to information from the Army, forward sections of the 5th Parachute Infantry Division are quickly thrusting forward to the Bastogne–Martelange highway via Lutremange–Harlange. No enemy forces opposite the right wing of the Seventh [sic] Army. Utmost speed is imperative for exploitation of the initial success.

Kokott was being marginally optimistic, but he had underestimated the defenders quite significantly, because the 5th Army commander, General von Manteuffel, didn't think the counteroffensive was proceeding as well as expected. One result was that the success of the 5th Panzer Army's initial attack had introduced an unofficial demarcation line that had isolated the northern sector from General Middleton's control of the VIII Corps line. Eisenhower made the controversial decision to appoint command of the northern half of the bulge to Field Marshal Montgomery, which in effect left Gen. Omar Bradley in charge of the area south of Bastogne. When Eisenhower imparted this news to his generals, it did not go down well. Montgomery remained impervious as always, but stating the line between him and Bradley wasn't very good was an understatement:

SHAEF STAFF MESSAGE CONTROL [redacted]
URGENT
FROM: EXFOR TAC, FROM FIELD MARSHAL MONTGOMERY
TO: SHAEF MAIN, FOR GENERAL EISENHOWER FOR HIS EYES ONLY
REF NO: 1-384, 20 December 1944
On receiving your instructions to take over command of the Northern Front I held a conference at 1400 hours today with HODGES and SIMPSON at Headquarters First Army and examined the battle situation. The front was in need of reorganization and I issued orders on this subject. I have arranged with BRADLEY that the boundary between us shall be the line GIVET PRUM: both places inclusive to me and I would be glad if you would confirm this with him as the line was not very good when I spoke. I have every hope that we shall be able to restore the situation and I see no need at present to give up any of the ground that has been gained in the last few weeks by such hard fighting.

Corporal William J. Stone, Battery B, 321st Glider Field Artillery Battalion, 101st Airborne, said:

The defense of Noville gave the other battalions of the 506th time to occupy and improve their positions astride the Bastogne–Noville Road just south of Foy. At 1:15 P.M. the order for the withdrawal came down to us on the artillery radio and we relayed it to the commander of the 1st Battalion. The German attack around the southern side of Noville was rapidly becoming more successful. Because of this, the Noville force was in danger of being cut off from the rest of the 506th and so there was little time to plan the withdrawal. Shortly after it began, we came under observation and direct artillery fire by the Germans on the high ground to the east. By this time we were traveling with the battalion commander. We told him that we could get artillery fire from the 321st on the enemy position. He told us to do it. (Note: I know that other measures were being taken at this time but I did not know of them and cannot describe them here.) We sent the fire mission down and while the fire was on the way, the battalion commander ordered the battalion to leave the road and continue the withdrawal on the western side of the road which was low ground, so low that it was not visible to the enemy. There was no clearly defined German front line and as I looked at the high ground to the east of the road, three German soldiers emerged from the woods 100 yards away. When they saw me they immediately surrendered.

Middleton had somewhat reluctantly agreed to a conditional withdrawal from Noville but only as far as Foy, which is closer to Bastogne. After Team Hustead returned to Bastogne, the 506th PIR was ordered to remain in Foy for the duration. The Noville garrison had lost 11 of its original 15 tanks, but in the process had inflicted terrible damage on the attacking German units and had held their ground for 48 pivotal hours. Out east, the remainder of Task Force Ryerson (formerly Team Cherry, Colonel Cherry was wounded in action) withdrew to the 501st PIR lines. The village of Neff was the scene of some vicious fighting but the 501st, assisted by tank destroyers, stopped the Germans in their tracks and inflicted some heavy casualties. German tanks and infantry had repeatedly attempted to take Marvie, where Team O'Hara and the 327th Glider Infantry Regiment were ensconced, but were repeatedly driven out. From December 20, all units within the perimeter of Bastogne were assigned to McAuliffe by General Middleton. There was still a hard fight ahead, ammunition was running low, along with all other supplies, and the skies above Bastogne stubbornly refused to clear.

CHAPTER NINE

We're Running Out of Everything

But our most critical concern was that our ammunition had dropped to a dangerous
level, which drastically curtailed fire missions.

THADDEUS KRASNOBORSKI, HQ, 420TH ARMORED FIELD ARTILLERY BATTALION

Two tank destroyers of the 2nd Platoon, C Company, 705th Tank Destroyer
Battalion, positioned to the south and southeast of Noville heard the rumble of
German tracks but couldn't discern where the noise was coming from. Then, as
suddenly as it had descended, the fog lifted, revealing what the defenders of Noville
had suspected. Fifteen German tanks were moving in for the kill from about a
1,000-yard range. The 705th immediately got to work and soon disabled four of
them. This all too brief clear spell also revealed German vehicles in proximity to Foy
and Recogne, effectively blocking the return route south to Bastogne.

The 506th Parachute Infantry Regiment (PIR) launched a diversionary attack on
Foy to provide the defenders of Noville an escape route south. While C Company
assumed reserve positions south of Noville with three tanks to support them, A
Company would lead the breakout to Bastogne; B Company, commanded by Capt.
George Primrose, remained behind. Priority was given to the wounded who occupied
the lead vehicles. Major Charles Hustead insisted on being the last person to leave
the village. Before he left, he and Lieutenant Frank, an officer from the engineers,
gathered as much unused ammunition as they could and stacked it against an empty
building. The purpose was to demolish an already teetering structure and block the
main road through Noville. Then, as the fog closed in again, and the column moved
south, a huge explosion was heard, signaling that the arms dump had detonated.

The first opposition the column encountered came from a small group of German
infantry hunkered down in a farmhouse astride the Bastogne–Houffalize highway
that ran through Noville. Hustead's lead vehicle received a barrage of small-arms fire
and "potato-masher" grenades from the farmhouse, which completely shattered the
windscreen of the lead half-track, before the other American half-tracks responded
with their .50-cal machine guns, terminating the exchange in about ten minutes.
When Hustead dispatched two Shermans to finish off the farmhouse, he could

clearly hear an exchange of fire almost directly south of their position, which led him to assume the way ahead was still going to be difficult.

As the column prepared to continue heading south, three German tanks appeared on a low ridge to the east and disabled two of Hustead's lead Shermans. A tank destroyer of the 705th drove up to assist the temporarily stalled column and return fire. In the process, the crew being so eager to join the fight as they maneuvered into position, it almost flattened an American jeep. Meanwhile, the Germans destroyed four of Hustead's tanks and left the fifth one bereft of a driver. The tank destroyer's crew's nerves jangled as the turret of one of the Shermans was completely blown off nearby. The paratroopers in the column dismounted their vehicles and walked towards Foy astride both sides of the highway. The line on the left didn't get much further than the farmhouse, but the group on the right comfortably reached Foy, and even took a few German prisoners while they were at it. Sergeant Carl Dickinson, part of the 327th Medical Detachment, remembered:

> Our aid station was full, and we opened another cellar. It was obvious that our losses were making gaps in our line which could not be plugged. The Command Post personnel, switchboard operators, clerks, also slightly wounded men, were sent to the companies. There was a lull, but we could see the tanks reforming. We had no communication with Bastogne. A half-track, which contained radio equipment that wouldn't work, was loaded with several badly wounded men, who were obviously going to die without attention, and was ordered to try to force the way back to Bastogne. The message I sent was: "Casualties heavy. No more armor-piercing ammunition. Request reinforcements, ammunition, and medic supplies. The vehicle left but did not return, although I found out later that it had forced the road block and gotten through.
>
> About 10 o'clock we briefly contacted the regiment by radio. I was afraid to tell our true situation over the air, and the message we received was "Hold at all costs." That cost began to mount then, with a tank attack right down the road. Part of our infantry positions were lost, but the tank destroyers got their 20th tank, which burned at the edge of town setting fire to one of the few whole buildings. The situation was now so acute that I called in the company and tank commanders. Another attack, surely two would end the affair for us. We drew up plans to fight a withdrawal. A jeep with two wounded men and a messenger who volunteered was sent down the road. The message was to General McAuliffe. It just said: "We can hold out but not indefinitely." There was no answer. About 1230 a radio operator in a tank picked up a message telling the armored units to assist the infantry in fighting it out.

There were many acts of bravery performed during this tactical retreat. German infantry had surreptitiously entered Foy during the night, isolating the Noville garrison, so they could deliver a withering fusillade of machine-gun fire over the path of their retreat. Shrapnel from exploding mortar shells reduced nearby trees to matchwood and caused a lot of GIs to hit the deck or dive into roadside ditches. The small-arms fire intensified as the head of the column, moving down both sides of the highway, reached Foy. The column returned fire but something more was required.

This was the cue for Capt. Rennie Tye to execute a suicidal dash through the temporarily German-held village. As described in a *The Saturday Evening Post* article of the time:

Lying flat on the hood of a speeding jeep with an automatic in his hand, Tye raced through Foy, firing until his ammunition was expended. One of two wounded men in the jeep was killed outright by a German machine gunner, but Tye remained untouched, and within an hour a rescue battalion had stormed Foy from the south and freed the trapped column.

This daring action allowed the column to continue to Bastogne. Corps headquarters called Gen. Anthony McAuliffe to inform him he could use the Neufchâteau road to retreat if necessary; the general laughed raucously at the mere suggestion and hung up. When word came to Lt. Col. Paul Danahy, the division intelligence man, that Bastogne could be surrounded, "the irrepressible young staff officer cracked, 'Good. Now we can attack in any direction.'"

> After Action report Company C, 609th TD Battalion. December 20, 1944.
> The Third Platoon assisted in repulsing enemy attacks on Noville by destroying 11 Mk V tanks and 1 Mk VI Tiger. An estimated 45 enemy tanks took part in the attack. In addition the destroyers fired numerous rounds of 76mm HE [High Explosive] and 50 cal HMG into woods at enemy infantry and MG's. The platoon acted as rear guard upon the evacuation of Noville and fought a continuously delaying action to Foy, causing considerable casualties to enemy infantry. The platoon returned to Bastogne. One Destroyer was lost to enemy AT Fire. One man killed and 6 wounded. The Second Platoon remained in position SE of Bastogne. Rcn Platoon was ordered to place a road block supporting the Second Platoon. Both platoons received heavy artillery, mortar and high velocity fire.

After evacuating south under fire from Noville, Combat Command B (CCB) set up an aid station on the southwest side of Bastogne in a three-story building with a grocery store named "Sarma," located just a few yards from the city's main square on Rue Neufchâteau. The aid station had lost much of its equipment and supplies, so it lacked even necessities such as scalpels, antiseptic, and morphine. The medical personnel scavenged some meager medical supplies and acquired two Belgian nurses who volunteered to help. The surgeons could only treat walking wounded and less serious cases since none had the training to perform major surgery. "The patients who had head, chest, and abdominal wounds could only face certain slow death," remembered battalion surgeon 1Lt. John "Jack" Prior.

December 20, out in Marvie, Team O'Hara had been actively engaged attempting to repulse successive German attacks throughout the day, which had started early, when enemy artillery shells began exploding close by O'Hara's positions. Marvie was occupied at the time by the 326th Airborne Engineer Battalion, which was establishing roadblocks at access points to the village. The unit had been augmented by the 2nd Battalion, 327th Glider Infantry Regiment (GIR), by the time the first serious attack happened.

German troops assaulted the village with elements of the Panzer-Lehr Division that attacked from the southeast; both sides physically clashed in the center of Marvie. Counterattacks by the Americans, however, succeeded in repulsing the German troops and enabled most civilians to evacuate the village. This act of

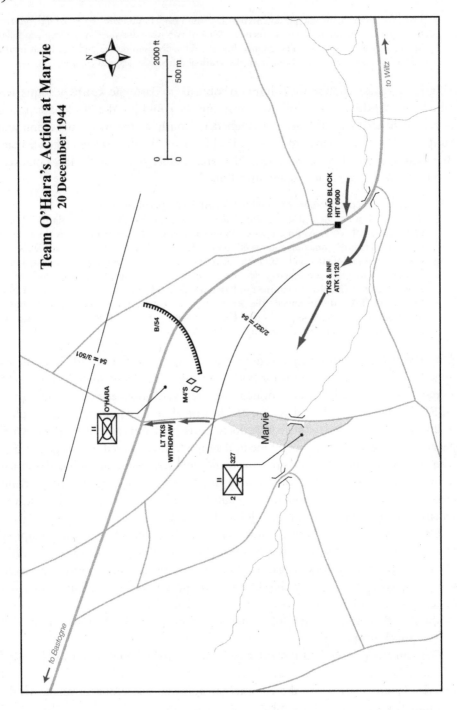

Team O'Hara's Action at Marvie
20 December 1944

humanity on behalf of the 101st Airborne Division greatly endeared the locals to these baggy-trousered soldiers, even though most of their homes were reduced to ashes and rubble. Thankfully, most of the civilians had already left thanks to the local priest mentioned earlier.

Like the team up in Noville, all actions and encounters were hampered by poor visibility. At 11:00 am, the 327th GIR's 2nd Battalion was attempting to relieve the 326th Engineers when it began to receive a barrage of incoming artillery. Shortly after, four Mark IV tanks, a self-propelled 75-mm gun, and six half-tracks carrying infantry emerged from the woods just east of Marvie. Lieutenant Colonel James O'Hara replied by sending his M5 Stuart tanks, which were equipped with 37-mm guns that proved largely ineffectual against German armor. Meanwhile, he had positioned two medium tanks on a nearby hillside just to the south that held their fire in anticipation of a broader German advance. The Stuarts hadn't really helped the glider men, in fact they proved to be more of a hindrance than an asset as the Germans directed fire against them.

As the 327th men attempted to evade the incoming German armor inside Marvie, the light tank commander realized his vehicles were doing more harm than good and, on that premise, and with O'Hara's express permission, decided to retreat to a safer position. This drew the German tanks out into the open as O'Hara had expected and was the opportunity he had been waiting for. O'Hara's Sherman M4s on the hillside opened up with a withering broadside against the Mark IVs and half-tracks, at a range of roughly seven hundred yards. The ensuing fight lasted for over two hours, with the 327th fighting literally from house to house. By the time the firing dissipated, 30 German soldiers had been killed and the rest taken prisoner. This attack was effectively repulsed but complacency wasn't on the agenda, because more hell was on the way.

By midnight December 20, once the road to Neufchâteau had been severed by the Germans, Bastogne became a city surrounded. The following morning, the encirclement was complete. This didn't come as a particular surprise for the defenders, but from this point on there was no physical contact with Allied forces outside the newly established perimeter. The strategic situation for the Airborne was that the 502nd PIR now occupied the northern area, which extended west where it joined the 327th GIR and east to the 506th PIR. Bordering the 506th was the 501st PIR, which effectively sealed any remaining gaps with the 327th GIR.

The following entry is from the 506th PIR's regimental diary:

DECLASSIFIED December 20/21, 1944[1]
Withdrew to the northeast. At 1130 hours, at 560555, four German tanks, a number of half-tracks, and at length 100 infantry, supported by artillery fire, attacked the Second Battalion. At 1245 hours the enemy withdrew. They had lost two tanks and one half-track. This battalion then occupied Marvie, Belgium (575560). The rest of the day, Germans on the Second

---

[1] Museum Copy. Provided by official 101st Airborne Historian Patrick Seeling.

Battalion front appeared to be organizing and consolidating for attacks with armor and infantry. Only intermittent enemy artillery fire and small arms fire were encountered until morning, 21 December. Eighteen prisoners had been taken on 20 December by the Second Battalion. On 20 December all roads leading from Bastogne were cut by the Germans and American forces in the Bastogne area were completely surrounded. By the morning of 21 December the Regiment had been entirely committed, each battalion fighting, separately. The First Battalion was with the 501 Parachute Infantry; the Second Battalion was at Marvie, and the Third Battalion was still holding the road and surrounding area where they had been sent the night before, about six miles northwest of Bastogne. No definite enemy line could be reported on the Third Battalion sector, but German troops and armor were seen at Givroulle (4864), and at Salle (469639). Company "B," Third Battalion had been sent two miles northwest of the other companies of the battalion to hold a road block and to "assist the Division medical Company" which had been attacked. The Salle concentration was confirmed when at 0330 hours German forces advanced against Company "B" but the enemy met intense resistance. After the Germans lost two tanks, four half-tracks, and three personnel carriers, they withdrew to the east.

On the Second Battalion front the German line could be rather definitely established, generally along coordinates from 587553 southwest to 577543 and west to 565543. They shelled Marvie heavily at 1300 hours and again at 1350 hours. Intermittent shelling was continuous. A strong German force attempted to drive around the right flank of the Second Battalion, but a platoon of Company "G" was sent there where it repulsed the attack. Meanwhile enemy movements threatened to cut off the road the Third Battalion was astride, this blocking the battalion's progress to Bastogne. Company "C," Third Battalion was moved with two attached tank destroyers to meet the attack but it did not develop. However, at this time Company "B" of this battalion was attacked by a patrol from the east at a cross-road at 448630. They repulsed the attack, took two prisoners, and then, on Division orders, moved back to join the Third Battalion.

The 506th PIR occupied the woods at a place called Bois Jacques, which is on the left side of a small road that runs between Bizory and Foy. Precisely who "Jacques" was, and why this small wood was named after him, has never been definitively ascertained, but it's rumored he might have been a local farmer. The 506th had the 501st PIR on its right flank and was directly across the road from the German positions. The 3rd Battalion of the 506th was directly on E Company's left flank and "Easy," "Fox," and "Dog" Companies occupied the center and right flank of the line during the battle. Captain Richard Winters established the 2nd Battalion command post far enough behind the line to prevent harassment from small-arms fire, but in close enough proximity to maintain contact with the ebb and flow of the battle.

The whole perimeter was supported by armor and field artillery provided by the remnants of the three teams. The 326th Combat Engineers and 54th Armored Infantry Battalion reinforced the center of the 327th GIR's lines. The supply situation for all units was reaching critical proportions. As early as December 21, urgent radio messages were dispatched from the 101st headquarters in Bastogne to VIII Corps requesting an urgent resupply air drop. In his memoirs, General Eisenhower stated, "As long as the weather kept our planes on the ground it would be an ally of the enemy worth many additional divisions." Technical Sergeant Thaddeus Krasnoborski, 420th Armored Field Artillery Battalion, remembered the situation only too well:

Headquarters was set up in a large well-constructed barn just west of Bastogne. I remember steel beams and concrete in some sections. There was a large hayloft overhead. (For the life of me I can't remember sleeping there.) This location turned out to be our final move from whence we fought the rest of the battle. We were running out of food and the most foul C-rations I had ever tasted (which I could not eat) was all that was available. Finally the cooks liberated the farmer's entire chicken coop and we had one decent meal. But our most critical concern was that our ammunition had dropped to a dangerous level, which drastically curtailed fire missions.

The grave site of one Airborne soldier was adopted by a German person, who cares for it to this day. Private Charles L. Hunt, Headquarters Company, 3rd Battalion, 506th PIR, 101st Airborne Division, jumped off the back of a truck at Champs, Belgium, during the early morning of December 19. Marching into Bastogne and further north towards Noville, Pvt. Hunt took part in defending the town of Foy. In the course of the German attack on Foy on December 21, Hunt was reported missing in action. This was not recorded in the company's morning report before January 5, 1945. His young wife was notified on January 20. The exact location of his loss is not given in his military records, however, within the historical context, he made the ultimate sacrifice somewhere around Route Madame between Foy and Recogne during a German artillery barrage. He was hit by shrapnel from an artillery shell.

It remains unknown when he was recovered from the battlefield, but Pvt. Hunt was buried on February 20, 1945, at the American cemetery at Foy. A memorial in front of the field where the cemetery was remembers the 2,701 American servicemen once buried there. In 1949, Pvt. Hunt had found his final resting place at Henri-Chapelle American Cemetery, Belgium.[2]

The remarkable fact that emerges on December 21 is that, although many previous books on the subject claim there wasn't much enemy activity on this date, the Germans continued to send in probing attacks, which were all successfully repulsed before they could gain any ground. Many previous books almost discount December 21 as a day when not much happened. Shrinking the perimeter had been an intelligent and necessary move to shore up the defenses, and despite fuel, ammunition, and medical shortages, the Germans weren't having it all their own way by a long chalk.

Fuel was a constantly mitigating factor for all three attacking armies. Hardly any of the German units had received their promised provision. Although some fuel was captured from the Americans, it was nowhere near enough to maintain momentum.

December 21 saw the 2nd Panzer Division fail to make a bridgehead at the village of Tenneville, just a few miles northwest of Bastogne, due to ongoing fuel shortages. German supply vehicles were also experiencing significant problems when they attempted to provide fuel to units in the field by night. In many cases, they failed to locate the units and were frequently delayed by self-imposed gridlocks. German high command had decided Bastogne must be taken by December 22. General Heinrich von Lüttwitz, commander of the Panzer Corps, regarded this

---

[2] Information provided by Carsten Krikorka.

request as perfectly feasible. For this purpose, the 26th Volksgrenadier Division would be augmented by 15 Panther tanks provided by Gen. Fritz Bayerlein's Panzer-Lehr Division, which would also release the 901st Regiment along with additional artillery support and the 5th Fallschirmjäger Division. The decision was made to attack from the west, which the Germans considered less well defended, although the line of defense hadn't been broken there. General Hasso von Manteuffel made a formal request for reinforcements to achieve this aim, but therein lay the problem. His request fell on deaf ears because OB West (Oberbefehlshaber—high commander—West) refused to authorize the release of sufficient additional forces to capture Bastogne and keep the vacillating offensive alive.

By this time, the 327th GIR was now covering almost half of the Bastogne perimeter, which qualified the unit to receive armor reinforcements from CCB along with a few tank destroyers. Still holding on in the east, O'Hara closed the circle on his right flank when he connected with Lt. Col. Julian Ewell's 501st PIR.

Although American forces were now decisively surrounded, it should be noted this was a regular state of affairs for an Airborne unit. Stephen Ambrose wrote a quote in his famous book *Band of Brothers*—"They've got us surrounded, the poor bastards"—but this was probably jingoistic conjecture, because he didn't attribute it to any one person. Apparently, it was made by a medic who was telling an injured corporal why none of the wounded had been evacuated.

Sergeant Robert T. Harrison, 3rd Battalion, 502nd PIR, 101st Airborne Division, remembered the conditions and the supply issues. His narrative is a little eclectic, but this an abridged version:

> They'd moved our base camp from England to France, and our camp was at Mourmelon. Not too far from Rheims [*sic*]. What they moved us to was an old French army fort. It was nice, brick buildings, they moved us into these brick buildings, and they moved us into these buildings, we weren't there very long. They were sending a company of men every three days to Paris for R&R. Take up a load, three days then bring back a load. I was supposed to go to Paris this one day. So that day we pressed our uniforms, shined our boots, because before all our uniforms were packed into duffel bags all the time we was in Holland. First four days in Holland we lost 420 men killed and 29 officers, and probably three times that many was wounded. That was for four days fighting in Holland.
>
> The first day in Bastogne the Germans captured our hospital unit. They took everything, took the doctors, the medicines, everything, all the medical help, took them all prisoner. They shot some of them. So that left us without a hospital. So the men that was getting wounded was just getting first aid, there wasn't much more they could do for them. The guys in my regiment were hauled back to regiment, there was a big barn there. They laid them out on the floor in the barn, and it was cold. It got down to 10, 20c below zero, and we're outside in the foxholes at 20c below zero. In the daytime maybe you could build a fire, get warm and then run back to your foxhole. But at night you couldn't make no fires so you just had to put up with the cold. A lot of guys had frostbitten hands, feet, everybody had cold feet. This went on for a while. We couldn't get no supplies. The weather had closed in. They couldn't fly planes, we couldn't get nothing.

In my platoon, where we were at was by a farm and there was a razorback hog there. We killed the hog and hung him in a tree. We had a little frying pan, a skillet, and the farmer had potatoes buried, if you ever see them. They put them up in a mound, put straw over them and put dirt on them. Well we'd dig potatoes out of that potato mound, take them down to the run [stream], wash em off. Had to break the ice in the run. We didn't peel them, we just sliced them in there. Broke a piece of that pork off, the fat, and put it in that skillet on a wood fire and put a piece of meat in there with it. Let them cook for a little bit, dump it into your mess gear, then let somebody else use the skillet. We had to keep passing it around. That's all we'd get to eat all day long. We had no salt and pepper, no butter, no bread, no coffee. All we had was that little piece of meat and some fried potatoes, that is what we had to eat. Then somebody got the word, regiment got the word. Somebody found out that we had a hog and potato mound. So they sent a truck up and said, if you guys got to eat, everybody's got eat. So they took our hog and took our potatoes. Then they'd make like a stew out of it. Once a day they'd bring that stew up, but by the time it got to us it was cold. We were running out of ammunition, medical supplies, running out of supplies, running out of everything. I never even seen Bastogne until the day we left.

All American units in the field and in Bastogne were running out of supplies; the 463rd Parachute Field Artillery stated that supplies of high-explosive ammunition had dwindled to the point where they were insufficient to support heavy indirect-fire missions. Fortunately, the 463rd still had some armor-piercing ammunition it had obtained in Italy. This ammunition had not been listed on unit ammunition reports but would come in handy. Emergency messages were sent to VIII Corps headquarters to provide a resupply air drop. The message was then passed along to the Third Army with a veritable shopping list of urgently needed provisions. This was passed on to IX Troop Carrier Command in England, but air resupply couldn't happen until the skies were clear and conducive for such an operation. So, for the time being, the defenders of Bastogne had to bite the bullet and hold on with every sinew and every ounce of courage they could muster.

CHAPTER TEN

The Value of Momentum

Clean or dry socks became a rarity and although all commanders tried to prevent frozen feet and trench foot some cases developed later. However the men withstood a tremendous amount of cold and pain with very little complaint.

ROBERT B. GALBRAITH, 2ND BATTALION, 327TH GLIDER INFANTRY REGIMENT, 101ST AIRBORNE DIVISION

During the night of December 20, the first significant snowfall occurred, which turned the ground from wet and mud bound to insensibly frozen. This proved somewhat advantageous for the defenders who discovered it was easier to displace armor across the frozen earth. But the all-consuming cold also debilitated many. Those defenders were rightfully jealous of the insulated German white camouflage suits, which also allowed the wearer free movement and provided tactical advantage in snowy conditions.

By December 21, the 101st Airborne Division and subordinate units were completely surrounded. German forces that hadn't been ordered to head west continued to send in armor and infantry and, in some cases, they made incursions into the American lines, but these sporadic attacks actually worked to the defenders' advantage. It provided both 101st Airborne's infantry and artillery battalions the opportunity to concentrate their fire on a single area; even though ammunition supply was running dangerously low, they still managed to successfully resist all attacks.

Landlines to VIII Corps in Neufchâteau had been severed, but radio communications were still possible. In addition, radio-link equipment provided by VIII Corps' signal company preserved radio-telephone and teletype facilities for the duration of the siege. Thanks to this, the 101st in Bastogne was indeed surrounded but never completely isolated.

December 21 didn't see a great deal of activity. Major Robert B. Galbraith, 2nd Battalion, 327th Glider Infantry Regiment (GIR), reported that:

Some patrolling was felt by the 2d Battalion. K rations were supplemented by potatoes and hams found in Marvie. Fire units from field ranges were used in the company areas in an effort to provide some facilities for hot food and water. Plans were made to bring a few men at a

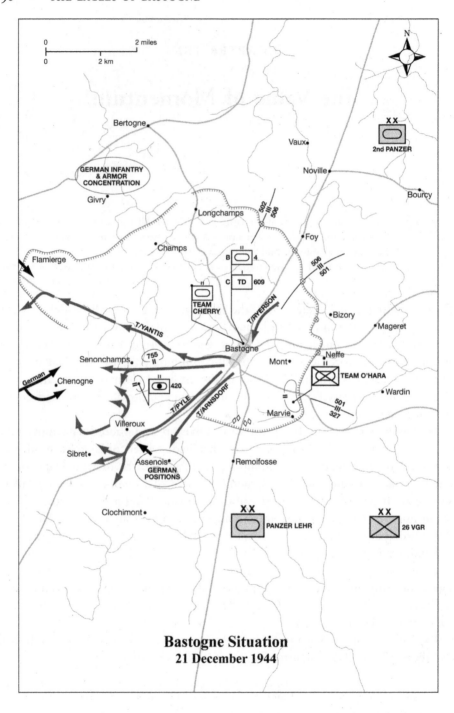

Bastogne Situation
21 December 1944

time into houses to warm themselves and dry out their shoes and clothing. Clean or dry socks became a rarity and although all commanders tried to prevent frozen feet and trench foot some cases developed later. However the men withstood a tremendous amount of cold and pain with very little complaint. The right flank of the battalion was given additional strength by attaching the platoon of G Company which had been held in reserve, to F Company in order to protect the right flank of the battalion.

The 326th Airborne Engineer Battalion was covering part of a gap which extended to the northwest. Neither they nor the 2d Battalion had sufficient troops to close it. Good firm contact was never made here although the ground was open and during the day could be covered by fire, at night some contact patrolling was possible though difficult through the snow drifts. The battalion reserve now consisted of administrative and supply personnel.

While some German officers said Bastogne didn't really need to be captured, and that it would have been sufficient to maintain the city under siege and circumnavigate it, others regarded it as integral for the delivery of supplies to front-line German divisions. They thought it would be sufficient to simply keep the supply lines to Germany open. During the Battle of the Bulge, a similar situation had evolved in the north with the town of Malmedy, where the 1st Division SS "Leibstandarte Adolf Hitler" ("personal bodyguard …") had gone around the city and saved expending troops on its capture. But Malmedy wasn't as integral to the German attack as Bastogne was at the time.

Many previous volumes on the subject claim Gen. Hasso von Manteuffel, the 5th Army commander, regarded Bastogne's actual capture as a secondary consideration, but he also knew full well how to follow orders, even when they didn't correspond with his preferences. He claimed his 5th Panzer Army was falling behind schedule and would later state, in no uncertain terms, that the combined German panzer armies had begun to lose momentum as early as December 18. His primary consideration at the outset was the capture of Sankt Vith, not Bastogne.

By December 21, his army in the field was also suffering from supply issues and von Manteuffel complained bitterly that he only received one-and-a-half units of fuel to sustain his forces for the duration. He realized it would be difficult to bring forward artillery and rocket artillery after the offensive started. The lack of ammunition, and lack of precise knowledge of American positions, meant 5th Army artillery batteries were compelled to confine their fire to recognized, and clearly identified, American positions where opposing batteries were located. The problem with this directive was that most of the American artillery was mobile, with the exception of the 155s, but even some of those could be redeployed where they were required.

The German units instructed to head west were strung out along various roads and had, in some cases, been compelled to use secondary routes where they faced serious opposition, which further depleted their ammunition and reduced the vital but limited fuel resources available.

Meanwhile, the 3rd Battalion of the 327th GIR was causing even more significant headaches for the Germans attempting to strike west. According to the unit's regimental diary, by the morning of December 21, the regiment had been entirely committed, each battalion fighting separately. The 1st Battalion was with the 501st Parachute Infantry Regiment (PIR). The 2nd Battalion was at Marvie, and the 3rd Battalion was still holding the road and surrounding area where it had initially been sent, roughly six miles northwest of Bastogne. No enemy infantry line was seen in the 3rd Battalion sector, but German troops and armor were identified at Givroulle and at Salle. This was the furthest, and one of the best, western outposts of the 101st, where the 327th executed what could be aptly described as the "perfect ambush."

The B Company men were well hidden on a small rise astride the highway when the Germans approached. They allowed the enemy to reach within twenty-five yards of their position before giving the order to open fire with every weapon at their disposal. The result was entirely predictable and within minutes smoldering hulks of German vehicles stood abandoned, surrounded by the bodies of around fifty dead and mutilated German infantry. The Americans didn't concede a single casualty on that occasion but, despite this, B Company was ordered to retreat east, where it could be closer to Bastogne.

The German officer at the vanguard of his unit sent an alarming message to his superiors describing the roadblock as being held by a very powerful and significant force. His apprehension, and complete overestimation of the situation, cost his comrades valuable time, time they could ill afford to lose. One of the reasons for this assessment was that the attacking troops had been subjected to the "Meat Chopper," among other things.

The M45 Quadmount (nicknamed the "Quad 50" and "Meat Chopper" for its high rate of fire) was introduced in 1943. It had four standard Browning .50-caliber M2 heavy barrel, turret-type machine guns, operated electrically by a single gunner firing a murderous 1,600 rounds per minute, with ammunition fed by outboard magazines (trunnions). With a rate of fire that intense, it wasn't unusual for the operators to sustain first and third degree burns when changing out the barrels, but it did considerably more damage to the Germans. Modern soldiers describe a single M2 .50-cal as turning cover into concealment. Four of these guns have the potential to turn almost any area into a killing field.

Major Robert J. MacDonald, who was with the 3rd Battalion, reported that:

> Lieutenant Colonel Allen said to dig in and hold the road junction at all costs. By 0800 we were dug in and prepared to carry out our mission. In this position we were over 4000 yards from the closest friendly troops with no artillery until an observer from the 333rd Artillery reported to me. This officer was not in contact with division artillery but offered his services in any way he could help. By 1000 fog came in so thick that visibility wasn't over thirty feet. Two Mark-V tanks rumbled towards our position from the direction of Salle. They stopped fifty yards from the road junction, pulled off the road, fired all their machine gun ammunition over our heads, waited, turned around, and left. Still we had no casualties. Apparently the Kraut tankers weren't too anxious to find out whether we were still at the junction or not after taking such a sound shellacking the night before. Dawn brought forth a dirty grey misting day. It would be another one without the P-47s we all knew. Some men were moving about and

others merely stayed in their holes cooking their K rations. I was in the Command Post when all in a sudden hell broke loose.

All the shooting was taking place in the area of the third platoon. I ran to a spot where I could see what was going on. It was a good sight, the best my eyes had seen in a long time. Those men had trapped a German convoy of nine flak wagons towing artillery pieces moving across their front. They were literally cutting it to ribbons as it sat there helplessly 75 yards directly in front of them. They had battle-wise non-coms and they were all experts at their business. They had initially knocked out the lead vehicle and the last. The rest couldn't move so they picked them off one by one at their leisure. When the last vehicle had been demolished I notified Lt. Col Allen what had taken place. He was jubilant, as was General McAuliffe when he got the news. Incidentally, we felt pretty good about it ourselves.

One hour later two tanks approached from the direction of Marche. A very unique anti-tank defense was worked successfully by two bazooka teams of the company on these tanks. It went something like this. The leading tank would shoot up the road toward our position. The instant that the shell would explode one rocket launcher team -would rush out on the road and fire at the tank. As soon as they had fired they would rush back off the road. The tank would again fire and then the second rocket launcher team would double time out on the road and shoot. Considering that they were firing at a range of two hundred yards, I think it is quite an amazing feat that they knocked the leading tank out on the third round.

Shortly after 1200 we repulsed another probing infantry tank attack with severe losses to the enemy infantry. At this time we were ordered to pull back to the battalion perimeter some three miles to the rear. This was accomplished in thirty minutes by using the transportation we had captured at the roadblock.

Shrinking the defensive perimeter had been a tactically sound move at all levels. The CCB (Combat Command B) teams, with assistance from the 101st Airborne, had done their jobs and caused havoc among the attackers; now American defenders had the opportunity to displace when and where required, and harass the Germans from any chosen direction. The initial response to the emerging crisis in the Belgian Ardennes may have been a little lethargic in some respects, but now it was seriously getting into gear. The 50 tanks the 101st had at its disposal could be effectively employed as a mobile counterattack force. The carefully selected string of Airborne foxhole networks had been positioned with good fields of fire, which constantly frustrated German infantry attacks, without requiring assistance from the CCB Sherman tanks or available tank destroyers.

First Lieutenant Fred A. Bahlau, a double Silver Star recipient and member of H Company, 506th PIR, 101st Airborne Division, was part of the defense:

The big old problem, the big one that was up at Bastogne. Who in the world had ever heard of Bastogne, or Belgium really. Nobody. The Germans had to get through there, they had a lot of troops over there. There was 7 different roads, I did know that for a long time. I don't think the general knew a lot more than us. General McAuliffe was there. Our real general, he was back in the states. We had to spread them out so we were forming a circle right around Bastogne. We formed a ring and they could not break us.

Von Manteuffel had exacerbated his growing logistical conundrums by instructing his two strongest units, the 116th and 2nd Panzer Divisions to forget Bastogne and head west. But while Bastogne remained in American hands, they were forced to take circuitous routes north and south of the city respectively. This saddled the 26th Volksgrenadier and Panzer-Lehr Divisions with the daunting task of attempting to secure and neutralize the city. Those two German divisions had neither the resources nor the ability to capture Bastogne without the 116th and 2nd Panzer; even then it's highly debatable it could have been achieved. The most serious weakness of the German forces in the west was not confined to the shortage of men and materiel, but the general absence of a unified command. While Gen. Gerd von Rundstedt's name was linked to the Battle of the Bulge, his influence at that stage in the war was negligible and far from adequate to tackle the job in hand.

As early as December 17, Gen. Troy Middleton's VIII Corps had absorbed the brunt of the 5th Panzer Army's attack. Granted, in those first few days, there was complacency on both sides, but once the 10th Armored Division's CCB had arrived and once the 101st Airborne Division managed to retain and reinforce an expertly layered defense in depth surrounding Bastogne, the Germans never really had a realistic chance of capturing and occupying the city.

Fuel remained a pervasive and debilitating problem for all German units in the field. Unterscharführer (junior squad leader) Hans Baumann, 12th SS Division "Hitler Jugend," had been fighting on the northern shoulder. He was sent to Noville after it was captured to procure fuel for his newly acquired JagdPanzer IV. His first one had taken a direct hit at Rochrath; he was the only survivor. When he arrived in Noville, he literally begged officers from the 2nd Panzer Division but discovered, to his great disappointment, there was absolutely none to spare. So, he abandoned the vehicle and walked back to Germany.

The 5th Panzer Army was advancing roughly eight-and-a-half miles per day, which would culminate in around sixty miles in seven days, nowhere near fast enough for the purpose. Getting to Antwerp was a pipedream that could never have been accomplished without sufficient fuel. Moreover, the stressed importance of Bastogne at that juncture badly constricted the style of Field Marshal Walter Model's initial plan of attack.

Gefreite (private) Jürgen Tegethoff, 3rd Company, Schwere Panzer-Abteilung 506, said:

> At 18 I was assigned to a company as a lieutenant. The army was held together with command and obedience, when I said something had to be done, then that was done. We had something called "Panzerschokolade" [Tank chocolate]. It was provided in case we were trapped in our tanks, but that was never the case. In fact we ate it as soon as it was given. We thought, what's the point in saving this if we get shot up. Eating any rations in advance was strictly forbidden but we did it anyway. I preferred "soft targets" infantry units or houses or such like. I would give the order, then the gunner rotated the turret, and then I said: "Aim and fire at will."

"Panzerschokolade," was distributed to Wehrmacht soldiers. This so-called chocolate was laced with the stimulant Pervitin, which was used by German forces ubiquitously in World War II. Pervitin tablets were very popular in Germany and could be purchased without a prescription in pharmacies. One could even buy boxed chocolates spiked with this methamphetamine. The purpose was to keep them focused and wide awake. The modern equivalent today is known as crystal meth. It was the first large-scale use of a synthetic performance-enhancing drug. To what extent Wehrmacht soldiers received Pervitin is unclear. However, it is clear this particular tank commander enjoyed his ration, whenever it was supplied.

In the spring of 1943, Tegethoff was deployed to the Eastern Front near Stalingrad, where he was badly wounded. In the summer of 1944, he returned to Paderborn in Germany to take charge of a new tank. Then he experienced the Battle of the Bulge full on and was present at the siege of Bastogne.

It wasn't just the Germans who used performance-enhancing drugs. Admittedly, Benzedrine wasn't as dangerous as Pervitin, but the drug still carried risks. Both British and American armed forces embraced amphetamine use even though, at the time, the drug had not been adequately proven to boost performance in fatigued subjects. These days, amphetamines are recognized as having a high risk of addiction and abuse but, in 1940s scientific literature, experts utterly dismissed this notion.

Thankfully, the Airborne men defending Bastogne would have been largely oblivious to the fact they were possibly being assaulted by drug-addled soldiers; they had other matters to contend with. Morale remained relatively high among the troops guarding the perimeter, but they weren't all doing things by the book. One particular paratrooper from the 502nd PIR had discipline and kleptomaniacal issues. Staff Sergeant Earl R. Kelly, I Company, 3rd Battalion, said:

> I told them before when we went into Bastogne, the problem I had, stealing jeeps and that. The Military Police were looking for the driver, I gave it to them, which was comical and that was the kind of stuff I did. Like beating a 1st Sergeant up, and I'm not proud of that but I did it, real bad. Everybody else liked it. Everybody hated him but I was the only one who did anything about it. I said to my buddy, "I feel really bad about that," he said, "Why feel bad about it. You saved his life," "How did I save his life," I asked? "Because I would have killed him," my buddy replied. I talked to another buddy, Chester Elliot who told me the same thing, "I was gonna kill him," and they would have.

On December 21, 2Lt. Robert Potach, Headquarters Company, 2nd Battalion, 502nd PIR, celebrated his 21st birthday in a foxhole outside Bastogne. During the fighting, as he recounted earlier, he became part of an 81-mm mortar team, which left him deaf in one ear. He recalled:

> I was a replacement for those who were lost; the rate of losses in the airborne were [sic] high. My first exposure to combat was at Bastogne, outside in the snow with German troops surrounding us. Our winter gear came the following March, when it's spring in Belgium, it would have been very welcome, but I don't know where it was. We didn't have it. That's when I decided I was never going to live where it was cold. I don't know how many weeks it was until we saw the interior of a structure; we were out in the open all of the time. We weren't dressed for it, we had regular gloves and regular shoes, which were jump boots. They made you a little taller, but

> not warmer. It was months before I had a change of underwear or socks. We had K-rations so
> often because we were out and didn't have a full kitchen. Every single one of them had cigarettes
> in them, so if you were sitting out in the middle of nowhere and you were cold and there was
> nothing going on, if you had cigarettes, you used them.

Before Bastogne, Robert hadn't been a slave to nicotine.

Rogues and heroes aside, the people of Bastogne were suffering badly, and a serious number of them hadn't been able to evacuate the city. The streets were festooned with Christmas decorations at the time in preparation for the yuletide activities. When the occupying forces had left in September, they left with the ominous prediction that someday they would return. This close-knit community had only one consideration in mind at the onset of the German offensive—will they attack Bastogne? They didn't have to wait long to discover the answer. As American vehicles rolled into Bastogne, the locals were disturbed by the sounds of tracks and wheels on frozen roads, and in the distance the sound of war was coming unerringly closer.

To reduce the risk to the population, resident American military authorities imposed a curfew, insisting the streets be empty by 6:00 pm every evening. When the electricity was disconnected, the blackout lasted four months. Every night, the skies to the north and east were illuminated by lights and spotlights reflected on the low, pregnant clouds. By December 21, the city was a hive of activity as tanks, jeeps, trucks, and half-tracks returned from the front lines.

It was on that day that von Manteuffel received the order from von Rundstedt to take Bastogne. The former had already demonstrated his capacity to evolve his plans in sync with the evolving situation as he adapted his attack to correspond to the actual conditions and elements he had to contend with. This meant his 5th Panzer Army became the main attacking force with the most realistic chance of reaching the River Meuse. Reaching the Meuse was one thing, crossing it would be another matter entirely.

Aerial reconnaissance photo of Bastogne. (Filip Willems personal archive via Ronald Stassen)

General McAuliffe in 1941.

Men of "Easy" Company, 2nd Battalion, 501st Parachute Infantry Regiment, 101st Airborne Division, boarding 6×6 transports before heading to Bastogne.

Sergeant Lee Weaver, 502nd Parachute Infantry Regiment, stands in deep snow near Château Rolley.

The Germans named it "Gerold Kazerne." Heintz Barracks, Bastogne, 1944, the location of the 101st Airborne Division's headquarters. A wireman from the signal corps is stringing communication cables while three American soldiers keep guard under their "homemade" shelter.

The commanding officer of the 506th Parachute Infantry Regiment, Col. Robert Sink, and Maj. Gen. Maxwell Taylor, the commanding officer of the 101st Airborne Division, at Zell am See, Austria, in July 1945. (Private First Class Richard David Moellenkamp, "Dog" Company, 506th Parachute Infantry Regiment, via Ronald Stassen personal archive)

Corporal Jesse Donahue and Lieutenant Robert W. Mayer examine a German StG-44 abandoned in the woods near Monaville, January 11, 1945. Both are members of the 609th Tank Destroyer Battalion.

In their attempt to stem the German breakthrough, the 101st Airborne Division marches in the direction of Foy, Belgium, December 19, 1944.

Sergeant Harold J. Sloan, from Akron, Ohio, a member of the 101st Airborne Division, fills his canteen cup with clean snow to make coffee in the forest near Foy on January 11, 1945.

Following a night skirmish near Bastogne, three members of the 101st Airborne Division set out to find and rejoin their unit. Left to right: Private First Class M. L. Dickman, East Omaha, Nebraska; Private Sunny Sundquist, Bremerton, Washington; and Sergeant Francis H. McCann, Middleton, Connecticut.

Sergeant Lee Weaver, 502nd Parachute Infantry Regiment, holds a Belgian child near Bastogne.

The heavily damaged church of Noville after the battles on December 19 and 20, 1944, and January 15, 1945. B Company, 1st Battalion, 506th Parachute Infantry Regiment blew away a part of the tower while retreating on December 20.

Positions of the 3rd Battalion, 506th Parachute Infantry Regiment, at Bois Champay near Foy. Lieutenant Colonel Lloyd Patch, commander of 3-506th, established his CP nearby.

A paratrooper cleaning his M1 Garand in Bois Jacques.

Members of the 777th Anti-Aircraft Artillery Battalion and 101st Airborne Division warm up around a fire on the outskirts of Bastogne, December 31, 1944. They are, left to right, Private First Class Calvin C. Bates, Private Charles Doocly, Private Donald Loelson, Private First Class Leonard Madrid, and Private O. P. Cove. The last three named are members of the 101st.

Members of the 501st Parachute Infantry Regiment counterattack the Germans near Bastogne astride a tank of the 10th Armored Division.

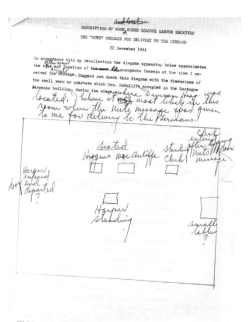

Wounded German soldier being brought to the division aid station in Bastogne by members of the 502nd Parachute Infantry Regiment on December 21, 1944.

Major General Harper's description of personnel locations in the 101st Airborne Division headquarters when the "Nuts" message was delivered.

German prisoners being marched to the rear by members of the 326th Airborne Engineer Battalion near Bastogne late in December 1944.

Two members of the 101st Airborne Division retrieving medical supplies air-dropped to the besieged 101st Airborne Division on December 23, 1944.

A C-47 en route to Bastogne.

C-47s dropping supplies into Bastogne.

Nurse Augusta Chiwy (second from right) and friends in the downed C-47 flown by Captain Ernest Turner. It hit the ground near the positions of the 321st Glider Field Artillery Battalion. The aircraft was called *The Stardust*. (Martin King personal archive)

Color-coded parachutes descend upon Bastogne during a resupply drop.

A glider brings in 155-mm ammunition for the 969th Field Artillery Battalion on December 26, 1944. The 969th was attached to the 101st Airborne Division at Bastogne.

Belgian refugees at a roadblock, manned by soldiers of B Company, 1st Battalion, 502nd Parachute Infantry Regiment, at the culvert underneath the N834 between Savy and Longchamps.

C-47s fly over Bastogne after dropping their supplies.

A jeep belonging to the 502nd Parachute Infantry Regiment shortly after being destroyed by a German land mine near Bastogne.

German prisoners, guarded by members of the 101st Airborne Division Military Police Company, clean up rubble from what seems to be the hospital where Nurse Renée Lemaire was killed during the air raid on December 24, 1944.

War Correspondent Gary Seahan, of the *Chicago Tribune*, interviews a paratrooper of the 2nd Battalion, 506th Parachute Infantry Regiment, on December 27, 1944.

The 502nd Parachute Infantry Regiment's staff at Bastogne on December 28, 1944. Left to right: Captain Eldia R. Haire, S-4; Major James J. Hatch, S-3; Captain Robert Clements, S-2; and Captain Hugh Roberts, S-1.

German prisoners of war, captured by the 502nd Parachute Infantry Regiment, being escorted out of the woods near Bastogne in December 1944.

Near Bastogne, a member of the 53rd Infantry Regiment, 4th Armored Division, escorts German prisoners suffering from exposure.

Members of C Battery, 463rd Parachute Field Artillery Battalion, send a round on the way just outside Bastogne on January 6, 1945.

A member of the 101st Airborne Division probing for land mines on the road between Bastogne and Foy in December 1944.

Members of the 326th Airborne Medical Company rush bundles of medical supplies off the drop zone after the first aerial resupply mission on December 23, 1944.

General Taylor confers with some officers after arriving in Bastogne on December 27, 1944.

A soldier of the 101st Airborne Division pulls security from his foxhole in the snow near Bastogne.

Bastogne in ruins, 1945. (Martin King personal archive)

German prisoners, guarded by members of the 101st Airborne Division Military Police Company, dig graves to bury the paratroopers who didn't survive the siege of Bastogne.

Bastogne refugees leaving the city via Rue du Marche on December 30, 1944. The high building in the middle of the picture is the former hardware store of Renée Lemaire's parents.

Lieutenant General George S. Patton (right) confers with Brig. Gen. Anthony C. McAuliffe and Lt. Col. Steve Chappuis shortly after awarding them each the Distinguished Service Cross for their actions in the defense of Bastogne.

A member of the 501st Parachute Infantry Regiment passes out cigarettes to German prisoners awaiting interrogation at Bastogne.

Parachute infantrymen of the 101st Airborne Division in Belgium search for their size in a pile of overshoes needed to combat deep snow and cold weather. Left to right: Staff Sergeant Charles L. Hettel, of Toledo, Ohio; Private George Barnett, of Ironton; and Private Francis Snow, of Newmarket, New Hampshire.

A dead Airborne soldier who fell while driving entrenched German soldiers from a heavily wooded area, Bois Jacques, near Bastogne.

Private First Class Frank Vukasin, 83rd Infantry Division, from Great Falls, Montana, stops to load a clip in his rifle while advancing in the snow-covered front-line sector at Houffalize. The two bodies are of German soldiers wearing camouflage snow suits.

Members of the 501st Parachute Infantry Regiment move across snow-covered fields.

Members of the 327th Glider Infantry Regiment pack up and move out of Bastogne shortly after being relieved on January 18, 1945.

Paratroopers from the 2nd Battalion, 502nd Parachute Infantry Regiment, maintaining security on the perimeter at Longchamps.

Two members of the 501st Parachute Infantry Regiment demolition platoon searching for land mines near Bastogne in December 1944.

A room in the division command post hit by artillery fire. Blankets cover two dead headquarters men.

Lieutenant Colonel Steve Chappuis, commander of the 502nd Parachute Infantry Regiment, and Lt. Col. Patrick Cassidy, Executive Officer of the 502nd, near the 502nd's command post at Château Rolley in January 1945.

The village of Foy shortly after its recapture by the 506th Parachute Infantry Regiment on January 14, 1945. Note the livestock still wandering about the streets.

CHAPTER ELEVEN

He Said What?

I met Patton, Eisenhower, Montgomery, Bradley.
He [McAuliffe] was the only general, including Monty, who never used profane language.
Never used a cuss word the whole time I knew him, he never used it in his whole life.
VINCENT B. VICARI, 101ST AIRBORNE DIVISION ARTILLERY HEADQUARTERS STAFF

Between 3:30 and 4:30 am on that bitterly cold morning of December 22, various reports of enemy activity were reaching the 101st Airborne's headquarters in Bastogne. It was still very foggy, but auditory evidence of German troop movements could be ascertained in most sectors, particularly out east on the right flank of the 2nd Battalion, 327th Glider Infantry Regiment (GIR), where the Americans reported hearing enemy troops digging in, accompanied by the movement of motor vehicles, horses, and wagons. By 9:00 am, the Germans had blocked the road at Mont, just a few miles directly east, prompting the 3rd Battalion to act and effectively remove this impertinent obstruction, and capture 25 prisoners in the process. Late on the previous evening, the 26th Volksgrenadier Division had captured the villages of Assenois and Sibret, effectively severing the last two roads that led to Bastogne and completing the encirclement.

By December 22, Col. Meinrad Lauchert's 2nd Panzer Division remained relatively static because its tanks had run dry and were forced to wait for fuel deliveries. When the advance west resumed at nightfall, it encountered stiff resistance at Marche from the 84th Infantry Division. General Heinrich von Lüttwitz, leading the Panzer Corps, ordered Lauchert to turn the bulk of his strength west towards Dinant and the River Meuse, and to leave only a token blocking force near Marche. Too much time had elapsed for the Germans to cross the river and seize the bridges but some of their commanders appeared to be in denial. Some were prepared to use any tactic at all to persuade the defenders to throw in the towel and surrender Bastogne.

Sergeant Tom Rice headed towards Belgium feeling a bit unprepared. "I had my sub-machine gun," he remembered. "But little, if any, ammunition. I didn't have a jacket. I had no gloves. I might have had a K-ration or two in my pocket, that's about it." He arrived in Bastogne late in the evening of December 18 on

Rue de Marche, not far from the city center. On the 19th, he was part of the 1st Battalion, leaving the R&R area at around 6:00 am for Neffe. The 1st Battalion was stopped by a German tank of the 130th Regiment just 500 yards west of Neffe. C Company occupied the high ground and, during the night of December 21/22, retired about two-thirds of the way up the hill. On the 22nd, Rice was sent out on a six-man patrol. When he recognized the potential for an ambush of his squad, he stood up to communicate his concerns, making him a target for enemy weapons. "I knew the risk I was taking," he recalled. Hit in his left leg, he called over another man to administer morphine, then decided to stand again to see if the leg was broken. Again, Rice presented a clean target and, this time, an enemy bullet hit his right arm. As he went back down into a frozen ditch, he heard another round "pop" just inches from his ear. Rice sent the rest of the men back to safety, while he hid behind a frozen haystack for hours, hoping the Germans wouldn't set it on fire. He eventually made it back to safety and received medical attention, thanks to the courage of a fellow paratrooper named John W. Curtis, who came to Rice's aid and helped drag him along the frozen ditch until they reached a jeep.

Rice and Curtis drove to the sisters of Notre-Dame convent in Bastogne where they could get the medical attention they needed. While he was lying on the stretcher, the medical personnel asked if there was anything they could do for him; he replied, "Yes, can you bring me a sandwich?" He was attended to by nuns until transferred to the 121st Field Hospital on December 28.

The snowfall that occurred during the previous night had covered the whole area, but this was no winter wonderland; it was a pockmarked battleground where black earth indiscriminately rimmed shell holes and bomb craters in all directions. A few rogue flakes were still spiraling to the frozen earth when, at 11:30 am on December 22, 327th GIR Sergeants Oswald Butler and Carl Dickinson, and Pfc. Ernest Premetz, 327th Medical Detachment, had cause to furrow their brows and ask, "What the hell is this?" At that moment, they were uncomfortably ensconced in a foxhole smoking, talking, complaining about the freezing weather, and very occasionally looking toward the German lines. The past few hours had been relatively quiet, but experience had taught them this was rarely a good sign. They knew there was a farm nearby, but this detail wasn't regarded as anything special either; the whole area was dotted with farms. This particular one was the former residence of a Mr. Kessler, after whom the farm was named. At the time, that area to the southwest was occupied by Germans.

Emerging from the haze, the paratroopers gazed with incredulity as they observed four Germans approaching from Remoifosse, a diminutive village just southeast of Bastogne. They appeared to be carrying a sizable white flag of surrender as they tenuously approached the 2nd Battalion's lines from an area the American artillery had already zeroed. The 327th guys cautiously crawled out of their foxhole and, keeping low, went out to meet this impromptu delegation, which comprised Lt. Helmuth Henke, Maj. Wagner (a Panzer-Lehr officer on von Lüttwitz's 47th Panzer Corps staff), and two enlisted men. When Carl Dickinson wrote his account of the event, he said there were three enlisted men:

> My most noted experience came late in the morning of December 22nd. While covering the Arlon road we observed five German soldiers approaching up the road about 300–400 yards away. There were three soldiers followed by two officers. The soldiers were displaying one large white flag and two smaller ones. As they came closer, I asked my BAR [Browning automatic rifle] man to cover me as I left my position to meet the Germans. Although the regular soldiers wore standard coats, the officers were very sharp, wearing long leather coats and polished boots. One of the German officers spoke English. He stated that according to The Hague and Geneva Conventions they had a right to deliver an ultimatum. He then asked to be taken to my commanding officer. The German officers each produced a white handkerchief. The English speaking officer blindfolded the other officer with one of the handkerchiefs and I blindfolded the English speaking officer.
>
> I was just finishing when Pfc. Ernest Premetz arrived. Premetz could speak German and thought he could be of some help. Premetz and I escorted the two officers to the rear, leaving the three soldiers behind at the BAR position. When we walked by a farm building housing the platoon command post, Tech Sergeant Butler and Lieutenant Smith were looking out the doorway. When Sgt. Butler asked what was happening, I told them that the Germans asked to be taken to our commanding officer. Butler told us to escort the officers to the company command post, which was about a quarter mile to the rear. Contrary to most historical references to the initial meeting, neither Lieutenant Smith nor Sgt. Butler was present at the first contact and neither of them was a participant in the escort. Premetz and I walked the officers in a round-about fashion so as not to give away headquarters' position. When we arrived at the company CP [command post] in the woods the Germans wanted to know why the CP was not in a building. When they were told that there was no building, the officers replied that they understood because they had just come from the Russian front. We turned the German officers over to officers at the CP where they delivered their message. Later, Colonel Harper arrived at the company CP in a jeep to deliver the response from acting commander General McAuliffe. After speaking with the Germans, Harper escorted them back to the American lines in his jeep. There was no room in the jeep for me so I had to walk back to my platoon's position. I was never interviewed about my initial meeting with the German ultimatum delegation. Others, with only peripheral knowledge of the initial meeting were interviewed shortly after the event.

Their story and/or the interpretation of the story by the interviewer resulted in incorrect versions being penned into history. These incorrect versions continue to appear in publications and film to this day.

Premetz spoke passable German, but he wouldn't need his language skills on this occasion. Keeping his finger on the trigger of his M1 carbine, he motioned the Germans to move closer. Henke, the apparent leader of the small group, had a very decent command of the English language; he looked at Sergeant Butler and said in measured tones, "We are parlementaires," which was an unusual turn of phrase, as it's a French word that means parliamentarians, but these paratroopers were not there to practice diplomacy; either way they got the gist of it. The Germans had been sent out to negotiate.

The surrender demand read:

> To the U.S.A. Commander of the encircled town of Bastogne.
>
> The fortune of war is changing. This time the U.S.A. forces in or near Bastogne have been encircled by strong German armored units. More German armored units have crossed the river Ourthe near Ourtheuville, have taken Marvie and reached St. Hubert by passing through Hompre–Sibret–Tillet. Libramont is in German hands.
>
> There is only one possibility to save the encircled U.S.A. troops from total annihilation: that is the honorable surrender of the encircled town. In order to think it over a term of two hours will be granted beginning with the presentation of this note.
>
> If this proposal should be rejected one German Artillery Corps and six heavy A.A. Battalions are ready to annihilate the U.S.A. troops in and near Bastogne. The order for firing will be given immediately after this two hours' term.
>
> All serious civilian losses caused by this artillery fire would not correspond with the wellborn American humanity.
>
> The German Commander.

There was nothing veiled about this threat of imminent destruction, but there's no other way to describe it than a bare-faced German bluff. After the ultimatum was presented, company commander Capt. James F. Adams ordered the enlisted men to be detained while the officers were blindfolded. The message, and the German officers, were then transported to the division headquarters in Marvie by Maj. Alvin Jones (S-3, operations), and Col. Joseph H. Harper, the regimental commander. The Division Operations Officer (G-3), Lt. Col. Harry H. Kinnard, recalled that Gen. Anthony McAuliffe initially asked, "They want to surrender?" Lieutenant Colonel Ned Moore, the division's acting chief of staff, told him, "No, sir, they want us to surrender." This is where Texan Harry Kinnard picks up the story:

> They brought the message to me, the G-3, and Paul Danahy, the G-2. My first reaction was that this was a German ruse, designed to get our men out of their fox holes. But be that as it might, we agreed that we needed to take the message up the line. We took it first to the acting Chief of Staff of the Division, Lt. Col. Ned Moore. With him, we took the message to the acting Division Commander General Tony McAuliffe. Moore told General McAuliffe that we had a German surrender ultimatum.
>
> The General's first reaction was that the Germans wanted to surrender to us. Col. Moore quickly disabused him of that notion and explained that the German's [sic] demanded our surrender. When McAuliffe heard that he laughed and said, "'Us surrender? Aw, nuts." Then he pondered for a few minutes and then told the staff, "Well, I don't know what to tell them." He then asked the staff what they thought, and I spoke up, saying, "That first remark of yours would be hard to beat." McAuliffe said, "What do you mean?" I answered, "Sir, you said, 'Nuts'." All members of the staff enthusiastically agreed. McAuliffe then wrote down: "To the German Commander, Nuts! The American Commander."

Apparently, McAuliffe looked somewhat perplexed when he first read the ultimatum, because he didn't think there was any serious cause for consternation at the time. He gaged the situation perfectly, as he handed his reply to Colonel Harper, adding, "See that this is given to the Germans," to which Harper immediately replied, "I'll hand it over myself with the greatest of pleasure."

Sergeant Paul Bebout, 1st Battalion, 501st Parachute Infantry Regiment (PIR), 101st Airborne, Division said,

> We all laughed when we heard what McAuliffe had said to the Germans. That was something. They come with a jeep and white flag and a colonel of the 327th met them. They wanted to see the commander. So they brought them in to meet our commander. They wanted to know when we were going to surrender. At first they didn't know what to do. Another executive officer there said it's getting close to Christmas; that's why the boss said "Nuts." That was a good idea. So McAuliffe wrote it on a piece of paper and gave it to them but they didn't understand what "Nuts" meant. We explained that [it] means "Go to hell." McAuliffe had his hands full; he was completely surrounded. I saw him but I never had the pleasure of talking to him.

The 327th's commander, Colonel Harper, later recalled the circuitous route the notorious surrender note had to travel before it reached its intended target:

> At the time the four Germans with the surrender message approached Co F outpost along the Arlon road, I was in my jeep inspecting a portion of the regiment line. The Germans blindfolded were first taken to Lt. Smith's CP [command post] in a nearby farmhouse and from there to Captain J. F. Adams in a pine woods about 200 yards northeast of this farmhouse. The Germans gave the surrender message to Capt. Adams, initially. He read it and then called 2nd Battalion CP in Marvie, and read it to the acting commander Major Galbraith. Major Galbraith then sent a messenger jeep to Capt. Adams CP, picked up the message and delivered it to the 327th regimental CP, which was in one of the Barracks in the compound, not far from Division CP. At regimental CP Major Jones, the S3 read the message and walked over to Div. CP and delivered it to Col. Ned Moore, the Chief of Staff.
>
> About this time I received a message by radio to report immediately to Gen. McAuliffe at Div. CP. When I arrived at Div. CP [...] I found General McAuliffe and Higgins seated in a small room. When I walked in and saluted, Gen. McAuliffe handed me the surrender message and asked if I had seen it. I said that I had not. Then he asked me to read it, and indicate to him how he would reply. His request surprised me and placed me in quandary as to how to frame a proper reply. Just at this moment a clerk typist (of about medium height and build) entered the room from a door on Gen. Mc's left and handed him the original typed "NUTS" message. Gen. Mc glanced at it then passed it to me, asking me what I thought of it as a proper reply. I read it and started laughing. I told the Gen that I thought it the perfect answer. He asked that I deliver it etc.
>
> As I stood facing Gen Mc A, McAuliffe, was to my right and Higgins to my left. However I do not remember seeing McAuliffe's bedding roll but it might have been there. It seems to me I entered a door from my left (Higgins' right). The clerk typist came in a door from Gen. Mc's left rear. No one else was in the room, except the four of us at the time the original "Nuts" message was handed to me to deliver to the Germans. After receiving the message, I saluted and left by the door to Higgins right. I did not see Major Jones at all at Div. CP. I assume that he walked back to Regiment after delivering the surrender message to Col. Moore, did not go back with me to Co. P. CP where the blind-folded German officers were waiting.

A little time later, at F Company's command post, Harper responded to the two German officers who were still under strict guard. He told them in no uncertain terms, "I have your answer from our commander." Then there was some verbal altercation as one of the German officers enquired if the response was verbal or in writing.

Without displaying any sign of jocularity, Harper reliably informed the officer it was a written reply. Then the officer enquired further as to the nature of the response from McAuliffe by asking if it was a negative or an affirmative reply. "Well, it isn't affirmative," replied Harper as he loaded the two officers in his jeep. A few minutes later, he stopped in front of the Kessler farm where the two enlisted men, complete with white flag, were patiently waiting.

They obviously didn't know what "Nuts" meant so Harper and Premetz briefly discussed how to explain the response. Harper suggested, "Tell them to take a flying shit." Premetz thought this a little abrasive so he turned to the Germans and said, "Du kannst zum Teufel gehen." He informed Harper this meant "You can go to Hell." Then Harper chipped in, "If you continue to attack, we will kill every goddamn German that tries to break into this city." Henke replied, "We will kill many Americans. This is war." Harper then said, "On your way, Bud, and good luck to you." He later thoroughly regretted wishing them good luck. The time was 1:50 pm.

Mr. Kessler was perfectly oblivious to the proceedings happening at his farm. He just bumbled around and simply regarded this temporary ceasefire as a suitable opportunity to feed his cattle.

The threatened annihilation of Bastogne mentioned in the German ultimatum didn't transpire, hence the defenders just sustained the routine daily dose of shelling. Then, around 4:00 pm, the Germans launched an attack against the 327th that again concluded in abject failure. Even when the enemy introduced tanks to the equation and forced a 150-yard breach, the situation was immediately checked and the line restored. The entire 26th Volksgrenadier Division, reinforced by 15 Panzer-Lehr tanks and its 901st Regiment, and artillery support and assistance from the 5th Fallschirmjäger Division, failed to break the line in the north and the east; the attempted incursion in the west didn't yield any positive results either. The ultimatum had indeed been nothing more than a calculated ruse.

Captain Vincent B. Vicari, 101st Airborne Division Artillery Headquarters Staff, remembered one of the first times he met General McAuliffe:

> I reported to General Mac, we started talking. He was the perfect gentleman, and spoke very quietly, never raised his voice. It was an honor. He told me to sit down and out of a clear blue sky he asked me, "How would you like to be my aid?" I replied "Yes, sir." I didn't know what an aid [sic] did, he taught me what the duties of an aid were. That was my first contact with the general. We built up a relationship that was fabulous. He was the only general that I came across and I met them all, I met Patton, Eisenhower, Montgomery, Bradley. He was the only general, including Monty, who never used profane language. Never used a cuss word the whole time I knew him, he never used it in his life. And when you were talking with him or discussing something with him he would say "Nuts" and that was the end of the conversation. Forget about it. If you persisted in continuing being that General Mac was Irish, he'd start to flush red from the neck up. If we were in the office with someone and he started to flush we would give them the hint to stop the conversation. But he would never raise his voice, never yelled at anyone in front of anybody.

While McAuliffe was making his historical riposte, continuous probes along the entire perimeter persisted, but there were only two attacks of any significance, and both were orchestrated by small enemy units that didn't exceed company size.

On December 21, while consolidating the Bastogne perimeter, the 327th had expertly placed its battalions precisely where they needed to be. While the 1st Battalion was out assisting the 501st PIR, as previously noted, the 2nd Battalion was at Marvie with Team O'Hara, and the 3rd Battalion was still holding the land and surrounding area roughly six miles northwest of Bastogne.

The 3rd Battalion sector observed enemy activity at Givroulle, and Salle on the extreme northwestern perimeter, around 12 miles away from Bastogne. Early on the morning of the 21st before daybreak, German forces advanced against B Company where they met intense resistance. It cost the Germans two tanks, four half-tracks, and three personnel carriers, which ultimately compelled them to retreat east.

Private First Class John G. Kutz, Sr., C Company, 326th Airborne Engineer Battalion, 101st Airborne Division, was at Marvie and a witness to the white-flag incident and the ensuing chaos that evening:

> It was about two miles out of Bastogne. We were out there nosing around. You could see the Germans there came out with a white flag. We thought they were coming to surrender. The couple of soldiers that they had with them, they took the Germans that were coming to surrender. One guy from the engineers, I don't know who it was, said, "Them dumb bastards, what they coming around here for? They're gonna get shot." When they went back they were going to open up with I don't know how many artillery pieces in this area and saturate us with shrapnel. Well we waited for it, and we waited for it. We dug a hole it was full of snow and ice. It never did come [the barrage]. We said "Boy McAuliffe musta really scared them." Then at that night. That's when they really opened up, that's when they come at us. That's when I got captured. It started at, oh I don't know what time it was and all. It started after supper, it was getting dark. We knew their tactics. The first thing they do is make light, they set a house or two on fire, a barn or two barns whatever. They light the whole area. I was in my foxhole on top of a hill, and down here was this house. My lieutenant was right by me, right by my hole and he hollered over, "Who's over there?" I replied, "Kutz and Alman." He said, "Come here the both of you. Go down the hill and see what's going on. We got a whole squad down there." It was on a corner, so we started down and my buddy said, "I'm not going down that road." I replied, "Neither am I." So I crawled into a ditch. We didn't fire anything. We crawled about 30 yards until I said I'm not going down any further. I could see our guys, we could tell who they were stood there with their hands up. I saw some guys laying there wounded. So we went back and to tell just what we saw. When we got up there we didn't find no lieutenant. Golly my buddy started running. I said, "Where you running?" He said, "I'm going in that house." So I was going to the CP to tell em but I couldn't find it. The CP was gone, it was empty. So I ran back up. Alman hollered from a window, "Kutz, come here." I said, "Who's with you?" He said, "Nobody." I just had a feeling that we just weren't alone. Then I heard a little noise in the house. I swear to God I said, "Somebody's in this house." He said, "Go upstairs and look." I said, "You go upstairs and look. I'll stay down here." So he went up there then a guy came down and walked out into the kitchen. "Who the hell are you?" "Lieutenant Kennedy." "What army?" "327th." "Oh, you're right next door to us." You didn't know all the guys from your outfit. He had all the right medals on except on the shoulders, he had captain's bars on but he was Lieutenant Kennedy? He called for artillery fire, but that was funny, our artillery

wouldn't fire on us. I crawled out of the house, he said, "You better get the hell out of here right now," then they captured us.

Out in Marvie, Team O'Hara and the 2nd Battalion were resisting a serious enemy artillery barrage. A well-equipped German force attempted to make an incursion around the battalion's right flank but, with assistance from G Company, the attack was successfully repulsed. There was marked consternation at the time because it was feared the Germans would attempt to sever the road beside the 3rd Battalion, but this never materialized. B Company got into a precarious firefight at a crossroads east of O'Hara's position, but held its ground again and captured two German prisoners before being ordered back west to reunite with the 3rd Battalion.

Some of the fighting on the 22nd centered around two battalions of armored field artillery. The 58th Armored Field Artillery Battalion moved to a location near Tillet to support the 101st Airborne and Lt. Col. Barry D. Browne's 420th Armored Field Artillery Battalion, now operating as a combined-arms team on a 4,000-yard perimeter in the neighborhood of Senonchamps. Tillet is about six miles west of Senonchamps. Some of the surrounding countryside to the west of Bastogne was in the hands of roving patrols from Panzer-Lehr, one of which had erected a strong roadblock midway between the two villages. Rumors were rampant regarding a potential German surrender.

Sergeant B. Vern Lieberman, 326th Medical Airborne Company, 101st Airborne Division, said:

> When General McAuliffe said "Nuts" to them, it sorta picked the men up we said, we can do this. It went all over the camps, it was something, word of mouth given all around. We heard the Germans wanted us to surrender and the general said "Nuts." I said, "That's my sentiments entirely." I would have said the same thing. I would fight to the last breath.

Meanwhile, although General von Manteuffel acknowledged Bastogne was a thorn in his side, he was more interested in striking out to the west. To achieve this, he was prepared to deviate from his orders to compensate for the actual conditions and elements. But the 5th Army commander reputedly said, "The importance of Bastogne was considerable. In enemy hands it must influence all the movements in the west, damage our supply system, and tie up considerable German forces. It was therefore essential that we capture it at once."

After the meeting with Harper and Premetz, the two German officers drove over to the 901st Panzergrenadier Regimental headquarters in nearby Lutrebois. After checking in, they went to the Panzer-Lehr Division's headquarters, less than a mile away. Moments before they reached their destination, they saw von Manteuffel's staff car parked beside a small copse. Major Wagner stopped and duly reported the day's proceedings to the general, who was allegedly outraged when he heard about the surrender ultimatum. He constantly denied he had any knowledge of it, but this was disputed by Panzer-Lehr commander Fritz Bayerlein, who said, "One part of the troops were to attack and another part push on toward the West. Through this decision no adequate attack was made. Then we tried to do it by appealing to the garrison to capitulate, the text being composed by Manteuffel and Luttwitz."

Von Manteuffel was perfectly aware his army didn't have sufficient artillery to effectively execute the threat included in the surrender proposal. Moreover, the threatened heavy artillery barrage that would annihilate Bastogne and bring the defenders to their knees never came because, by that time, the artillery had been moved to the west of Bastogne. Although 47th Panzer Corps commander von Lüttwitz later claimed he was solely responsible for dispatching the surrender ultimatum, there is sufficient evidence to suggest it came straight from OB West (Oberbefehlshaber—high commander—West), and was approved by von Manteuffel himself, even if he was only the messenger.

Generalmajor Heinz Kokott, the 26th Volksgrenadier Division commander, said:

> The enemy there had actually withdrawn in the direction of Bastogne. The 2nd Panzer Division had then, in accordance with instructions, turned in to the west and, with its bulk, was rolling in a westerly direction. Only weak security detachments had been left behind near Foy. In the course of the morning, corps had informed the division that, by orders of corps, a negotiator of the Panzer Lehr [sic] Division would be dispatched to Bastogne—who would ask the enemy forces there to surrender. News arrived from corps to the effect that the commander in charge of the Bastogne forces had declined a surrender with remarkable brevity. This response was fully in accord with the stubborn tenacity displayed by the defending forces.

McAuliffe later modestly extolled his humanity when he said, "I read it [the surrender ultimatum] and just said, 'Nuts.' That sentence about the civilians irritated me. The Germans had shown no concern for the civilians up to then."

Amid the chaos and the bloodshed, the fight would go on, but as von Manteuffel continued his push to the west with his best divisions, the 101st was never in any real danger of losing Bastogne. It just needed to receive, rather than procure, supplies to keep fighting. A resupply air drop was on the cards and would get underway as soon as the weather was conducive to such an operation.

CHAPTER TWELVE

Smiling at Me

We stole jeeps, we stole cranes, we blew up barracks; we blew down trees. And we stole the colonel's whiskey.

JAMES E. "JAKE/MCNASTY" MCNIECE. PATHFINDER, 101ST AIRBORNE DIVISION

Wrapped in multiple blankets and shivering almost uncontrollably, Sgt. Ralph K. Manley stirred from a fitful nap to the sound of raucous, bronchial coughing and retching coming from his foxhole, and others nearby. For some, those coughs were indications of imminent pneumonia and chronic bronchitis. For others, it was just the morning reaction to having smoked too many Lucky Strikes during the previous night. Cigarettes were always available in abundance, especially on the front lines.

Bleary eyed, Ralph scanned his immediate environment and noticed something he hadn't seen for several days. In the distance he thought he could see the faintest slither of sunlight cracking the dawn horizon. A hazy mist was still stubbornly clinging to the ground, but it was that bit of light that filled his heart with hope. There didn't appear to be any significant enemy activity at that time, but the Germans, and the prospect of reluctantly imbibing a fresh breath of hell, were never too far away. Ralph hadn't slept much; none of his comrades had either.

Nighttime was always the worst. All senses were operating on overdrive and the most innocent sounds, such as a lone fox, deer, or boar breaking twigs as it moved among the trees, had the potential to provoke an alert along the line. One corporal, driven by desperation and gnawing trepidation, had decided he couldn't take it anymore and shot himself in the head. They were all reaching, and some had reached, the pinnacle of human endurance. But the dawn of December 23 hailed the prospect of some meager relief for the besieged defenders of Bastogne. Captain Joseph S. Jenkins, 1st Battalion S-4 (logistics), 401st Glider Infantry Regiment (GIR), wrote:

> The night of 22/23 December was passed with anxiety and anticipation by the men of the various supply sections in the 101st Division, all were awaiting dawn to check for visibility and weather conditions. They were not disappointed, all of the elements of weather that had harassed the division since its arrival had disappeared and a perfect day was in the making. At 0930 hours, 23 December, the pathfinders landed and began the operation of their homing

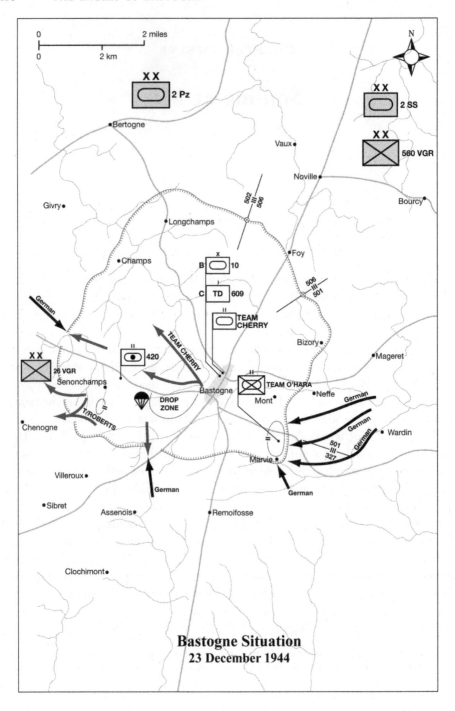

Bastogne Situation
23 December 1944

devices to bring the re-supply planes in "on the beam." Commencing at 1130 hours a steady stream of Army C-47s began to discharge a continuous flow of cargo parachutes containing ammunition, rations, gasoline, medical supplies and equipment. North of the "Drop Zone," a glider "LZ" [landing zone] had been marked and gliders bearing medical personnel and bulky supplies were being landed. In their zest to recover the much needed supplies being dropped the unit supply sections disregarded all safety precautions and a few casualties were inflicted on personnel and vehicles by malfunctions and improperly packed aerial containers falling unretarded to the ground. Spasmodic artillery fire fell within the limits of the drop zone, but it only hastened the efforts of the recovery teams to clear the area of the resupply bundles. By 1600 hours a total of 241 planes had been relieved of 1446 aerial containers containing 244 tons of gasoline, rations, medical supplies, ammunition and equipment.

Exhilaration ran rampant through the troops. Here was definite knowledge that they were not forgotten, here was something concrete to see and use. Morale increased a hundred-fold.

There appears to be some disparity regarding the amount of supplies dropped by the Ninth Air Force's IX Troop Carrier Command. According to their official reports, commencing December 22, 260 aircraft dropped 334 tons of materiel by color-coded parachute. The most urgently required ammunition supplies couldn't be dropped in parachute containers for fear of causing ground explosions. To get around this issue, gliders left over from the invasions of Normandy and the Netherlands were used to deliver the ammunition, mainly because they didn't require intricate container packaging. It culminated in the most accurate and effective air resupply mission of World War II. An unclassified document reveals:

> Two hundred and forty-one aircraft from the United Kingdom approached the "Drop Zone" at Bastogne from the South, using A-91 [airstrip] as their Initial Point. These aircraft approached A-91 direct from the United Kingdom.

During the night, a further six inches of snow had fallen and more was expected. In the military, the only thing that travels faster than the speed of light is bad news and, granted, the men of the 101st Airborne Division hadn't had much to cheer about up until that juncture. Thankfully, some good news arrived from the south when the 101st heard that Gen. George Patton's 4th Armored Division was moving up from the southwest to provide support. It was also reported that the 7th Armored Division was approaching from the northeast, where it had been fighting close by Sankt Vith. But the best news to raise a grin of optimism among the besieged troops was that a resupply air drop had been scheduled and would occur as soon as the skies cleared, whenever that would be. This "Hitler weather" had been persistent and temperatures had been plummeting even further.

The official weather report for southern Belgium, provided by the London Meteorological Office, Saturday, December 23, stated: "Heavy frost in all areas. Light mist in low lying areas clearing before noon. *Clear skies* [emphasis added]. Winds N/E 6 miles per hour. Temperature: –25° C."

The resupply, particularly of medical staff and equipment, could not come soon enough. Paratroopers out on the perimeter were not just prone to enemy fire; there were some blue-on-blue incidents, such as the one that temporarily disabled an incredibly lucky S/Sgt. Robert J. Noody, F Company, 506th Parachute Infantry Regiment (PIR), 101st Airborne Division:

> It was very damned cold. It wasn't just the snow, and it stayed that way for at least a month. When we went on these patrols it was very tough to keep your weapon from freezing up on you. Had to keep it dry all the time or else. I went on two different patrols, I didn't volunteer for them. They were generally nighttime. That's when I got hit by a grenade, it was a friendly grenade. Some jackass had pulled the pin on a grenade and couldn't get it back, and dropped it. I just got plastered with that cos [sic] I had my legs up. We were in a house at that time along the railroad track in Bastogne. Guarnere and Hefron and them, they were in the woods right there and we were with them. We were the left flank of Co E [...] They took me to the aid station and flattened me out on a big stretcher and I couldn't even stand the needle, so they kind of had to hold me down while they took out most of the shrapnel, most of it, I guess. Only a few pieces have surfaced since then. They patched me up. We were back in no time. Harry, a friend of mine from New York had 62 stitches, he had a darned mortar shell explode. He had a radio on his back and it completely ruined it. By God he lived through that, he came back. That was the end of my experiences in Bastogne. I had taken one of those patrols into Foy, they always sent you out in the field see. When you think about the number of people that were there it don't make a lotta sense to me, but apparently did to them. And that was right after that when I got hit with a grenade.

In light of mounting casualties and dwindling ammunition stores, although the Gen. Anthony McAuliffe never said as much, his situation was reaching its nadir. In a concerted effort to assist the beleaguered general and his men, American planners loaded gliders with surgeons, litters, and medicine and prepared to head to Bastogne. These gliders were originally in France, so were not encumbered by the same weather problems facing the transports scheduled to leave England. First, however, pathfinders would be parachuted in to mark the landing zones. Tech 4 Leon A. Jedziniak, a medic with A Company, 501st PIR, 101st Airborne Division, said:

> That day the airdrop was the most beautiful [sight] you could see. A hundred goddamn C-47s coming and dropping parachutes; they even dropped in doctors for the hospital. We were using [part of] the seminary for our aid station. The P-47s coming in [knocked] out the tanks too.

Major Robert F. Harwick, acting commander of the 506th's 1st Battalion, wrote:

> On the 23rd December some of our pathfinders jumped to us and set up markings for planes. That night a glider came in with surgeons, who were badly needed, as our wounded had started to die. Our artillery ammunition was down to eleven rounds per gun per day.

Over in England, Lt. Shrable D. Williams approached acting 1/Sgt. Jake McNiece and told him to prepare his stick (team) for a combat jump that afternoon. He said something to the effect of the 101st was isolated in Bastogne and in desperate need of supplies. Jake would be making his third combat jump as a pathfinder. The mission was going to be extremely precarious because the planes and paratroopers could be greeted with a barrage of flak and small-arms fire as soon as they approached Bastogne. Then there was also the additional danger of missing the target and landing on the heads of the Germans. Some even regarded it as positively suicidal.

Pathfinder Capt. Frank Brown had offered the sergeant stripes to Jake while they were in England. Jake wasn't impressed. He said he'd been in the military three years already and hadn't even made Private First Class. He also warned Frank, in no uncertain terms, that he didn't like military protocols; "I'm not First Sergeant material. I'm the biggest goof-off in the Army." Brown replied, "I'm in here for the same reason as you. I'm a goof-off. I don't care about military discipline, saluting or picking up cigarettes, and all that. We've got 400 goof-offs here."

There's no doubt Jake enjoyed his reputation as a lovable and courageous rogue, who enthusiastically extolled the fact that he detested military discipline at every level. His comrades had quite a reputation for having serious personal hygiene issues; they refused to wash for weeks while they were in England. This earned them the name "The Filthy Thirteen." Jake would often say the movie *The Dirty Dozen* was modelled on him and his Rabelaisian team. He reveled in being a rebel, but there's no detracting from the fact they were all incredibly brave, and extremely effective when in combat. He said, "We went AWOL every weekend that we wanted to, and we stayed as long as we wanted to. We stole jeeps; we stole cranes. We blew up barracks; we blew down trees. And we stole the colonel's whiskey."

Despite this, according to an Army University newsletter, they were everything you could want from a demolition squad on the front lines but, while in garrison, they were arguably among the most difficult, insubordinate, and undisciplined individuals in the U.S. Army. From today's perspective, Jake and his gang of delinquents were undisciplined and uncontrollable. It didn't stop them from being incredibly effective when required to be so. The following description clarifies the extreme danger they were being subjected to for this vital mission:

> Commanding General, XVIII Corps [Airborne]. Report on Pathfinder Drop and Resupply to 101st A/B Division, Bastogne Area, 22–27 December 1944 [provided by 1Lt Patrick Seeling].
>
> Airborne Pathfinder Detachment was alerted for a two-stick Pathfinder Mission at 11.30 hours, 22 December 44 via orders from Lt. Col. Juice T. Blair, Executive Officer, 1X TCC [Troop Carrier Command] Pathfinder Group.
>
> Attention is invited to the fact that Airborne Pathfinders participating in this operation are not permanently assigned to IX TCC Pathfinder Group but were on temporary duty while attending school for a period of two weeks. It was merely a coincidence that sufficient Airborne Pathfinders to accomplish the mission were available at this base at the time the mission was received!
>
> a) First decision was to commit one stick, one officer and nine enlisted men to mark the DZ. Due to the fact that the DZ was known to be surrounded by the enemy and considering the effect of small arms fire on C-47 type aircraft at jump altitude [400–600 feet]. The Ex-Officer, IX TCC Pathfinder Gp and XVIII Corps [Airborne Pathfinder Officer] felt that two identical teams should be committed. A telephone [scrambler] request to commit two teams was approved by IX Troop Carrier Command.

b) Coordinates of DZ with as much intelligence data as was available were telephoned [scrambler] to IX TCC Pathfinder Gp at 1330 hours with instructions to have personnel airborne at 1400 hours to facilitate checking of teams and equipment on the round during daylight hours.

c) Airborne Pathfinder Teams were equipped with weapons and combat equipment by the Group S-4, Smoke and panels have been predrawn and are available in the XVIII Corps supply room. Radar equipment was set up and checked. Due to limited time all enlisted men belonging to the Airborne Pathfinder teams were dispatched to the Dispersal Areas to load at 1330. Officer jumpmasters reported to Group Operations for Pilot–Jumpmaster Briefing at this time.

d) Intelligence reports relative to enemy and friendly situations on the ground indicated that the situation in the area was fluid and a close map reconnaissance of the DZ was impossible due to lack of large scale [1:25000] maps. Airborne Pathfinders were furnished with 1:100000 maps of the area, the time limit from receipt to necessary information to take off [thirty minutes] did not allow time for proper briefing, plotting of course and emergency operation under the circumstances. Combined Air Corps and Airborne teams took off at 1452 hours.

The first attempt was aborted on the orders of Captain Brown, but the following morning, December 23, at precisely 6:45 am, the pathfinders set off to a very uncertain future. Both teams would land exactly on target and open smoke canisters to indicate to other aircraft the sticks had landed safely, and were precisely where they should be, but the flight in was nothing short of absolutely terrifying.

As the planes drew near to Bastogne, the co-pilot on McNiece's plane switched on the red light, indicating that the pathfinders had to stand and hook-up to the static line. At exactly the same moment, the Germans opened up with 88-mm antiaircraft fire. Amid the engine noise and turbulence, an 88-mm round blew a hole clean through the airplane's fuselage right between McNiece and his friend Sgt. Cleo Merz. There was a serious danger of the aircraft being completely destroyed before the pathfinders could bail out and achieve their objective. As the flak became more intense, the pilot decided to lower his altitude to tree-top level, whereupon it was actually grazing the tops of some of the snow-covered conifers. By this time, Jake and his companions were lying on the floor, but as the airplane began to climb to jump height, Jake told the men to hook up again and prepare to disembark. He saw a cemetery, which is still there today. Jake had seen it indicated on maps, so decided it was time to go. The green light illuminated, and he and Sergeant Merz were out of the first plane.

After landing and gathering his parachute, Jake immediately started cracking orange smoke canisters so the 10 pathfinders in the second aircraft could zero in on the target. They all landed safely within the city perimeter, almost directly opposite the 101st Airborne Division's command post, but it had been a hairy, scary flight. They had also landed near Col. Joseph Harper's 2nd Battalion. Within seconds, this bunch of undisciplined rabble became a finely tuned machine as they set to work setting up Eureka beacons and marker panels. The drop zone was established between Senonchamps and Bastogne. Harper's men were quick to leave their foxholes and offer protection to the pathfinders, who reliably informed them supply planes were on their way and would arrive over Bastogne in roughly ninety minutes. They were the only Airborne unit to parachute into Bastogne throughout the time the 101st was there. It was a truly momentous day on the Bastogne calendar. Ducking sniper fire, the 101st Airborne men managed to successfully retrieve over ninety-five percent of the air-dropped cargo, making it one of the most successful air resupply missions of the war.

> 327th Glider S2 report:
> On 23 December, resupply was dropped to the Division by parachute at 1155 hours, 1400 hours and 1410 hours. At 1350 Company "C" Third Battalion, was attacked by five German tanks and infantry. Again at 1400 hours, ten German tanks and infantry attacked Company "C" from the south. The Third Battalion was forced to give up Flamierge, but no further ground was lost as a result of that attack.

A military policeman on duty that morning at the entrance to the division's command post at the Heintz Barracks noted several large aircraft circling the area. First Lieutenant Earl E. Rigsby from IX TCC Pathfinder School (Prov) was one of the pilots who took off from Chalgrove for Membury airfield fully loaded with para-packs and re-supply bundles for Bastogne. They began departing the East Devon airfield in small groups. After the first waves of C-47s had dropped their supplies, the German antiaircraft batteries really got to work. The remaining C-47s were hit hard by flak. First Lieutenant Robert Anstey, 327th GIR, reported a crashed C-47 near Savy. Luckily, no aircraft were shot down over Bastogne, but many had to perform emergency landings at various Allied airfields.

Private First Class Bruce Middough, C Battery, 463rd Parachute Field Artillery Battalion, near Savy, witnessed the shooting down of one of the resupply aircraft on December 24:

> During the resupply mission, one C-47 had been hit by antiaircraft fire and the whole tail assembly was engulfed in flames. The plane was flying on a course from west to east about a half mile south of Hemroulle. I watched the plane as it approached and saw one, then another, and a third crew member bail out. Their chutes all opened without any trouble and they all landed within the perimeter very near "A" Battery's gun position. The plane continued on for a few seconds but was beginning to lose altitude rapidly. Then the fourth crew member bailed out. He didn't wait for the count of four but pulled it immediately upon departing the plane. The chute was just beginning to deploy when the tail assembly of the aircraft broke off and the plane went straight in exploding upon impact. The crew members' chute opened O.K, and he came to ground on the hillside just southeast of Hemroulle.
>
> I watched him through binoculars and observed that he just lay in the snow without moving. Shortly thereafter two troopers went down the hillside to where he lay. They stood near him for a few minutes. Then one of the troopers cut his parachute off, bundled it up and both returned to their positions. I continued to watch the crew member who was still laying in the snow, but thought he must be dead. Thinking that it was odd that the troopers didn't carry him back toward their positions, several of us in the farmhouse were a little upset at the C-47 crew member being left in the snow and as we were talking about it the crewman got up out of the snow and started walking toward the direction the troopers had come from. I never did talk to anyone who knew the full story of what occurred that day, but only surmise that the C-47 crew member had had such a harrowing experience those last few minutes before his

plane went in and he was so thankful just to be alive that he just wanted to lay there in the snow and appreciate having made it.

The 441st Troop Carrier Group left its airfield at Dreux, France, at 9:58 am. The aircraft flew in following the N4, the (still there today) Bastogne–Marche highway, at an altitude of 900 feet. A Panzer division was also occupying the highway as it drove to Rochefort. The C-47s began receiving heavy small-arms fire and flak, mostly from the 2nd Panzer Division. The 302nd Troop Carrier Squadron was leading the formation; it was the second ship, piloted by 1Lt. Robert L. Anstey and co-piloted by 2Lt. Raymond G. Wiethorn, that became the first aircraft of the formation to be destroyed by flak. Thankfully, the crew, minus Anstey, managed to bail out and were subsequently taken prisoner by the Germans.

The remaining aircraft unloaded directly on the red smoke set out by the pathfinders. The C-47s were accompanied by P-47 Thunderbolts from the 509th and 510th Fighter Squadrons, which were under strict orders to protect the cargo aircraft from any potential Luftwaffe threats; none transpired on the first day of the resupply mission.

Lieutenant Joseph W. Lyons of the 463rd Parachute Field Artillery Battalion recalled a close encounter with P-47 Thunderbolt fighter-bombers in a letter:

This was to be a memorable day for the 463rd Parachute Field Artillery. It started with an all-out German attack designed to wipe out the "doughnut." Everyone was prepared for the worst. The barracks bags with our belongings were piled ready to be burned and the cannoneers were oiling their rifles and carbines in case we were overrun by the enemy. General McAuliffe had told them "nuts" and they were going to finish us. D Battery, 463rd, was the only battery in the division firing. Because of our position, we were the only battery capable of firing anywhere on the perimeter of the "doughnut." Therefore, all the remaining ammunition in the division was assigned to us. The other batteries of the 463rd were deployed in anti-tank positions. After a morning that saw B Battery repulse a tank attack and capture 4 of them, we were catching our breath from the busy morning. Suddenly we heard familiar airplane motors in the distance, and then the sky was full of supply parachutes, our aerial resupply was here. The sky had cleared for the first time. We also heard guns; in the distance which meant our relief was approaching.

While this aerial display was occurring, one of the C-47 cargo planes became disabled and landed in the creek bed fifty yards from D Battery gun position. The occupants of the plane came out with their hands in the air yelling "Kamerad," but were relieved to find they had landed among friends. Miraculously, no one was seriously injured. After we took care of them and sent them to the rear, the rest of the Air Force appeared. 3 P-47s circled us and, after a round of tracer was fired by some trigger happy antiaircraft gunner up on the hill, they came at us in dive formation. I told my ack ack gunners to fire on them, which drove them off. I assume they realized we were Americans after they got close. We'll never know.

In a letter to a friend, Lyons described how desperate they were for resupply:

This incident takes place in Bastogne, Belgium. You must remember that my unit was composed of a group of cocky, arrogant, and confident paratroopers. When the breakthrough at Bastogne came, we were ordered to take positions around Bastogne. After digging in we were ordered again to move to new positions and then ordered to make a perimeter defense. Now I realized that something was amiss, especially when I heard a rumor that we were surrounded, but no worry, cocky, arrogant, confident me. We had our supply of ammunition and food, and for the most part they were plentiful. In fact there were wrapped crackers in my 8 rations that I disliked, so instead of eating them, I threw them in a hole with other refuse. Well as the days went by and getting no resupply, due to being surrounded, and no air drop because of bad weather, our supplies began to dwindle. I still had my confidence, arrogance, and cockiness, but I now added on hunger. My eyes kept going to that refuse hole where I threw those crackers I disliked, I finally weakened and dug them up. A short time after a delicious meal of soggy crackers, we were resupplied by airdrop and the hunger was erased. To this day, I find very few crackers that I dislike enough to throw away.

Another element of the resupply mission often omitted, but alluded to above, is the group of five doctors and four medical technicians that volunteered to go into Bastogne via glider. Major General Maxwell D. Taylor, the absent commander of the 101st Airborne Division for whom Gen. Anthony McAuliffe was acting, said he'd rather jump in using a parachute than go in by glider. This didn't seem to bother the medical team. Doctor Lamar Soutter, the leader of the group, later said, "This was something we felt we absolutely had to do."

The medical team flew into Bastogne on December 26 along with 10 other gliders carrying almost 3,000 gallons of 80-octane fuel. Although this was an especially hazardous mission, all the gliders landed without incident.

The 3rd Auxiliary Surgical Team at Bastogne reported:

> The large-scale airdrop, which began on 23 December, alleviated most medical supply deficiencies. Penicillin and other medicines, plasma, Vaseline gauze, anesthetics, morphine, distilled water, syringes, sterilizers, litters, and blankets arrived in the parachuted bundles. The parachute cloth itself, and the wrapping of the bundles, went to the hospitals to provide additional warm covering for patients. Whole blood also was among the air-delivered supplies, but the bottles broke on landing or were destroyed when a German shell blew up the room where they were stored.

Realizing they were losing momentum, some German officers began to question the competence of Adolf Hitler and the resolution of the Luftwaffe to provide effective support for the offensive. Lieutenant Wingolf Scherer, 5th Panzer Army, said:

> The initial euphoria with the powerful German artillery subsided very quickly. I heard a general tell his staff officer how an idiot ordered an offensive. The "idiot" of course meant Adolf Hitler, who, as many times before, ignored the advice of experienced military advisers and ordered a suicide attack. We had no information about the enemy, or how many there were or where they were stationed. We practically rushed into the battle blindly. Our decimated Luftwaffe, which four years earlier had controlled the airspace, provided very little assistance.

Many of the men on the ground described seeing the resupply air drop as one of the most, if not the most, heartening spectacle of the whole siege.

Major General Taylor said:

> Air supply performed an important role in support of the Division in HOLLAND and BASTOGNE. It was established conclusively that supplies dropped by parachute from C-47s

were put down in a much better pattern than those from bombers. Also the glider is definitely a better way of landing Airborne supplies than parachute. The procedure marking fields and homing aircraft bringing in supplies would be the same as the procedure for putting down Airborne troops.

The take-off and order of resupply drop over the Bastogne drop zone was performed by:

1) 12:28 pm: 41 C-47s from the 437th Troop Carrier Group (TCG)
2) 12:45 pm: 50 C-47s from the 434th TCG (drop altitude 500 feet)
3) 12:45 pm: 46 C-47s from the 436th TCG (drop altitude: 500–700 feet)
4) 12:50 pm: 43 C-47s from the 435th TCG (drop altitude 700 feet)
5) 12:59 pm: 43 C-47s from the 438th TCG (drop altitude 380 feet)

By the end of the day, 249 C-47 loads had been dropped for the cost of eight lost due to enemy action. The first stage of the resupply mission had been a resounding success. Jake McNiece and his comrades were recommended for Silver Stars, but this was subject to the approval of Col. Robert Sink, 506th PIR commander, who refused the recommendations and downgraded them to Bronze Stars. Sink's excuse was that none of the group had been to Pathfinder School, but he insisted they should all be integrated into the 506th.

Meanwhile, the Germans were continuing to push beyond the besieged city. General Heinrich von Lüttwitz wrote:

> On the 23–24 Dec 44, I personally drove up to the point of the Division and discovered that the road block consisted only of thin barricades. I saw that there were no enemy forces and later had to clear the matter by a court-martial. I then got the Division moving, but we had proceeded northwest only a short distance when we came to a small river crossing. At that place, the whole road was blown up. It was an exceptionally good piece of work by the American engineers. We reconnoitered a bypass and the Division then moved rapidly on to Marche. I had counted on the enemy building up a new defensive position on the line Rochefort–Marche; therefore, I tried to pass this line as quickly as possible. In the late afternoon of 23 or 24 Dec 44, while still southeast of Marche, contact was made with the enemy. I ordered the Division only to screen against Marche, while the bulk of the Division was to make a breakthrough at Hargimont. I had had command of this Division before I assumed command of XLVII Pz Corps.

The defenders had received 230 tons of supplies that constituted ammunition, medical supplies, and rations. The following day, 50 more gliders lifted off behind their tugs and headed for Bastogne, 35 of which landed close enough to directly assist the defenders. By the end of the resupply mission, gliders alone delivered 106,291 pounds of cargo, and the medical personnel flown in saved innumerable lives during those horrific days and nights. That air drop made it imperative for General von Manteuffel to turn some of his precious armor around to send it back to Bastogne, in the vain hope of destroying the American defense, but the momentum had already been lost. Those blue skies didn't just open for the Allied air forces, though; the defenders would learn soon enough that they opened for the Luftwaffe too.

CHAPTER THIRTEEN

What's Merry About All This?

We have stopped cold everything that has been thrown at us from the North, East, South and West.

ANTHONY MCAULIFFE, ACTING COMMANDER, 101ST AIRBORNE DIVISION

Many veterans of the battle to hold Bastogne mentioned they heard Bing Crosby's "White Christmas" crackling mockingly from a requisitioned gramophone. At that moment it was difficult to imagine that less than a week ago the place had been festooned with decorations in anticipation of the approaching festivities. Now the illuminations were dead, due to the electricity being disconnected, and paper bunting was scattered like discarded confetti around the shell holes and debris that littered the sidewalks and roads in Bastogne. Paratroopers out on the perimeter huddled in their foxholes and acknowledged the low resonant booms of artillery exchanges. These percussive blasts no longer induced any fear in a lot of the men. They were too preoccupied with attempting to stave off the bitter cold and stay alive in the inhuman conditions.

Sergeant Robert Minnich, 907th Glider Field Artillery Battalion, 101st Airborne Division, wrote a letter home:

Dear Mom,

I don't know how long it will take for this letter to reach you, but being Xmas, I wanted to drop a line to let you know I'm thinking of you on this day. It wasn't much of a holiday for us, as you can guess. I spent Christmas eve in a foxhole, trying my best to keep warm. I got relieved today and came back to a whole quart of champagne as a Christmas present to myself. I went to Holy Communion this afternoon and had a prayer said by the Chaplain. The service took place in a barn, but to us the presence of God is all that matters.

Some provisions were still low; this made it necessary to requisition yet more supplies from the civilian population, who were, as always, willing to share whatever they had. While white bed sheets were used as ad hoc ponchos, pillowcases covered a lot of the American helmets, and burlap bags were wrapped around those indolent paratrooper "jump boots." Throughout this whole period, a trickle of refugees was still arriving in Bastogne.

Refugees had begun to vacate the city as early as December 16, and this exodus continued practically unabated throughout Tuesday morning when shells began landing on both civilian and military targets smack in the center of the city. The flow was reduced to an intermittent trickle by Wednesday, and by Thursday there was no way out. For the thousands of rumbling stomachs of GIs both inside and on the perimeter, the military scavenged all the food it could find in the abandoned stores in the city. The American authorities, namely Captain Smith CAO (Chief Administrative Officer) and Lt. McGuire CIC (Counter Intelligence Corps) established a civilian government and appointed Mr. Jacqmin as mayor, and 25 assistants for the duration; the new mayor immediately mobilized the civilians, who volunteered in droves to do everything they could to alleviate the suffering. While they organized burial parties for civilian casualties, two local doctors and a veterinarian stepped up to take care of the sick and wounded in the cellars. A new curfew was imposed, allowing the civilians to scavenge between noon and 2:00 pm.

Although there had been a desperate shortage of some things, such as ammunition and medical supplies, the air resupply had helped a lot and, in retrospect, the food situation was not all that bad because Bastogne was a centrally located farming hub where all local farmers sold and traded their produce. Fresh meat was in abundance. A team of local volunteers, inspired by their culinary requirements, bravely ducked and dived between shells and bullets to recover animals from nearby farms, especially pigs, most of which had been abandoned in the pens and byres. Once acquired, these animals were taken to a communal abattoir; despite the discomfort, despite the incessant shelling, despite the lack of hygiene, Belgians nurture deep and profound relationships with their stomachs, and nowhere more so than in Bastogne. When the animals had been slaughtered, the meat was then divided among civilians and military personnel in the overpopulated cellars.

December 24, the Bastogne garrison welcomed another supply drop. At 3:40 pm, 160 C-47s dropped an estimated 139-and-a-half tons of ammunition and three tons of signal equipment by parachute. These supplies were flown in from the Airborne camp at Mourmelon-le-Grand. This was also the date the Luftwaffe began a four-night bombing assault against Bastogne. A squadron of bombers left Dedelstorf, just over the German border, heading west. Despite smaller bomb loads, stripping down to the bare essentials of equipment, and cleaning up the fuselages to improve streamlining to increase range, the Junkers Ju 88s were already down to a little over half their fuel reserve. They flew low, following the road network while maintaining strict radio silence. They carried 500-pound purveyors of death.

During the early evening, the Junkers encroached on the cold skies above Bastogne. It was claimed the overhead drone was so resonant that buildings shook with the vibration. Within moments they were unleashing their deadly cargo on the population below. The first wave dropped incendiary munitions, spewing flames as they detonated, igniting and reducing an already-wrecked city to a hellish inferno.

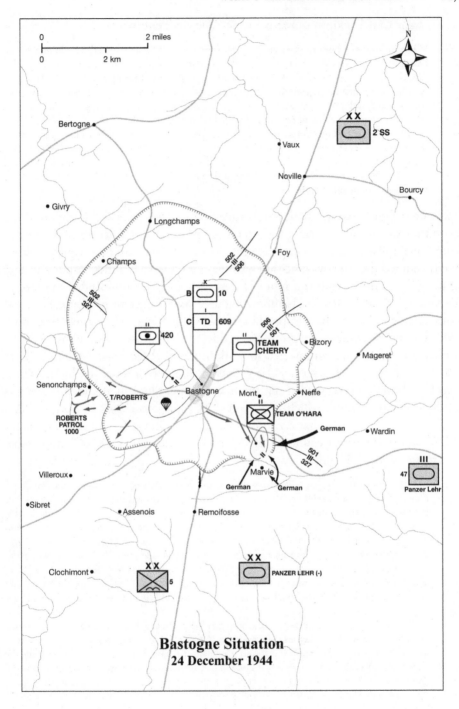

Bastogne Situation
24 December 1944

Sergeant Carl Dickinson, 327th Medical Detachment, wrote:

> While in Bastogne I got to sleep on the bare wood floor of a warehouse type building with no heat and no blankets. My foxhole was more comfortable than that place. It was also no safer. The German Luftwaffe bombed the village while I was there, causing considerable damage. I was, however, able to acquire some additional uniform parts in Bastogne including another pair of pants and another shirt. I had also gotten into the habit of rotating my socks putting the wet ones on my chest to dry while I wore dry ones.
>
> The cold was bad and the snow was getting deeper, but wearing three pairs of pants, three shirts and dry socks helped take the edge off. It was during this action to close the bulge that I was struck in the right shoulder by a bullet. It knocked me down but I didn't initially feel any pain. Pfc. Premetz, who was also the company medic, patched me up. The captain directed me to walk to an aid station.

Most remaining "Bastognards," numbering around three thousand (opinions differ as to the exact number), had given up on the prospect of Christmas and taken to communal cellars, some holding between 30 and 50 civilians. Consequently, hundreds endured the siege with neither washing nor sanitary facilities. Around twenty senior citizens died as a direct result of these extremely uncomfortable conditions. Despite the almost relentless bombing endured by the citizens of Bastogne, it was considerably worse for those trapped in surrounding villages where shells from both sides devastated centuries-old properties, reducing them to ashes and rubble. Augusta Chiwy, the nurse who volunteered to work in Combat Command B's (CCB) aid station on Rue Neufchâteau, regularly dodged shrapnel to reach her home, which was just a few hundred yards from the main square. She had attended the Sisters of Notre-Dame School, which had opened its capacious cellars to both civilians and military personnel. One Airborne soldier, Sgt. George Mullins, C Company, 327th Glider Infantry Regiment (GIR), had firsthand experience of hard combat and those cellars. He said:

> It begins to snow with large flakes coming down. Two inches of snow are on the ground at present. The guys all assemble after mass, and we move out toward the crest of the hill. Private Robert E. Johnston from Indiana and another trooper are in front with me as we approach some small trees that surround a flat place. There is a low drop along the lower edge. A lieutenant lies motionless here in this small clearing of the woods. "He was killed a few minutes ago," says a paratrooper who is standing near him, looking very sad. He says, "He was my lieutenant, my friend." I can see movement and hear the roar of engines in the valley, even though it is about five-hundred yards away. I have no idea what's going on. One of our Sherman tanks approaches quickly from the small field at the top of this hill. It stops at the crest with a better view of the valley.
>
> The tank crew wastes no time and begins zeroing in on the enemy. This tank concerns me because there must be numerous German tanks in the valley with their wicked 88s, also zeroing in. The Sherman is a fine tank, but it's no match for the 88mm and its crew. The 88 beats the Sherman to the draw, taking it out with one shot. I am standing with my friend, Johnston, and another man when the Sherman tank crew exits their disabled tank, running at lighting speed right past me. The Jerrys down in the valley waste no time reloading. We are the next target. I hear the sound of the 88 as the round leaves the barrel of this massive gun.

This must be the largest, fastest round that has ever been fired at me! In an instant, it hits a tree nearby with an explosive force splintering the tree tops. Fortunately for me, I was quick to move and get just far enough away to avoid impact. The troopers with me weren't so lucky. As soon as the round left the gun five hundred yards away the three of us were long gone on our way to the low place at the edge of the clearing, just ten feet away: I am certain that none of our boots touched the ground as we ran to the low spot. As the round explodes, all I can see are these two big guys, Johnston and the other trooper, as they fall on top of me. They aren't as lucky as I am. I can see blood running down from Johnston's and the other mans' bodies in front of my face. They are mumbling something. I'm pretty sure they're praying, as I probably should be.

I manage to free myself from the weight of these two men. I think I'm okay, but everything is blurry, and I'm having a hard time getting my eyes to focus, I move a few steps backward. I see Sergeant Whalen, then Parker, and a couple more troopers. They are taking cover in a small ditch near trees that are along the trail. Slowly make my way to the ditch. It's not quite dark yet but its close. I hear no artillery, rifle fire, machine gunfire, or explosions from tanks. It's cold and snowing heavily; I don't know how much time has passed, but there are at least eight inches of snow on the ground.

An ambulance arrives with a couple of medics. I'm having a bad time seeing as they help me climb into the ambulance. Through blurry eyes I can see some wounded soldiers, men I have been with before I arrived at this God forsaken place. It feels as if I am living in a dream. I don't remember where or how these guys got wounded. As I ride along, the ambulance wheels are spinning, dipping and siding. It seems like only a few minutes but I am certain it is longer before we stop in front of a very large building, the school the Sisters of Notre Dame. A soldier says to me, "You get out here." It concerns me that I am the only one getting dropped off here, but I exit the truck and enter the building. It takes a moment for my eyes to adjust because there is very little light. There are a few combat soldiers with their rifles standing nearby as the wounded are being treated. The room is dim except for one corner where there is something going on. A doctor and couple of medics are attempting to remove shrapnel from a soldier's head.

Captain Morton J. Smith, C and Headquarters Company, 502nd Parachute Infantry Regiment, wrote a letter to a friend in which he mentioned that at the time he was aware of 158 wounded soldiers languishing in the Bastogne cellars with civilians. Many of the wounds became gangrenous and amputated limbs were just thrown onto a pile. Soldiers and civilians suffered together; there's nothing that draws people together stronger than shared adversity, and a mutual hatred of a third party. That's why the bond remains strong today. It has passed on to other generations, who nurtured it with the same respect and love.

By this time, the town had been under siege for almost four days. Although reports about Gen. George Patton's advancing Third Army were encouraging, it brought little comfort to those having to fight both inside and outside the perimeter. Nazi propaganda minister Josef Goebbels wrote in his diary, "The situation cannot be regarded as too rosy for us. The German 2nd Panzer Division covered almost a hundred kilometers in a week, but didn't succeed in reaching the River Meuse."

The 2nd SS Panzer Division was transferred to the 5th Army to facilitate the capture of Bastogne but was unable to redeploy because the roads were completely gridlocked by the 116th Volksgrenadier Division and the Führer-Begleit-Brigade

(Führer Escort Brigade). In the west, the 116th Panzer and 2nd Panzer Divisions were encountering problems.

The 5th Panzer Army commander, General Hasso von Manteuffel, noted in his diary on December 24:

> The attack led by the 116th Panzer Division was unsuccessful. The desired breakthrough was not achieved. In the evening there was a local incursion in the area to the northwest of Vardenne that succeeded and was able to fire down Hotton Street, Marche. Another division battle group, with its Panzer Regiment managed to take Vardenne and to gain the area north and northeast of the town. The enemy was present in the entire LVIII section. Attacks by the 116th Panzer Division continue because it was necessary to support the 2nd Army, which had advanced far to the west to bring relief to the Panzer Division. The bloody losses of the division on December 24, 1944 were considerable. The Corps applied to the army for the addition of the Führer-Begleit, Führer Escort Brigade, and intended to place them on the south bank of the Ourthe to be used initially against the long-contested town of Hotton, and proceed with the 116th Panzer Division's attack. December 24th, 1944 was all about activity, more specifically, the fighter [jabo] actions of the enemy.

General von Manteuffel implored Hitler's military adjutant for a cessation of all offensive operations in the west, and a full retreat back behind the Siegfried Line. Hitler refused point blank. He had very little or no consideration for how many Germans would die in this vain, deluded attempt to reach Antwerp.

It's often said the only two certainties in life are death and taxes; this applied to serving soldiers too. Fiscal considerations were probably the least of a soldier's worries when he was fighting off repeated attacks from well-armed Germans. One paratrooper told a story about a letter he received from the Internal Revenue Service. It stated clearly that he owed $171 and if he didn't pay they would come to take him to jail. He said, "I took all the money I had, French, Belgian, Dutch, and put it in an envelope. I told them I'm in a foxhole in Bastogne and they can come get me if they want. I never heard anything back from them."

One of the distinct highlights of December 24 was the Christmas message distributed to the troops by the division commander. In an attempt to raise the flagging spirits of his troops, unencumbered by hubris or arrogance, Gen. Anthony McAuliffe, acting commander, 101st Airborne Division, wrote an excellent morale-boosting yuletide note. All the defenders received a hectographed Christmas message from McAuliffe:

> Office of the Division Commander.
> HEADQUARTERS 101ST AIRBORNE DIVISION.
> 24 December 1944.
> What's Merry about all this, you ask? We're fighting, it's cold, we aren't home. All true but what has the proud Eagle Division accomplished with its worthy comrades the 10th Armored Division, the 705th Tank Destroyer Battalion and all the rest? Just this: We have stopped cold everything that has been thrown at us from the North, East, South and West. We have identifications from four German Panzer Divisions, two German Infantry Divisions and one German Parachute Division. These units, spearheading the last desperate German lunge,

were headed straight west for key points when the Eagle Division was hurriedly ordered to stem the advance. How effectively this was done will be written in history; not alone in our Division's glorious history but in World history. The Germans actually did surround us, their radios blared our doom. Their Commander demanded our surrender in the following imprudent arrogance:

"To the U. S. A. Commander of the encircled town of Bastogne.

The fortune of war is changing. This time the U. S. A. forces in and near Bastogne have been encircled by strong German armored units. More German armored units have crossed the river Ourthe near Ortheuville, have taken Marche and reached St. Hubert by passing through Hompres-Sibret-Tillet. Libramont is in German hands.

There is only one possibility to save the encircled U. S. A. Troops from total annihilation: that is the honorable surrender of the encircled town. In order to think it over a term of two hours will be granted beginning with the presentation of this note.

If this proposal should be rejected the German Artillery Corps and six heavy A. A. Battalions are ready to annihilate the U. S. A. Troops in and near Bastogne. The order for firing will be given immediately after this two hour's term.

All the serious civilian losses caused by this Artillery fire would not correspond with the well known American humanity.

The German Commander"

The German Commander received the following reply:
22 December 1944
"To the German Commander:
N U T S !
The American Commander"

Allied Troops are counterattacking in force. We continue to hold Bastogne. By holding Bastogne we assure the success of the Allied Armies. We know that our Division Commander, General Taylor, will say: "Well Done!"

We are giving our country and our loved ones at home a worthy Christmas present and being privileged to take part in this gallant feat of arms are truly making for ourselves a Merry Christmas.

A. C. McAuliffe

Life in Bastogne had long since lost any semblance of normality. It was now a scene of utter desolation and destruction, a mere shell of its former self. Dead bodies and limbs lay everywhere, some covered, some exposed, their frozen forms accentuated against the unremitting snow and cold. Smoke billowed from the ruins of now-unrecognizable structures. It was difficult to discern which buildings had been shops and which had been civilian domiciles. Burned-out hulks of abandoned vehicles were scattered intermittently along the entire main street, and outside one aid station the frozen cadavers of soldiers were stacked upright against the wall.

Bastogne felt like a ghost town. Only the occasional thunder flashes of artillery followed by agonized screams gave any indication there were still people alive there. The scarred and battered ruins appeared to be at the point of total collapse, as if they would shake off what little cement was holding their bricks together and implode in a cloud of choking dust at any moment. To the observer, it seemed like everything within Bastogne's perimeter was dying a wretched and protracted death. As the situation deteriorated, the city had indeed suffered terribly, but it hadn't succumbed, and along the rest of the line marginal successes had been noted.

The SHAEF (Supreme Headquarters Allied Expeditionary Force) report from December 24 leant towards a favorable outcome:

> The great weakness of the enemy's forces, [such as] lack of training, has made itself apparent in the infantry divisions. The enemy staff work has shown care and ability of a very high order in planning and his intelligence has foreseen every move in the game of a continental battle of maneuver, over terrain familiar to German strategists for centuries. But the execution by undertrained formations, is not faultless. Supply difficulties have arisen and will grow. Much of the petrol carefully hoarded on the start line has been expended without the capture [one of the major hazards] of Allied stocks, the communications net in the EIFEL and ARDENNES is poor, and, with clearing weather will be at the mercy of Allied air superiority.
>
> In fact the plan worked in general well in the center, where 5th Panzer Army reached its first bound along the road and railway through MARCHE without mishap, the infantry following up comparatively stoutly: BASTOGNE, however, was not taken and remained, though surrounded, a galling commitment in the middle of the Army's line of communication, while 11 Panzer Division, late at the start line, was in trouble with Allied forces at LAROCHE. In the South the Volksgrenadiers led off with some limited advances, but were soon stopped and even driven back, suffering unwelcome casualties. But it was in the north, where much the greatest weight had been placed, that things went most seriously wrong from the start. Between Fifth and Sixth Panzer Armies was an infantry corps [LXVI] which had the mission of seizing the key communications center St. Vith: in this it failed over a crucial period of five days, and a firm Allied salient was maintained, thrusting deep into the center of the enemy's advance. If the Meuse had been reached in the first four or five days Allied stocks would have been captured and Allied positions would have been turned before their forces could have been mustered and regrouped. But it was NOT. The enemy is far from beaten yet. For the last time he has accumulated men and machines in Teutonic mass, by draining all sectors of the West, even the most vital and the whole Fatherland, of all reserves. This mass will fight on, dragging in even the last panzer or Volksgrenadier from the North and South and East, to exhaustion. It can never be reproduced, it has gone on too far to draw back.

Surgeon Jack Prior of the 20th Armored Infantry Brigade, CCB, now under the command of the 101st Airborne Division, was operating with his nurse volunteers Augusta Chiwy and Renée Lemaire. They all looked up as the sound of aircraft engines began to fill the night sky. They assumed they were C-47s making another drop, but it was difficult to discern. When Jack and Augusta went next door to enjoy a festive glass of champagne, they were oblivious to the situation developing at the aid station.

A few incendiary bombs had already fallen and a small fire had ignited at the back of the building. These bombs were probably intended as target markers for the following wave of bombers. Renée began attempting to douse the flames with melted snow but was unsuccessful. She was seen running out into the street looking for assistance. As she returned to the aid station on Rue Neufchâteau, a 500-lb bomb impacted the building, blowing Augusta Chiwy clean through a glass partition wall. The aid station was completely demolished. Augusta sustained bruises and cuts but, despite her injuries, she continued to work. She was later made an honorary member of the 327th GIR.

Renée Lemaire has quite wrongly become connected to the 101st Airborne. She was tragically killed on December 24 while serving at the aid station in Bastogne. In the series *Band of Brothers*, she was shown tending wounded and interacting with "Doc Roe," a 101st Airborne medic. This was purely contrived in Hollywood to give a minor romantic interlude to the series. The fact is, she never worked with E company or the 101st Airborne in any capacity and would have been more or less oblivious of them. It's incredible how fact and fiction can become blurred.

Three Bastogne nurses worked at the 101st Airborne facility located at the former "Riding Hall" of the Heintz Barracks, which had been requisitioned to serve as the 101st's headquarters/command post. They were Andrée Giroux, Blanche Dombier-Hardy and Augusta Chiwy. They all pulled 18- and 20-hour shifts in an attempt to clear the backlog of wounded, some of whom had been waiting for up to eight days for surgical intervention. They also performed many necessary amputations. Working with Dr. Prior and the 101st surgeons, they managed to complete 50 operations in one day, incurring only three postoperative deaths. There would be more fighting, and more casualties because the Germans, who place such importance on the Weihnachten, were apparently not in a very festive mood. The following day, Bastogne would be the target of yet another desperate attempt to dislodge its defenders.

CHAPTER FOURTEEN

The Proud Eagle Division

I know that times, I remember, the crying, in pain. So it's not Supermen. Humans, willing to go that extra mile, that's what it was.

EDUARDO PENICHE, C BATTERY, 81ST AIRBORNE ANTI-AIRCRAFT BATTALION,
101ST AIRBORNE DIVISION

Christmas Day is always an emotional time for soldiers far from home, and the paratroopers of the 101st Airborne Division were no exception, but there wouldn't be much time to celebrate. They had an inkling the Germans were planning something big on the day. The area in and around Champs to the northwest of Bastogne was not a good place to be, but those Airborne men would rise to the challenge.

German command had decided that, on Christmas Day, the village of Champs would be the prime target for their yuletide assault. Generalmajor Heinz Kokott, commander of the 26th Volksgrenadier Division (VGD), assembled battalions of the 15th Panzergrenadier Division and the 26th VGD in the region of Fays and Rouette, and they had no intention of waiting until daybreak. He issued orders to the effect that Bastogne would have to be taken before 8:00 pm. It was a tall order, and he knew it. He planned a classic pincer movement and would strike at the 502nd Parachute Infantry Regiment (PIR) in the château from the small breach between the 327th Glider Infantry Regiment on the left and the 506th PIR on the right.

It appeared Kokott was relatively impervious to the fact that most of his troops were cold, exhausted, and operating on empty stomachs. He regarded this opportunity as the last chance to effectively take Bastogne. The attack commenced at 2:45 am with a powerful barrage by the entire artillery battalion of the 26th VGD. This was quickly followed at 3:30 am by an attack orchestrated by the 115th Panzergrenadier Regiment, 15th Panzergrenadier Division, led by Col. Wolfgang Maucke, and supported by two battalions of the 77th Regiment of the 26th VGD.

Kokott said:

> I was to participate in an attack on Bastogne on 25 Dec 44 and, in preparation, I moved my Command Post to Gives on 24 Dec 44. Just before I departed, I left a few guards and directed the placing of some antiaircraft guns on the heights around Hompre. There was only one good

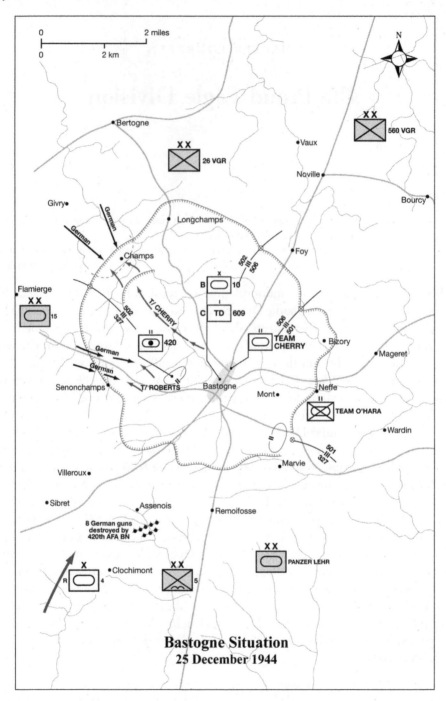

Bastogne Situation
25 December 1944

thing about 5 FS Div [5th Paratroop Division]: it was heavily equipped with weapons. I assisted by giving instructions as to how some of these weapons could be used to the best advantage.

On Dec 25th, 44 I made a trip around the perimeter defense of Bastogne and did not return to my Command Post until 2100 hours. I knew nothing more about the situation to the south, although my troops at Assenois had reported much artillery fire. I talked to Gen Pz von Manteuffel on the telephone. I told him that I could not watch two fronts, and that the southern situation was most dangerous. I did not think that 5 FS Div could hold.

During the previous evening, officers from the 502nd PIR, commanded by the very capable Lieutenant Colonel Steve Chappuis, attended midnight mass within the walls of the beautiful Château de Rolley (previously spelled "Rolle"), which is in a small, wooded area just east of the village. The château was selected because of its remote, hidden position and proximity to Bastogne. Its thick walls and adjacent buildings, including the stables, served as a sturdy command post for the 502nd, complete with radio room. Moreover, it was a relatively comfortable barracks that doubled as an aid station, a kitchen, and weapons depot. The 502nd had established its headquarters there, although somewhat out on a limb, consciously in proximity to Lt. Col. Ray Allen's 401st Glider Infantry Regiment (GIR) troops who were working in conjunction with M18 tank destroyers of the 705th Tank Destroyer Battalion.

At 3:30 am, Capt. Wallace A. Swanson, A Company, 502nd PIR, informed his superior officer, Lieutenant Colonel Patrick J. Cassidy, that the Germans were in the vicinity of Champs. The main German attack went in around 9:00 am and A Company became embroiled in a vicious hand-to-hand fight for every building in the village. The company had taken up position while it was still coal black outside; the only illumination was provided by muzzle flashes and artillery explosions. The château came under intense small-arms fire from the right and center.

Major Ivan G. Phillips, Communications Officer, 502nd PIR, wrote:

> The Regimental Commander, Lieutenant Colonel Steve A. Chappuis, was awakened and given a resume of the situation by Colonel Cassidy. Colonel Chappuis then called Major John D. Hanlon, 1st Battalion Commanding Officer, by radio to alert his battalion and report to the Rolle [sic] CP [command post] at once. By this time it was evident to all CP personnel at Rolle what was happening. The artillery barrage had lifted to the CP at Rolle. For fifteen minutes the outside was untenable. As the artillery fire calmed down, the Commandant, Regimental Headquarters Company, alerted all troops under his command to move out and occupy the high ground in the vicinity of the motor pool.
>
> The Demolition Platoon Leader, Lieutenant Laurence A. Hughes, influenced a change of these orders because of darkness and the lack of positions to occupy. Headquarters Commandant was also alerted later to occupy Road Block No. 3. The 2d Platoon of Company B, manning a third road block on the Longchamps–Bastogne Road, was sent by Colonel Steve A. Chappuis to fill the gap that existed between Company A and the 2d Battalion. Lieutenant Stewart, Platoon Leader of this 2d Platoon of B Company, moved up the draw through regiment and into position near the woods by the No. 2 bridge and occupied the position. Major Hanlon [1st Battalion Commanding Officer] reported to the command post at Rolle for further orders. Upon learning that contact had been lost with Company A, he wanted to go forward to Champs and report back the situation. Colonel Chappuis [Commanding Officer] and Colonel Cassidy

[Executive Officer] had made an estimate of the situation, thinking the main effort would either be at Champs or west of Champs, which later proved correct.

Before Major Hanlon had left for Champs, he was ordered to send Company B forward to the vicinity of the road block and report to regiment when they arrived. Major Hanlon then ordered Company B to move forward to Bridge No. 1. After giving this order by radio, he proceeded to Champs to find Company A swarmed with enemy. The US Forces were firing at everything that moved from their dug-in foxhole positions outside of the buildings. The enemy was so stunned to find the American troops not occupying the houses in the freezing weather that it completely confused them. The enemy was all over the position, yet not an inch of ground was gained by the Germans.

Fierce fighting ensued in the vicinity of Champs, and on the road between Champs and Hemroulle, but the American forces repulsed every single attempt to break through to Bastogne. At dawn, a force of 18 German tanks got ahead of their infantry and attacked east from Flamizoulle (Flamisoulle), actually reaching the headquarters of the glider infantry's 3rd Battalion.

In one particularly nerve-racking incident, the glider men on the front lines, no doubt recognizing their weapons would have little effect on the German tanks, hunkered down in their foxholes and allowed them to drive right over. The German infantry was then left without tank support and was mowed down by the glider men. At the end of the day, the survivors of that German unit were commanded by a 19-year-old lieutenant, a bad day for the unit but likely good for that officer's career prospects if he survived.

One particularly disorientated German tank commander reported that, according to his map coordinates, he had reached the perimeter of Bastogne itself, but he was wrong. While the Germans were fervently attempting to hit out to the north to try to isolate Chappuis, they dangerously exposed their right flank to the mercy of a force of M18 tank destroyers from the 705th concealed in nearby woods. On this occasion, they put six German tanks out of action—three were destroyed by the tank destroyers, three by bazookas. Between December 19 and 26, the 705th gunners destroyed 39 German tanks, three half-tracks, three trucks, an armored car, three antitank guns and four other vehicles. They also accounted for innumerable enemy casualties.

The 12 remaining German tanks made a further attempt to reach Bastogne; 11 were completely destroyed and one was captured. The proud "Eagle" Division had succeeded again.

Major Phillips wrote:

In counting the casualties at Champ, there were 98 German dead, 8 American paratroopers dead, with 15 US casualties and 81 Germans, including two officers who were captured. Over in the 3d Battalion area of the 327th Glider Regiment where the German tank-infantry teams had broken through, eleven other tanks had been knocked out by the combined efforts of the tank destroyers and the 463d Field Artillery Battalion firing direct fire. Front-line companies of the 3d Battalion, 327th, had made a tenacious stand to stop the infantry troops and tanks without moving from their dug-in foxhole position.

Eighteen enemy tanks in all were knocked out in this Christmas morning action. Information contained in captured enemy document showed the 115th Panzergrenadier Regiment [recently brought up from Italy] and two battalions of the 77th Volksgrenadier Regiment supported by the 26th Volksgrenadier Division Artillery had participated in the German attack. Later reports revealed that two regiments of the 15th Panzer Grenadier [sic] Division had gotten off to a poor start in the 327th Sector, while the 77th Regiment made an attack on the east side of Champs., The Reconnaissance Battalion of the 15th Panzer Grenadier had hit the 327th Glider Regiment lines farther south.

The 327th GIR's after-action report for Christmas Day read:

Early Christmas morning two enemy planes again bombed Bastogne and the city was shelled with heavy artillery. German infantry attacked Champs at 0330 hours. At 0530 the 326th Airborne Engineer position received small arms and mortar fire, and at 0710 hours German tanks and infantry made a strong attack on Companies "A" and "B" of the Third Battalion. At 0720 hours these German tanks broke through to meet point blank fire from friendly artillery. The tanks withdrew and tried again, only to be repulsed. Meanwhile other German tanks had broken through at Champs between the Third Battalion and the 502nd Parachute Infantry. Five out of eight of these tanks were knocked out. Fighting continued to flare up all day in the Champs sector but at 1030 hours it diminished in the First Battalion sector. That day German prisoners taken totaled 117 during the fight around Champs. All ground lost early in the battle was retaken.

By noon all the German tanks had been knocked out and the enemy infantry was forced back. The enemy also attacked along the main south road into Bastogne against Company B and continued their attack on a light scale Christmas day. Artillery fire and mortar fire fell only intermittently in the southern sector.

ANALYSIS AND CRITICISM

For the purposes of clarity this Christmas day action was explained in four separate individual actions. Actually the enemy had made a double envelopment on Champs with the plan of capturing the American Forces' CP at Rolle [sic].

The initial attack in the wooded draw between Champs and Longchamps failed in the initial stages because of the effective fire laid down by Company F's two light machine guns and the speed in which 2d Battalion mortars had brought the enemy under accurate fire. The fact that the concentration was tree burst was not planned, it just happened. As the enemy attacking at Champs moved in with assurance as to the lay of the position. The buildings were occupied without a great deal of opposition; however, when Company A road blocks and dug-in positions opened up with accurate, well-aimed fire on the enemy outside the buildings, it completely confused the German commander.

The excellent targets for the tank destroyers were made by the enemy occupying the houses. It is apparent that Company A was fighting in all directions and firing at all moving targets. In this particular situation, it worked without firing into their own troops. Had the enemy that penetrated over the entire village of Champ employed armor, there is no doubt that the Champs position could have been taken. In the combined tank and infantry battle at Rolle CP, it may appear that the reserve was committed piecemeal; however, it was not. Company C quickly took up positions in the woods and was reinforced by regiment along with Company E.

The action of the tank destroyers was an effective morale booster to the troops, plus the fact they accounted for a considerable amount of enemy armor knocked out. The running battle of the two tanks which destroyed three enemy tanks before they themselves were destroyed is an example of the tank destroyers' actions. The enemy riding the tanks were quickly cleared and the enemy tanks deprived of infantry. For this reason, the tanks were in no position to have any further firefight since they were buttoned up. The success of this combined action was a direct result of the regimental commander and executive officer making a correct estimate of the enemy capabilities.

Reading the extent of the excellent coordination between artillery, armor, and infantry, a picture emerges of the incredibly high level of reliability and cooperation between the different units defending Bastogne. General Anthony McAuliffe was an artilleryman who fully comprehended the necessity of cohesive efforts among all the units under his command in resisting the Germans. When the American artillery units received an urgent fire mission from an air observer of the 420th Armored Field Artillery Battalion around 10:30 am on Christmas Day, Captain Murray, the assistant S-3 (operations) and Colonel McElroy, immediately set out in an M3 half-track to reconnoiter the situation. They didn't have any other option because communications were down; they provided a radio to help coordinate the artillery barrage, which resulted in highly effective salvos being landed precisely where they needed to be—on the heads of the attackers, many of whom scattered in disarray.

This type of coordination had become a specialty of the 101st by this point in the war. Major General Maxwell Taylor had frequently formed ad hoc task forces led by McAuliffe or one of his regimental commanders. These task forces typically involved elements of multiple regiments with additional artillery or armored units attached. Such ad hoc formations had performed well at Carentan, Best, and in countless other engagements.

One of the artillery units under McAuliffe's command was the African American 333rd Field Artillery Battalion, which had initially been attached to the 2nd Infantry Division until that unit was replaced by the ill-fated 106th Infantry Division on December 14 (ill-fated because two of its three regiments were captured out on a salient in the Schnee Eifel in the largest surrender of American troops in Europe during World War II). The 333rd only managed to escape that debacle with five working 155-mm artillery pieces, which they put to very good use in conjunction with the other highly effective artillery units within the perimeter of Bastogne.

Before they reached Bastogne, and merged with 969th Field Artillery Battalion, 11 members of the 333rd were captured and murdered in a most horrific manner by members of the 1st Division SS.

A combination of sheer determination, excellent leadership and courage had repelled the Germans at Champs, leaving Kokott feeling distinctly disadvantaged. The lay of the land there is particularly conducive to a defensive action. Quite steep rolling hills and wooded areas provided excellent cover for the 502nd PIR and elements of the 327th GIR. They used the environment to their advantage, by choosing the ground, and displaying a remarkable capacity to gauge the strength and direction of the German attack. The Rolley Château was a classic Belgian design, not unlike the château/farm at Hougoumont, which was a pivotal feature during the Battle of Waterloo, and there are parallels. They both held, and both managed to repel the attackers without having to squander reserves in the process.

The after-action report of the 705th Tank Destroyer Battalion for December 25 read:

> Throughout the early morning hours there were marked indications of an enemy armored build up in the northwest, and western sections of the perimeter. About 0400 in the morning, after some preparation of mortar fire the enemy attacked in great forces, their armor preceding infantry by about 200 yards. The infantry of the 101st Airborne Division permitted the tanks to pass through them, and then effectively stopped the following infantry. Their own infantry were excellent targets for the anti-tank defenses of all arms of the division as well as our own guns. In some instances our guns permitted the tanks to pass them and were enabled to place effective fire on their flanks and rear. In places the enemy armor was enabled to penetrate the MLR [major line of resistance] but denuded of their own infantry were excellent targets for the antiaircraft defenses of all areas of the division as well as our own guns. In several instances the Tank Destroyers were able to effectively assist friendly infantry by M5 and .50 caliber machine gun fire on the enemy infantry. It is believed that the high degree of coordination between the infantry and tank destroyer commanders was largely responsible for the success enjoyed this day.

The action at Champs effectively proved a fairly sizable division could remain operable and effective thanks to air resupply. As long as the skies remained clear, the tactical advantage remained with the defenders. The favorable weather also allowed Third Army surgeon Maj. Howard Serrel to fly an L-4 Grasshopper into Bastogne. It was noted he had medical provisions for 60 wounded, when provisions for 600 had been requested. He assisted the medical personnel and performed 15 surgical procedures in 36 hours. Meanwhile, the audacious response McAuliffe had given to the German surrender ultimatum continued to resonate among his men.

Second Lieutenant Robert Potach, Headquarters Company, 2nd Battalion, 502nd PIR, said:

> You respected [McAuliffe] more, he gave the answer that I think 90 percent of us would have given. We weren't about to surrender. Our training didn't include any prep for that. The spirit of the Airborne was different than a lot of the rest of [the Army].

Standing a diminutive 5' 5", Pfc. Eduardo Peniche, C Battery, 81st Airborne Anti-Aircraft Battalion, 101st Airborne Division, participated in the action at Champs. He was a proud Mexican American. After his discharge, he returned to his native Mexico because his visa had expired while he was fighting in Europe; he refused to reside in the United States illegally. Before his departure, he was told that, by virtue of his military service, he was entitled to apply for a permanent visa. He was an exemplary soldier, who became a patriot. He fought through Normandy and Operation *Market Garden*, but nothing prepared him for the deprivations he faced in the Ardennes:

> I am from the Yucatan. To be ten below zero, my biggest fear was that I was not going to wake up. The enemy fire would not let up. But the cold was torturing you day and night. And I was panic-stricken. If I fall asleep, I'll never wake up. Foxholes didn't provide much protection. It was snowing. We had, in some places, two feet of snow. And then, when you are in the foxhole

and the heat, your body heat, melts all that snow. So in the bottom of the foxhole, you have a puddle of water. I saw some German prisoners. They were purple, their faces, their arms. And Americans that died of frostbite.

There is nothing taller than a short paratrooper, I felt 10 feet tall. You know why? Because I had confidence. And I felt welcome. Our leaders, from generals to sergeants, were superb. We were well trained, but the esprit d' corps of the Airborne helped us to overcome all challenges. Do you measure up? Can you measure up? Can you give all you have? Can you stand tall? Can you go all the way? All these are icons, you might say, icon words. But you live up to it because you reach down deep. We were not Supermen. Of course, we were not. I saw the troopers dead. That's not Supermen. I know, I know that times, I remember, the crying, in pain. So it's not Supermen. Humans, willing to go that extra mile, that's what it was.

As an addendum to Ed Peniche's story; in 1952 he returned to the United States, rejoining the U.S. Army, and became a loyal citizen because he wanted to live in a land where merit counted more than class and where commitment to freedom was more than a slogan. He married Miss Deanie Baggett from Paducah, Kentucky. While serving in the Army, he learned to speak French, Portuguese, and Vietnamese; the latter served him well when he became an advisor and translator, first during the Vietnam War, and then as a translator for the Inter-American Defense College. In the process, he became an honorary professor after being awarded degrees from George Washington University and the University of Nebraska.

Generalmajor Kokott noted:

> I was in no position to prevent a breakthrough. Manteuffel told me to forget about 4 Armored Div [U.S.], that it was quiet for the moment. The only solution to the problem was to attack Bastogne, he directed that I stop worrying and devote all my efforts to the attack from the northwest. I followed his advice, but the situation was most "disagreeable." It was this situation which precipitated our attack on Bastogne at 0300 on 25 Dec 44. I was busy all day with the attack. That night, Obstlt Kaufmann, Commander of 39 Grenadier Regt, asked to move his Command Post from Assenois. He said that the situation was most dangerous. I refused his request. The breakthrough would come from CCB, 4 Armored Div [U.S.].

Sergeant Paul Bebout, 1st Battalion, 501st PIR, remembered:

> Patton was the only help we could get. We was [sic] attacked by three armored divisions. It got you to thinking, *If I'm gonna get out of here, we got to end this.* Patton saw us and said he never commanded such a brave bunch of men in his life. He decided to take us, so from then on the 501st Regiment, 101st Airborne, was with Patton.

December 26 was to be a seminal day in the history of the 101st Division at Bastogne. General George S. Patton's lead unit, the 4th Armored Division, had advanced along the Neufchâteau–Bastogne highway on Christmas Day and was already in the vicinity of Nives and Cobreville, on a direct line south of Assenois. One paratrooper wrote to his mother, "McAuliffe said Patton didn't rescue the 101st, instead [he] interrupted us in our revenge on the dastardly Boche. We didn't need him as long as the Allied headquarters had C-47 airplanes to throw away every day. After midnight I take a dim view of almost anything. It is now already morning. Love Richard."

Sergeant Robert Minnich, 907th Glider Field Artillery Battalion, 101st Airborne Division, wrote:

> During the evening of the 25th, one enemy bomber made a pass over Bastogne, discharging between eight and ten bombs in regular quarter-mile intervals. Lieutenant Jack Washichek and other members of the battalion air section heard "Twilight Charlie" approaching, and, by the fourth or fifth bomb, they were heading for the dank potato cellar in the house they were occupying. Lieutenant Washichek recalls how tough it was for six guys to get through the cellar door at the same time. They wound up with more injuries from the wild scramble than from the bombing.

Combat teams from the 502nd and 327th, in combination with the amazing tank destroyers, and well-targeted artillery support, had endured and survived a really tough battle and, even though their perimeter had been breached, it was restored by noon on Christmas Day. For the remainder of the day, they received some sporadic shelling, but there was still time to enjoy a Christmas dinner, even when it fell well below stateside standards.

Speaking of which, General McAuliffe and his fellow officers enjoyed an ad hoc Christmas dinner of canned salmon—some say it was sardines—and biscuits, complete with a rather sad-looking Christmas tree assembled from spruce branches. But he received an encouraging phone call from General Patton, informing him the Third Army was close by, which could have been arguably the best Christmas present he could have received. However, the final word of this chapter belongs to 502nd PIR paratrooper Pfc. Stanley J. Pazik who said, "You never even thought about Christmas. I never had a watch. I didn't know the time or the day."

CHAPTER FIFTEEN

A Winter's Tale

Patton's tanks arrived on December 26. As soon as it is safe to travel, the wounded are evacuated. When I sleep, I shiver to prevent myself from freezing to death. As long as the shivering continues to keep my blood flowing, I know I'm okay.

GEORGE MULLINS, C COMPANY, 327TH GLIDER INFANTRY REGIMENT

The Germans were proving to be as unimaginative and intransigent in their tactical approach as they had been the previous day, and on previous occasions. It didn't take a rocket scientist to figure out each attack followed more or less the same pattern. First their tanks would appear, preceding infantry by roughly 200 yards. The American tank destroyers would allow the infantry to pass unmolested, while remaining concealed, the hills around Champs and the château were particularly conducive to this approach; at just the right moment the tank destroyers would open up with their cannons and .50-cal machine guns and chew up the German infantry up en masse. The excellent level of coordination with the paratroopers proved to be a worthy deterrent, but although this punitive approach had worked successfully on almost every occasion, it didn't prevent a further German attack occurring on December 26, the day Gen. George Patton broke through the encirclement. While some paratroopers were largely oblivious to this momentous breakthrough, some, such as Capt. James Adams, F Company, 327th Glider Infantry Regiment (GIR), were eagerly anticipating Patton's arrival.

Adams reported that:

Company F spent a relatively quiet morning that day. The men were rotated so they could spend some time indoors getting warm and making coffee. Enemy artillery and mortar fire fell mostly in the rear areas, but heavy fighting could be clearly heard along the western sector of division, several miles to the south, and southwest. Heavy firing gave hope of an early breakthrough by the 4th Armored Division. At 15:00 medical personnel landed by glider on the drop zone just west of Bastogne. A resupply by parachute was dropped at 15:20. A portion of the last serial fell outside the perimeter. At 16:50 amid a great deal of firing five tanks could be seen breaking out of the woods 1500 yards due west of the company F command post. Observed through field glasses they were found to bear the white star of friendly tanks. Regiment called Company F Command Post at 17:30 hours to officially confirm the arrival of five friendly tanks

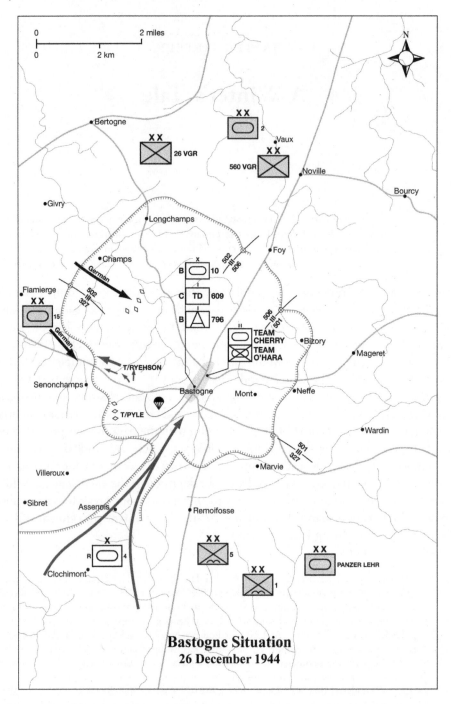

Bastogne Situation
26 December 1944

in the area of 326th Airborne Engineer Battalion. Regiment also instructed that yellow panels would be displayed marking our forward positions on the main road. The main elements of the 4th Armored Division were expected to enter Bastogne via this road on the following day. Company F then settled down for the night. Nevertheless strong security was maintained. No chance could be taken even with relief promised for the morrow. The enemy still manned his positions and, while in them, was a constant threat.

The most pervasive question that always arises at this point of the siege of Bastogne is did the 101st Airborne Division really need rescuing? On the basis of the evidence presented so far, there's some ambiguity and contention regarding the word "rescuing." Although it was later claimed Patton's Third Army rescued the 101st, not a single member of the division ever admitted to needing it.

Up until December 26, and despite numerous attempts, the Germans forces had failed to dislodge the paratroopers in Bastogne. It should also be acknowledged that the main German force designated with the task of capturing Bastogne at this juncture was Generalmajor Heinz Kokott's 26th Volksgrenadier Division, which wasn't really up to the standard of either the 116th or 2nd Panzer Divisions. Moreover, they were fighting battle-hardened, experienced paratroopers reinforced with armor and artillery. When it dawned on German commanders at OB West (Oberbefehlshaber—high commander—West) that a quick capture was no longer feasible, they sent some tanks to assist, but the best German divisions had headed west, even though they were going to be recalled, and lost both momentum and impetus, along with a significant amount of strength.

By December 26, the attacking forces were getting critically short of ammunition and fuel, the underlying problem of this ill-conceived German counteroffensive. During those first tumultuous days, they enjoyed a numerical advantage, but after conceding a considerable number of casualties in the course of the battle, this dissipated. The staunch and consistent defense of the 101st Airborne, and all subordinate units, had effectively deprived the Germans of any ability to use their numbers and mobility to their advantage. There was never really a danger of the 101st conceding Bastogne. The air resupply had restored the imbalance and bolstered the stability of the defensive perimeter.

The significance and importance of Bastogne, as a strategically crucial road junction, has been consistently overstated in other published historical accounts. There's no doubt it was an important road junction in its area, but the main thrust of the German armor was not, and was never intended to be, there. The spearhead was further north and that had been completely repulsed, by tough American divisions from the First Army and the 82nd Airborne Division, by Christmas Eve. Bastogne was on the southern flank of the 5th Panzer Army's attack. Due to its tenacious defense, its importance increased as the battle progressed. This was reflected most effectively by contemporary media of the day. The propaganda value of Bastogne greatly inspired the Allied cause. Hitler fully understood the value of propaganda, hence the importance of Bastogne intensified.

The 101st was fully aware Patton's Third Army was on the move and striking north. The level of discipline in the Third Army must have been quite phenomenal. The logistical challenges of disengaging an army of around 350,000 personnel from one front, turning 90 degrees, and advancing north, would have presented a gargantuan task for any commander, but Patton wasn't "any commander," hence he managed to accomplish this in a matter of days. For all his self-aggrandizing braggadocio, this was going to be his moment and he knew it. His Third Army had punched a corridor through German positions to the south and southeast of Bastogne. In some places, the corridor was only a mile wide, but that was sufficient to get the wounded out and supplies in. Patton was heard to say to a sergeant of the 101st Airborne, "It isn't over yet!"

Three designated combat command teams of the 4th Armored Division had been steadily edging their way toward Bastogne since 6:00 am on December 22. They had taken three separate routes from their assembly areas north of Arlon, but it was no easy task. Every stuttering advance was met with concerted resistance and they lost tanks and sustained many casualties. By 3:00 pm on December 26, CCR (Combat Command Reserve) had reached high ground close to Clochimont to prepare for the assault that would break the siege. After some military dithering, they took Sibret, which they had incorrectly assumed was well defended by the Germans. Although General Kokott was fully aware of the developing situation, in light of the attacks taking place to the northwest of Bastogne, there was very little he could do about it. Part of the advance was Pvt. James Richard Hendrix, who valiantly earned a Medal of Honor at Assenois. His citation read:

> On the night of 26 December 1944, near Assenois, Belgium, he was with the leading element engaged in the final thrust to break through to the besieged garrison at Bastogne when halted by a fierce combination of artillery and small-arms fire. He dismounted from his half-track and advanced against two 88-mm guns, and, by the ferocity of his rifle fire, compelled the gun crews to take cover and then to surrender. Later in the attack he again left his vehicle, voluntarily, to aid two wounded soldiers, helpless and exposed to intense machine-gun fire. Effectively silencing two hostile machine guns, he held off the enemy by his own fire until the wounded men were evacuated. Pvt. Hendrix again distinguished himself when he hastened to the aid of still another soldier who was trapped in a burning half-track. Braving enemy sniper fire and exploding mines and ammunition in the vehicle, he extricated the wounded man and extinguished his flaming clothing, thereby saving the life of his fellow soldier. Pvt. Hendrix, by his superb courage and heroism, exemplified the highest traditions of the military service.

At 3:20 pm, Lt. Col. Creighton W. Abrams Jr., commander of the 37th Tank Battalion, ordered his S-3 (operations), Capt. William A. Dwight, to take a team composed of tanks and infantry, and break northeast to the village of Assenois, with the direct order to keep moving until he reached the Bastogne perimeter. The artillery stood by with three battalions of 105mm and one 155mm ready to place a concentration on

Assenois as the CCR advanced toward the target, where they expected to be greeted by German antitank guns.

On that eventful day, at 4:00 pm, a highly qualified Third Army surgical team—consisting of Maj. Laman Soutter, Capt. Stanley Wesolowski, Capt. Foy H. Moody, Capt. Edward N. Zinschlag, Capt. Henri M. Mills, and four enlisted surgical assistants—was flown in to assist the overworked medics in the riding hall at the 101st Division's headquarters.

Sometime around noon, Gen. Anthony McAuliffe received word elements of the 326th Airborne Engineer Battalion were reporting contact with "three light tanks believed friendly." Along the ice-covered road from Assenois, just a few miles southeast of the Bastogne perimeter, three American Sherman tanks and a half-track rumbled forward, followed by two more Shermans sweeping the rear. The three lead Shermans were commanded by 1Lt. Charles P. Boggess and his crew—Cpl. Milton Dickerman and Privates James G. Murphy, Hubert S. Smith, and Harold Hafner. The half-track had inadvertently become attached to the tank column. As they rumbled forward, Boggess ordered covering fire into the tree line. During the ensuing melee, a 300-yard gap developed between the first three tanks and the last three vehicles, giving the enemy just enough time to throw a few mines out on the road in front of the half-track, which rolled over the first mine and exploded, throwing burning metal, shrapnel, and body parts into the grey skies and across the fresh snow.

Gunfire from turret-mounted .30-caliber machine guns saturated enemy positions with devastating speed and, after a short while, the two rear tank crews hastily disembarked, cleared the remaining mines, and then radioed for more elements of their column to follow on. At 4:50 pm (the time is indelibly recorded in 4th Armored Division dispatches), Boggess, commanding officer of C Company, 37th Tank Battalion, spied what turned out to be Airborne engineers from A Company of the 326th preparing to assault a pillbox near the highway (which is still there). Boggess told the driver of his Sherman to take his foot off the gas. As daylight dithered and the light faded, a single engineer from the 326th hollered, "I'm Lt. Webster, 326 Airborne Engineers. Glad to see you guys."

Patton had definitely broken through. The siege was now lifted, but it would take a few days to firm up the American lines to the south. The tank following Boggess in his personally nicknamed "Cobra King," radioed Abrams to bring up the remainder of the breakthrough team. They had Maj. Gen. Maxwell Taylor, commander of the 101st, with them. He had returned from the United States to join his division, even though they had been performing splendidly without him. He had left Paris by jeep, but when he and his driver, Sgt. Charles Karthus were nearing Bastogne, Maj. Gen. Hugh J. Gaffey, the 4th Armored Division commander, had suggested it would be safer to continue the rest of the journey by tank. Taylor thanked him but said he preferred the jeep. His journey across the Atlantic had, obviously, been a desperate one. Captain Thomas J. White was an artillery officer with the 506th

Parachute Infantry Regiment (PIR) when he was summoned to become an aide to Gen. Maxwell Taylor. He recounted his story in a letter to a friend:

> I was ordered to report to General Maxwell Taylor immediately. Taylor was the Major General in command of the 101st Airborne and I had been his aide through Africa, Sicily, Italy and Normandy. Because of this long past association he offered to take me back to the States for approximately two weeks to brief the Pentagon on airborne operations. We left the same day, December 20, 1944 and flew back to Washington via Prestwick, Scotland; Gander, Newfoundland and on to Washington. General Tony McAuliffe, famous for his response "Nuts" when the Germans demanded surrender on Christmas Day, assumed command of the Division in the absence of General Taylor. I was thrilled with the idea of being home for Christmas for the first time in many years. However, at midnight on December 23rd I received word from Washington to report back there immediately for return to Europe. I flew to Washington the morning of the 24th and then we waited all day for suitable weather. We departed, finally, at 10 p.m. on Christmas Eve despite the fairly heavy snow storm. Our route this time was Newfoundland, the Azores and then to Paris. We then had to motorcade back to Bastogne [he spelled Bastogne, incorrectly on the letter heading, and consistently throughout the letter].
>
> We joined up with General Patton's troops and were the first ones to make contact with the surrounded airborne troops on the evening of December 26th. During the night of the 26th I was trying to sleep in a damp, cold cellar at Bastogne while the Germans bombed the hell out of us. I had rejoined my old outfit and we fought and slept in the snow, trying to stay warm when possible in snow filled trenches. Within a week we conclusively defeated the Germans in that area.
>
> In summary, my most vivid memory is the warmth and cheer of a scotch and soda at the Statler Hilton in Washington on the 24th and the marked contrast of the cold, damp cellar and the German bombs on the night of the 26th. How I wished I was back in Washington.

Accompanied by his own aide, McAuliffe drove out in a jeep to see Patton's troops for himself. Captain William Dwight, the second soldier to arrive with his tank after 1st Lieutenant Boggess, scrambled out, saluted, and asked, "How are you, General?"

"Gee, I'm mighty glad to see you," said McAuliffe.

A mere 20 minutes later, Lieutenant Colonel Abrams was shaking hands with the general who insisted the 101st party was well turned out for the occasion. They all had to be well-dressed and clean-shaven in an effort to display that, with or without Patton, they had everything under control. The siege of Bastogne may have been over, but the battle was most definitely not. The remaining two combat commands of 4th Armored Division still had a tough fight ahead before they effectively reached the Bastogne perimeter, but they would eventually get there. Assenois was completely cleared by 8:00 pm; 428 prisoners were taken in the process. Before morning, the woods on both sides of the road running north from Assenois were cleared sufficiently to provide unhindered use of this vital line of communication.

Generalmajor Kokott's last concerted attempt to capture Bastogne had petered out and resulted in abject failure yet again. His intention had been to circle through the village of Savy into Bastogne. Even though the Germans managed to edge in between two companies of the 327th, they were caught in the open by American howitzers, which decimated the infantry assault. Four German tank destroyers continued toward Hemroulle but were finally brought to a halt by a large ditch. While they were in the process of maneuvering, all four were destroyed by close-range artillery and tank-destroyer fire. Seventeen glider men defending a roadblock on the western perimeter were attacked by two Mark IV tanks, a few half-tracks, and infantry. Near Hemroulle, Companies A and B of the 327th GIR defended against five tanks and a company of German infantry. The infantry were turned back and the tanks destroyed by a barrage of highly effective and accurate artillery fire.

By mid-afternoon, Kokott learned the German 5th Fallschirmjäger Division at Assenois, as well as the 39th Regiment, were under attack from Patton's 4th Armored Division. In the late afternoon, the commander of the 39th radioed the unwelcome information to the German commander that Patton had breached the German lines.

Nurse Augusta Chiwy, who had volunteered to assist the American medical personnel for the duration, asked a surgeon, "Who is this Patton and what has he broken?"

Kokott noted:

> I really don't remember, the situation was so bad, however, if I knew, I didn't pay any attention to it. There was nothing I could do about it anyway. My only hope was to continue with the attack on Bastogne. The 39 Gren Regt had its principal strength in Assenois, Salvacourt, and Sibret. I told Obstlt [1st Lieutenant] Kaufmann to continue facing toward Bastogne, and not to form a front to the south. I warned him, of course, to watch his rear and, when it became worse, to prepare an all-around defense, using all his anti-tank guns. When 4 Armd Div [U.S.] broke into Assenois in the afternoon, Kaufman called me. He said there were twelve enemy tanks in the village. The tanks were passing through Assenois and going to Bastogne.
>
> I knew it was all over. Kaufmann was told to just block the road. The corridor was still very small, the width of the road itself, and I hoped that with roadblocks and barriers, we could close the ring around Bastogne. It was a difficult task, however, because 39 Gren Regt had been scattered on both sides of the road by 4 Armd Div [U.S.] tanks, which were firing in all directions. Now it was difficult for 39 Gren Regt to fight back without firing at each other.
>
> We tried to get reinforcements there, but the troops of 26 Volks Gren [sic] Div were so tired from their fighting that they couldn't make the effort. The Fuhrer Begleit Brigade [sic] was ordered by the Corps to move to Sibret to close the circle, but it didn't get there in time. When it arrived, 4 Armd Div [U.S.] had already taken Sibret.

Although the 101st men insistently claimed they didn't need Patton or his Third Army, Sgt. Warren Swanquist, Headquarters, 3rd Tank Battalion, had another opinion entirely:

> This jeep came down the alley with flags waving away like crazy, it was General Patton! He had all his guns, his pearl-handled pistols. I was right next to him, I could've grabbed him I was so close. He was smiling, I rifle-saluted him and he hand-saluted me. He said something, but I cannot remember what it was. I think I took my first deep breath when the 4th Armored arrived. I was glad to see more people. I had figured I was dead.

To a large extent, the Germans can be blamed for underestimating the caliber and tenacity of the Airborne men in their foxholes. The level of determination and resolution in the division exceeded both the capabilities and the incentives of their attackers. During those failed attacks on Christmas Eve and Christmas Day, the defenders were actually numerically superior to the Germans, who may have been well disciplined and well-armed, but didn't appear to have enjoyed the same esprit de corps the 101st Airborne had. Believing you're the best, believing you are indomitable, and among like-minded individuals, adds greatly to morale, and morale is a mighty incentive. Most of the defenders were prepared to fight it out, irrespective of whether Patton arrived or not; for many it was business as usual, as Sgt. George Mullins, C Company, 327th GIR, explained in his diary:

Patton's tanks arrived on December 26. As soon as it is safe to travel, the wounded are evacuated. The commander of the ambulance service tells me to load up so we can leave. I tell him to go without me. I'm not going anywhere. The captain that has been doing all the operating here sends one of his orderlies to give me a message. The orderly approaches me and says "Trooper, the captain wants to see you." I enter the doctor's quarters and give him a salute. He says to me, "I see you didn't leave with the others. I want you to come with me." I reply, "Go with you?" He says, "Yes, I want you to work in the field hospitals with me. You can keep helping me as you have been here and not return to that world of ice-cold foxholes."

I pause for a second to take in the offer the doctor has just given me. My mind flashes back to the Douve River, the seventy-two days of death in bloody Holland, and then I see Parker, Lynn, Henn, and the rest of my friends that I have lived and fought beside these last few months. I see them cold, dirty, and hungry. The wear on their tired faces from combat is something that no one should visualize, and I dare not try to describe. I cannot let my big brother, Parker, and the rest of my company down by taking the easy way out. I say to the captain, "Thank you, but I cannot do that." He acknowledges my decision and shaking his head, he says, "There is a jeep waiting to return you to the lines."

I leave the building and climb onboard my ride back to the front line. The little jeep begins to make its way out of Bastogne. We travel through the snow up onto the railroad tracks. The tracks have been cut through the forest into a ravine. As we travel along the tracks, I notice that the snow is covered with black smoke. I know from past experience that a deadly battle has taken place here. At the top of the ravine, there is a flat area that has been cut out. There are many tank soldiers lying in a row. The driver stops. I climb up to the top of the bank and take a close look at these dead young men. They are all dressed in the same brown uniforms, the uniforms of our tank men. They are frozen solid, as cold as the ice and snow they lie in. Someone took the time to lay these men in this line. As I gaze down at them, I hear the doctor's voice saying, "I am well aware of a much different world out there."

I get back in the jeep and continue on my journey. We travel over some really rough terrain until we approach a hillside. The driver stops, I get out, and the jeep drives away in a hurry. I see a dugout on the side of the hill and walk toward it. I reach the dugout, a screaming Mimi [*Nebelwerfer* rocket artillery] is sent to welcome me back to my platoon. It comes in screaming across the battlefield. The sound of these monsters will send chills, like the ghosts of hell running up your spine. The enemy must not be happy to see me.

As I enter the dugout, I see this is Captain Miller's new company command post. Captain Miller is sitting in a makeshift chair that has been carved out of the steep ground. Inside his dugout in the dim light, I see the captain. I can tell that the winds of war are taking their toll on Captain Miller. He has always spoken to me with respect. He is a very special person. I think of all the responsibility he is burdened with, the life of each man in C Company.

Very few people will ever understand the life that this man is living. I respect him for being who he is with such a heavy responsibility. The captain, who seemed to me to always have a trembling voice, tells a runner to show me the way to the machine gun. The runner and I arrive at a foxhole about forty yards down the hill below Captain Miller, overlooking a ravine. As I get in the foxhole, I notice that this isn't my machine gun or my gunner. I don't know the man next to me, I have never seen him before. I keep looking for Parker and the Squad, I ask the gunner next to me. He replies by shrugging his shoulders, I must believe that Parker and the others are okay and manning my machine gun at an outpost nearby. It is my understanding that Risley was wounded in Bastogne so this must be his gun. Henn and Avila must be with Parker.

As I get settled in this foxhole, the guy tells me that a couple of hours ago a German half-track drove by just a few steps from where we are. I ask him which direction it was heading and if he opened fire on it. He tells me that he didn't. He says that the half-track went into the forest at the top of the hill across the canyon. He points to a location and tells me that just recently a German medic was moving out to aid a wounded comrade when our men opened fire, killing him. I ask if he was wearing the big red cross. "Yes," he said. "They were in plain sight on both sides of his helmet and on his shoulder." In my mind, I understand what goes on in this world between two enemies on the battlefield but killing a medic is the wrong thing to do.

Retaliation doesn't solve anything for either side. It only makes things worse, but I can't change the past. Before dark, we make an attack into the woods at the top the hill across the canyon. Talk about luck! The enemy has already made a run for it, leaving us with some of the nicest, ready-to-use foxholes, although it would have been nicer if they had taken the time to clear the two inches of ice that is frozen around the top edge of the foxholes, but I'm not complaining. We set up the machine gun and get comfortable for the long, cold night ahead. I'm hoping we don't freeze to death before morning. To keep my feet from freezing, I make it a point to wiggle my toes around in my boots every few minutes. I am lucky, as many of the guys are having issues from frozen feet and frostbite. I also have become, as nature will have it, an animal. When I sleep, I shiver to prevent myself from freezing to death. As long as the shivering continues to keep my blood flowing, I know I'm okay.

I make it through to the next morning. It's really cold when we move out. We are on our way down the hill when we come to a highway covered by the debris of a German convoy. This is massive destruction. The whole convoy is completely destroyed, thanks to the United States [Army] Air Force. From what I can see, the pilots of those fighter airplanes are doing a fine job destroying enemy convoys.

The narrow corridor hammered through the German lines by Patton's Third Army was wide enough to bring in fresh supplies and ferry out the badly wounded to safer areas down south, away from Bastogne, even if they did have to run the gauntlet to get there.

The 101st Airborne's ground communications with supply depots were restored, and medics at the Heintz Barracks breathed a sigh of relief when their American wounded were evacuated to the 635th Clearing Company at Villers-devant-Orval, Belgium. At 6:00 pm, 27 December, a convoy of 22 ambulances loaded with seriously wounded was followed by 10 "deuce-and-a-half" trucks (the GMC CCKW two-and-a-half-ton truck) loaded with less serious wounded and, by 7:00 pm on the 27th, a total of 652 wounded had been transported to Villers-devant-Orval. Men of the 635th unloaded the casualties, tagged them, and transferred them to 64th Medical Group ambulances for movement to evacuation hospitals. The vehicles from Bastogne then went back to the city for another load. The Bastogne garrison would now benefit from an unlimited overland supply of weapons and medical equipment.

Their positions were fortified with additional tanks and troops of the Third Army, further compromising vain German attempts to capture the city.

One after-action report stated unequivocally that the German High Command had evidently considered further extension to the west or north as being both logistically and strategically unsound unless Bastogne could be taken. The attacks in the north began to peter out, and in the west there was a limited withdrawal, which clearly exposed the German forces, rendering them vulnerable to both ground and air attack. Their anxiety over that position was completely justified. Meanwhile, 101st Division and Third Army commanders concluded the Germans would probably continue employing the same fruitless strategy until the Bastogne situation was resolved one way or another. The 705th Tank Destroyer Battalion didn't even mention General Patton in its daily after-action reports:

> 26 December. This day was a repetition of the previous day although enemy attacks were not nearly as intense as those of the 25th. They again employed the same tactics and were handled in precisely the same manner. On this day, however, enemy armor was not able to make any deep penetration into the perimeter.

Marjory Avery, who was working as a war correspondent for the *Free Detroit Press* at the time, recorded her first vivid impressions of a city in ruins. She wrote:

> I reached Bastogne the day after a relief column had battered its way into the city to make contact with American forces, which had been cut off for a week. How we got here and what we saw on the way a number of times when we detoured to avoid German pockets, doesn't enter into this story.
>
> The town is still burning from German bombing. There are the usual scenes of wreckage and desolation. Civilians are digging themselves out, picking up bits of junk and trying to salvage their homes. Bulldozers crashing along the streets are trying to clear passageways. There is constant jolting from passing heavy artillery, tanks and trucks. In a pile of rubble which had been an improvised hospital before bombs hit it Christmas Eve, German prisoners and medical corpsmen are searching for bodies. American troops stand or stroll along the street grinning and asking the outsiders for news about the war.
>
> "The Germans said Luxembourg had fallen," a Yank said, "but we didn't believe it."
>
> I was struck by remarks made by a soldier who looked like a character from a Mauldin cartoon, unshaved, grimy and hollow-eyed,
>
> "How do you like the town?" he asked me.
>
> "It's horrible," I said,
>
> He looked around him for a minute,
>
> "You know," he said, "it was real pretty before we dug in."

CHAPTER SIXTEEN

Hell is Freezing Over

The wounded sat stiffly in the trucks, and they rose tautly when they came to a
rut in the frozen road. The dust of the road had made their hair gray, but it did
not look strange because their faces were old with suffering and fatigue.

A *STARS AND STRIPES* CORRESPONDENT

The commanders at OKW (Oberkommando der Wehrmacht, German supreme
command) utterly rejected General Hasso von Manteuffel's advice to abandon the
offensive, and ordered the battle for Bastogne to continue with all divisions present.
At the time, both the Panzer-Lehr and 2nd Panzer Divisions had collectively lost two
thousand five hundred killed, a thousand men captured, and almost innumerable
wounded, along with the destruction of 81 tanks, 81 guns, and 674 vehicles. These
were crippling losses they couldn't replace. Just before sunset, the Germans launched
two consecutive attacks that squandered the lives of a further 200 grenadiers; three
more tanks were also put out of action. They were stopped in their tracks by American
artillery before they could even get close to the 327th Glider Infantry Regiment's
(GIR) lines. The proverbial "Battered Bastards of Bastogne" were protecting a city
that was just as battered, if not more so.

The whole area in and around Bastogne presented a scene of total carnage and
destruction, and the temperatures continued to drop. During the following days,
howling winds and blizzards prevented any air bombardment, or air support, but,
on December 27, it was still conducive to resupply by air.

On that date, the Führer-Begleit-Brigade (Führer Escort Brigade) was ordered
to stop its advance and head to Bastogne immediately, an order that allegedly came
from Hitler himself, who was well aware the Third Army had broken through. It
would be another excuse for him to indulge in his by now notorious paroxysms of
apoplectic rage, which rarely achieved anything. Hitler's utter failure to accept the
reality of the situation was incredibly detrimental to his troops doing the fighting.

Some tanks of the brigade were abandoned due to a lack of fuel. One by one,
these behemoths came to a shuddering, spluttering halt; most would never even reach
Bastogne. The idea had been to send the brigade in from the south in an attempt

to close the breach caused by the Third Army. This was completely unachievable. Moreover, to have any hope at all of accomplishing this, the brigade would require the 26th Volksgrenadier Division to protect its flanks but, due to being severely depleted by the preceding battles, the 26th was no longer in a position to provide effective support at any level. A distinct air of desperation began to filter through the rank and file of the attacking Germans, which severely afflicted their morale and fighting spirit. German Panzerkommandant and Panzer ace Ludwig Bauer, 9th Panzer Division, who was with von Manteuffel's 5th Army, said, "I was driving a Stug III in the Ardennes. You could take out a hundred Sherman tanks, but the Americans could provide 120 replacements."

General Maxwell Taylor said, "if you take prisoners, they will handicap our ability to perform our mission. We have to dispose of prisoners as we best see fit." Some GIs found that difficult to comply with because a significant number of German prisoners taken around Bastogne, and in other places, appeared to be little more than barely adolescent teenagers. Their faces, contorted in expressions of horrified confusion at what they had witnessed, were often streaked with trails of tears through the grime. Many 101st Airborne veterans observed that it was hard not to feel sorry for these young soldiers. They hadn't known anything but Hitler's dictatorship; they had been ostensibly raised on a diet of hate and xenophobia, believing they were destined to control the world. They would soon discover they couldn't even control their bodily functions when they came up against the 101st.

One unattributed German after-action report for December 1944 stated that the preoccupation with the key position of Bastogne dominated German strategy to such an extent it cost them the advantage of the initiative. The German high command evidently considered further extension to the west or north as both logistically and strategically unsound without possession of Bastogne, as the city overlooks the main roads and concentration areas of the spearheads. Meanwhile, a triumphalist attitude had begun to permeate the American ranks.

Despite this, the Germans doggedly refused to abandon the offensive. Meanwhile, Bastogne had taken on a new significance for German high command. The story of the siege had reached the newspapers on both sides of the Atlantic. While the 101st Airborne Division's commander, Gen. Maxwell Taylor, was preparing to enter the Bastogne perimeter, he had met with some important journalists—such as Joseph Driscoll of the *New York Herald Tribune*, Norman Clark of London's *News Chronicle*, Cornelius Ryan of the *Daily Telegraph*, and Walter Cronkite of *United Press*. These men were more than prepared to publish headlines extolling the bravery and tenacity of the 101st Airborne—such as, "Brave defenders of Bastogne," "Alamo in the Ardennes," and "Battered Bastards of Bastogne"—but while the fighting continued with such ferocity, they were reluctant to personally accompany Taylor to Gen. Anthony McAuliffe's headquarters.

The daily 327th GIR's S-2 (intelligence) report read:

> ... at 1215 approximately 50 gliders landed with resupply. 4 C-47s were shot down by the enemy. At 1230 the Cherry Team established an OP [observation post] at 518585 to be manned twenty-four hours a day. At 1430 and 1445 resupply was dropped by parachute. At 1430 a patrol from the 1st Battalion reached RJ at 5355 and contacted Company A and C of the 51st Armored Infantry. These companies were cleaning out woods in area and hoped to enter Villeroux. At 1510, 4 friendly SP [self-propelled] guns came through our line at 541559. At 1630 word was received that friendly units had taken Sibret and were advancing toward Villeroux. Company A [326th Engineers] was relieved from sector 538563-545560, at 27 1200 A. Headquarters and Service Company [326th Engineers] was relieved from road block at 515587 by Company A [326th Engineers] at 27 1300.

From the Axis perspective, General von Manteuffel was decidedly unhappy with the evolution of the battle. He believed the German leadership had missed a vital opportunity to order the transfer of the 6th Panzer Army to the 5th Panzer Army, after the advance in the north had completely stalled as early as Christmas Eve 1944. He thought taking Bastogne would have been perfectly feasible if this had occurred. He also blamed high command for failing to launch the offensive on time.

His plan had been to advance to the River Meuse and then turn north in order to isolate Allied forces east of the Meuse. He mentioned that, despite the exemplary dedication and bravery of his troops, they were simply not quick enough to act and win the decisive battle for Bastogne, even when supported with additional reserves. He also praised the American tactical defense of both Sankt Vith and Bastogne. He secretly admired how the defenders of Bastogne had managed to tailor the situation to their ultimate advantage. Owing to the fact it hadn't been possible to take possession of the city early on, the divisions he had used for this purpose were withdrawn to advance towards the River Meuse. This failure to capture Bastogne within the allocated time frame meant the primary forces used to encircle the city were withdrawn. He was also disappointed the divisions left with the task were unable to take advantage of the initial gains made by the 2nd Panzer Division. Generalmajor Heinz Kokott's ensuing, incessant, concentric attacks, and attempts to find weaknesses in the perimeter defenses actually achieved very little.

Sergeant Robert Minnich, 907th Glider Field Artillery Battalion, 101st Airborne, wrote:

> The next day [December 27] provided more of the same. Another attack to the west of the positions was driven back with the help of one tank company, and, during another air raid, the building housing the Headquarters. Battery radio equipment was destroyed.

Pfc. William Treadway recalled the planes coming over in the evening, laying their eggs, and then getting out. He also recalled the concussion from the bombs which jarred the nails loose from the kitchen walls. The following morning the cooks, in between meals, nonchalantly hammered them back in. That same evening the tank crews of General Patton's 4th Armored Division broke through, ending the total encirclement of Bastogne. Pfc. Merlin Vanderah of the Headquarters Battery happened to be making a repair on a telephone line when General Patton's jeep pulled up in front of the Division Headquarters. Vanderah remembers seeing several MPs in the jeep and that Patton's ever resplendent appearance was a sight to behold. With the road way open once again, supplies started to pour in and the wounded were evacuated.

Pfc. Robert Anderson, 150th Signal Company, Combat Command B (CCB), 10th Armored Division, said:

> There was no let-up in the fighting. The artillery bombardment of the town continued. The team's wire laying halftrack [*sic*] was parked next to the Hotel LeBrun on the street facing the town square. Because of the shortage of gasoline it hadn't been used too much. Shortly after the breakthrough the track sustained a direct hit from an 88 or larger shell. Goodbye track. Even though the vehicle was armored, with armor plate extended around the sides and hood, the shell plopped down in the middle of the vehicle. It was inoperable. Fortunately no one was in or immediately around the vehicle. But, that left the team with a peep [jeep] as the only vehicle around for laying wire. These halftracks were constructed with a rack on the side of the body, extending back from the driver's side door and the right hand seat door. Each rack was loaded with land mines; so, there were 6–10 mines on each side of the vehicle.

Why they were there Bob never knew and it is doubtful if anybody else knew. Maybe the crew chief had the knowledge to set them up in a defensive position if the situation called for it. The "grunts" certainly didn't know. In spite of terrific damage to the track the land mines did not explode. What a Boom that would have been; no doubt the building next to the vehicle would have sustained considerable damage.

> As a platoon attached to the Headquarters of CCB, the wire team took its order from the officer assigned to signal or communication duties. In our case the officer was a First Lieutenant. SSgt Andy may have known his name but those of us down the line only knew him by sight. There was no personal relationship. The Lieutenant wandered around the vicinity of the hotel headquarters. Somehow or other in his explorations he came up with a black top hat. Probably it came from one of the apartments in town. The prior owner must have been somebody of importance like the mayor.

According to Albert Einstein, the definition of insanity is doing the same thing over and over again but expecting different results. Generals Manteuffel, von Lüttwitz, Bayerlein, and Kokott were collectively culpable of failing to achieve their objectives, but the real blame lies ultimately with Hitler's abject failure to recognize imminent defeat, even when it was staring him in the face. The majority of the commanders at OKW had become little more than obsequious, nodding sycophants, who acquiesced to everything Hitler said.

There's no doubt Hitler had been in a volatile mood since the attempt on his life at the "Wolf's Lair" in July. The perpetrators of this attempt were all Wehrmacht/Heer officers, most of whom he no longer trusted, but he still had faith in the SS. This is why he allocated the best equipment and designated the spearhead to the Bavarian butcher's son, Gen. Josef "Sepp" Dietrich, in the north. Dietrich had been a diehard Nazi since the days of the Munich beer halls in the turbulent 1920s. By 1944, he was a mere shadow of his former self.

As early as Christmas Eve, the 6th Panzer Army's attack had imploded in Stoumont, on the northern shoulder and left Kampfgruppe Pieper bereft of armor and with a mere 800 men, who were left alone to make a beeline back to their own lines through the snow. That particular drive to the River Meuse had been beset with logistical problems from the outset.

In his personal memoirs, and subsequent interviews, von Manteuffel rarely referred to Bastogne as a singular objective; it was almost always mentioned in combination with Sankt Vith which, as previously mentioned, he regarded as equally important to the offensive. Furthermore, the 5th Army had the most traversable terrain, particularly to the west of Bastogne, where there wasn't much boreal forest and most of the woods were Scots Pines, which had been imported in the 19th century.

E Company hero Second Platoon Sergeant William Guarnere mentioned during a return visit that "Belgian woods are not like any other woods, the trees grow in straight lines." Nobody pointed out to the dear man they'd been planted like that. This meant that still today, in places such as Bois Jacques, from a certain angle, it's possible to see all the way through from one side of the woods to the other.

The siege of Bastogne had produced a plethora of heroes from the Airborne, the armor, and the artillery combined. The level of cohesion and autonomy the defenders benefitted from was not mirrored by the attacking German forces, who were often stumped when they had to operate at anything below regimental level; they could still cause havoc, though.

Tech 4 A. Jedziniak, a medic with A Company, 501st Parachute Infantry Regiment, 101st Airborne Division, said:

> The Germans knew where we were, even in the foxholes. I had one man get killed next to me by a shell. Later on, I had two young kids, sixteen or seventeen years old, who surrendered to me when I had a guy on my back, bringing him back to the aid station. I used them to carry the guy on my back. I found a rifle and I had one of the guys hold the muzzle and the other the stock until I found an MP [military policeman] to take the prisoners and the wounded to an aid station.
>
> The medical kits had been returned back to supply and we never got new ones. I wound up with an officer's aid kit; the morphine was frozen, and there were sulfa pills and other drugs. I carried the morphine under my armpit to keep it warm. Trench foot was rampant. Treating the wounded, you did the best that you could. I took clothes off dead soldiers to treat the wounded, and we did not have many litter bearers to help get wounded men. [After Patton arrived] We started to get some stuff, like the ten-in-one rations from those guys who came in with the tanks. We got the wounded out as quickly as we could when the road opened. The civilians came out finally; they had been hiding. I happened to be in a farmhouse the day before, and I had a Coleman stove, and the other guys had a crock of oleo and potatoes, and we had french-fried potatoes. For a long time we did not have food.

On December 27, the 3rd Auxiliary Surgical Team noted in its daily reports that all the accumulated casualties came out through Villers-devant-Orval. Elements of the provisional medical battalion had moved into the city to provide a clearing station and forward surgical support for the Airborne troops, who still were engaged in intense combat.

In the defense and relief of Bastogne, the field army, corps, and division medical services displayed a high degree of resourcefulness and adaptability. Medics inside the perimeter, after the initial disaster of the loss of the 101st Division clearing station, put together a new second-echelon facility in the midst of combat, using whatever human and material resources they had. They kept most of the casualties alive until evacuation. Medics outside the ring made every effort to send in needed supplies and to re-establish forward surgical support for the besieged troops; they lost no time in evacuating the Bastogne hospitals after the relief. For the casualties, nevertheless, the siege was an ordeal.

How many patients died in Bastogne for lack of early surgery or as the result of other deficiencies of the improvised hospitals cannot be determined from the fragmentary records of those ephemeral organizations. One firm figure is the 101st Airborne Division's report of 33 deaths under treatment in its facilities between December 19 and 31. The Third Army surgical consultant, after examining the wounded brought out of Bastogne, concluded that "other than the physical discomforts, the casualties had not unduly suffered for lack of Medical Department treatment and that the mortality [rate] was extremely low." Whatever the clinical verdict, a *Stars and Stripes* correspondent, who watched one of the first evacuation convoys come out of Bastogne, expressed the human reality of the siege:

> The convoy of wounded came out of Bastogne in a slow trickle. The day was beautiful if you like Belgium in the winter time. The snow on the hills glistened in the sun, and the planes towed vapor trails across the big, clean sky. The wounded sat stiffly in the trucks, and they rose tautly when they came to a rut in the frozen road. The dust of the road had made their hair gray, but it did not look strange because their faces were old with suffering and fatigue.

On December 28, the 969th Field Artillery Battalion became part of the 101st Airborne Division for the duration. Even with the German siege broken, the 969th continued to be involved in supporting actions, and ensuing attacks to retake the area surrounding Bastogne. As the numbers of the defenders steadily increased, plans were made to go on the offensive, but there was no hurry.

Giving Some Back

Here's all these guys, bloodied and wounded, shot, and nobody's moving. Nobody's making any groaning or hollering like you see in the movies, you know, all that. Not these guys.

VINCENT SPERANZA, 501ST PARACHUTE INFANTRY DIVISION,
101ST AIRBORNE DIVISION

The weather report for southern Belgium, from the London Meteorological Office, forecast fog possibly clearing by late afternoon. It also stated heavy snow showers could be expected in all areas with winds from the north at 15 miles per hour, increasing to 46 miles per hour by the end of the day. Weather forecasts were not exactly reliable, because the morning of December 29 dawned with a resplendent sunrise that may have warmed the hearts of the defenders of Bastogne but didn't do much for their frozen extremities. As the sunlight permeated the morning sky, low-lying mist evaporated quickly and visibility to all points of the compass was excellent. There was one recorded firefight when a handful of paratroopers, stationed at one of the 502nd Parachute Infantry Regiment's (PIR) outposts near Recogne (where the German cemetery is located today), encountered a small group of German infantry but it was regarded as a mere distraction that didn't amount to anything significant in anyone's opinion.

Men of the 101st Airborne Division continued to patrol around the perimeter in an attempt to prevent any further German incursions, but little transpired during the day. Just before dusk, at around 4:00 pm, E Company was the target of a lackluster German attack. At around the same time, the 801st Airborne Ordnance Maintenance Company, which had set off from Mourmelon-le-Grand for Bastogne on December 19, finally arrived. The reason for the delay was due to the unit being ambushed and quite badly mauled by the Germans roughly five miles southwest of Bastogne. After the attack, the company was requisitioned by VIII Corps, and held back until the situation was conducive to their arrival.

Generalmajor Heinz Kokott's 26th Volksgrenadier Division (VKD) was augmented by the 3rd Panzergrenadier Division. The additional unit meant additional antiaircraft batteries that hampered Allied reconnaissance flights; the defenders had antiaircraft batteries too, and just after sundown these were put to use against three Junkers aircraft, which destroyed an artillery piece, a light tank and two half-tracks, before one of them was shot out of the sky; the other two turned tail and, still flying at a vulnerable low altitude, headed back to Germany.

Now we arrive at the story of a 101st Airborne veteran that most of the authors of this volume spent time with. There are ubiquitous versions of this legendary tale out there, but this one can be regarded as quite reliable.

Vincent Speranza, quoted earlier, was born and raised in the Hell's Kitchen neighborhood of lower Manhattan. He was used to hard knocks and was as tough as they come. He was reluctantly drafted in 1943. During the battle for Bastogne, he was a private with H Company, 501st PIR, right in the thick of it, amid the chaos and mayhem. Many of the wounded paratroopers from his, and other, units were being tended to in the seminary chapel. Vincent had been sent to headquarters on an errand. As he walked down the street, he went to a tavern and found his best friend, Joe Willis, lying on the floor among the wounded. As Vincent carefully walked between them, he teared up:

> Here's all these guys, bloodied and wounded, shot, and nobody's moving. Nobody's making any groaning or hollering like you see in the movies, you know, all that. Not these guys. They're all sitting there, and they're huddled up in whatever we could wrap them with. So I walked over, I find Joe, and I said, "Joe, how you doing?" He said, "I'm okay. I just got a few pieces of shrapnel in my legs. I'll be out of here in a few days." I said, "Well, Joe, I'm sorry you got hit," and so on. I said, "What can I do for you?" He said, "Find me something to drink." I said, "Joe, where the hell am I going to find you something to drink." He said, "Go look, maybe the taverns that have gotten bombed out or something." I said, "Okay." If your best friend wants to drink, you go find him a drink. I didn't have any luck in the first tavern I visited, but in the second one, I looked around, and everything's shattered glass and broken, and there's nothing in it but the bar was intact, I pulled on one of the taps and beer came out, then I looked around for bottles or something to put the beer in and there was nothing.

That's when he decided to use his helmet to convey the precious amber liquid. He carefully removed the lining, filled the helmet with beer, and then brought it back to his friend at the seminary aid station. That's when he heard that other wounded men there wanted some too. So, he made a second excursion. This time, when Vincent stepped out of the tavern with the next helmet of beer, a shell landed nearby and blew him clean off his feet, causing him to spill most of the beer; he wasn't hurt, he just got up and went back to the seminary. This time he was accosted by one of the regimental surgeons who enquired as to what he was up to. "I'm bringing aid and comfort to the wounded," he replied. The surgeon wasn't impressed, "You stupid bastard, don't you know I have chest cases and stomach cases in there? You give them beer you'll kill them. Get out of here before I have you shot."

Vincent didn't wait around, promptly retreating to his foxhole on the outskirts of Bastogne. He survived the battle and lived to the grand old age of 98.

Meanwhile, there was a seemingly intermittent convoy of supplies (including bottles of beer) arriving on the open road to the south of the city. Two 101st Airborne regiments, the 506th and 501st PIRs respectively, received welcome reinforcements.

The role American artillery played during the siege and ensuing battle for Bastogne cannot be underestimated. Every deployed artillery battalion was shelled repeatedly, and had to displace on numerous occasions, regardless of the inclement weather, and terrain restrictions. The city remained under continuous shellfire from all calibers of German artillery for almost the whole duration. German artillery fire was good but it was lacking what the allies regarded as a "game changer." After the arrival of Patton and his Third Army, the overall situation for the Airborne men improved by the day; now they had an opportunity to marvel at one of the most effective military inventions introduced to the Allied forces during the Battle of the Bulge.

The "Pozit" was an artillery fuse that greatly inspired "Ol' Blood and guts" Gen. George Patton, when he said, "The new shell with the funny fuse is devastating. I'm glad you all thought of it first." The variable time (VT)/proximity fuse could turn near misses into kills. Detonating at a predetermined height above ground, it could spread shrapnel over large areas, causing devastation and destruction. One German prisoner described the attacks as being quick powerful bursts for which there was simply no recourse or defense. Thanks to this new invention, Allied antiaircraft artillery batteries accounted for the destruction of 417 German aircraft during the battle. These remarkable shells were finally authorized for ground warfare in 1944, and their high point occurred during the Battle of the Bulge, when Patton specifically ordered them to be used against concentrations of armor and infantry.

The rounds were set to go off approximately 50 feet above the ground. Shrapnel tore through men and light equipment and wrecked entire armored and infantry units due to the sheer number of casualties. With all their means of technical innovation, the Germans were not able to develop such a fuse for their artillery despite many fruitless attempts.

It was now late December; the Americans most definitely had the advantage, which they planned to capitalize on at the earliest possible opportunity. Most actions that occurred around the perimeter during those final days of the year didn't amount to much for the Germans, who remained persistent; the feeling they were on the wane was almost palpable for the defenders of Bastogne. They had never entertained the prospect of defeat, and now their unyielding tenacity was yielding positive results.

The after-action report for the 705th Tank Destroyer Battalion for December 28 read:

> At 1800 elements of Company A which had covered the Company march of the battalion and had later been prevented by heavy enemy strength surrounding Bastogne from marching, rejoined along route cleared by 4th Armored Division. Pioneer Platoon, Reconnaissance Company, arrived in Bastogne at 1800. As well as Headquarters Company and Company Battalion Trains which made at once to 535595, where vehicles were dispersed and camouflaged. Arrangements were made for the return of Hq. Co. and trains to Bouillon the following morning.

It was December 30 and, after an ominously quiet night, just before sunrise, the Germans subjected the defenders and the residents of a dying city to a furious barrage considered to have been the heaviest of the battle so far, shattering what windows were still intact. It was so powerful that terrified Bastogne residents were invited to take advantage of American deuce-and-a-half trucks leaving the city on the south road, which was still the only road open at the time. The previous day's patrolling by the 101st Airborne paid dividends, though, because they were all too aware another German attack was looming.

By now, Patton's reinforcements, namely the 11th Armored Division and the 87th Infantry Division, had effectively deployed and were attempting to give some back by striking out from the southwest, from Libramont and Vaux-les-Rosières, against German positions in the vicinity of Noville. The 101st Division's artillery offered support but didn't participate in that particular assault; it did, however, assist the 6th Armored Division on its right flank. In retrospect, the attack towards Noville may have been a little premature because, as things transpired, it didn't really work out as well as expected. General Patton was heard to quip it was the most decisive day of the whole battle so far, but he hadn't been there during the first few days.

On that same day, as expected, the 26th VGD and the Panzer-Lehr Division launched yet another attack against Bastogne. This time they were joined by some desultory remnants of the 1st SS Panzer Division, along with the 167th VGD and the Führer-Begleit-Brigade (Führer Escort Brigade). Both sides incurred terrible casualties, and there was more to follow. For the defenders, it was becoming a case of same old, same old. The 101st Airborne, and subordinate units that provided great artillery and armor support, had repeatedly broken up concerted German attacks, even when, during those first few days, the enemy had numerical superiority. Now augmented by Patton's armor and artillery divisions, the Germans never really had a chance of closing the perimeter and reestablishing a siege.

General Hasso von Manteuffel, the 5th Army commander, was becoming increasingly disillusioned with his superior officers back in Berlin. He was already allocating blame before the new offensive had started. He was surprised fresh divisions were sent to reinforce his attack, but deeply regretted they weren't available when he almost reached the River Meuse. OKW (Oberkommando der Wehrmacht, German supreme command) remained intransigent and still overwhelmingly convinced Bastogne could now be taken. Even after Field Marshal Walter Model ordered "All units to Bastogne," von Manteuffel remained unconvinced; he cast aspersions against his superiors when he wrote:

> It was the Generals who allegedly, against their better judgment, made themselves available to Hitler to carry out this supposedly senseless offensive. It should be noted that the German soldier, through the inevitability of the political events before the outbreak of this war, was forced into a situation for which he was not responsible, and he was forced to obey in war, as all soldiers in the world have to obey. I made the critical mistake of relying on promises made by General Jodl

concerning an increase of the combat power for the shock armies. In this sense, the troops and leadership were once again, with self-sacrificing devotion for the task ahead prepared to engage and in the hope of some success. The fact that Jodl did not keep his promises, was probably nothing to do with Hitler's interventions. This demonstrates the tragedy in the conflict between Hitler and those military advisors closest to him. The course of the offensive proved that the commanders in chief [OKW] had assessed the chances and possibilities better than Hitler and his military employees. We didn't even significantly weaken the opposition. The consequences of this costly offensive were felt stronger in the east before they were in the West. The wasteful use of these last significant German reserves primarily benefited the Soviets. The promise that this offensive would buy us time in the West turned out to be a terrible fallacy!

General Alfred Jodl summoned what courage he could muster and confronted Hitler to inform him that crossing the River Meuse and retaking Antwerp was no longer feasible. Along with Model, he proposed a limited objective strategy. It's safe to assume that news wasn't received too well by the leader of the Third Reich. As early as December 22, tank expert Gen. Heinz Guderian had the temerity to inform Hitler the offensive had been a failure. Would Guderian have been a more suitable commander for this offensive? It was unquestionable that he could execute a tank battle like a ballet; he wrote a significant book about armor, which some claim to have been a blueprint for the "Blitzkrieg" that conquered and subjugated Europe in 1940. By this stage in the war, however, he was mainly confined to a desk job in Berlin.

For the Americans, both in and around Bastogne, it was no time to get complacent about the ensuing fight. They may have received additional units—such as the 11th Armored Division, the 87th Infantry Division, and the 17th Airborne Division—but indications were that the German forces were gearing up for another fight, and they still had the capacity to inflict terrible carnage; according to Gen. Troy Middleton, who wasn't inclined to be pessimistic, the Germans could even take the city. Patton, who wasn't known to be pusillanimous, confided to his diary, "We can still lose this war."

There was no doubt among the Allies that the Germans generally had superior tanks and associated weaponry during the final years of World War II; some tanks were even equipped with a rudimentary version of "night vision." In 1942, an infrared gun sight for the 7.5cm Pak40 self-propelled gun had been developed and tested with favorable results. On the strength of this, sighting devices were installed in some German tanks which provided the potential to attack at night without being harassed by Allied aircraft. There was no such equivalent in the Allied armies. Some Allied tank crews in Normandy had succumbed to a condition referred to in dispatches as "Panzer phobia." But it didn't affect everyone, particularly the armored divisions in Bastogne where, during that first 10 days, the 10th Armored Division Shermans frequently squared off against Panther and Tiger tanks. One particular "tankie" from the 10th wasn't deterred in the slightest. Gunner Corporal Donald Nichols, C Company, 21st Tank Battalion, Combat Command B (CCB), wrote:

I saw a Tiger tank point its nose out of the pine woods about 600 yards to my front, fire and back up. I told other crew members but they were unable to see or identify it. After several times of this happening, the tank commander told me to fire at it and adjust my own fire. My first round was a little short, the Tiger, backed up again. My next rounds were over or ricocheted off the trees. One hit the Tiger turret, bounced off but did not explode. These were high explosive shells. I finally told the loader, Sgt. Bulano, to load the HEAT [high explosive antitank], fired and hit the Tiger as it was rolling back into its pine tree hideout. Saw black smoke and figured it was out. Did not see it or hear from it again. Kill was later confirmed.

The odds were incredibly stacked against us. Every unit in the area covered itself with glory, and no one division was the whole show. Combat Command B did not win the battle of Bastogne alone. But many military students believe that without our armor, Bastogne would have fallen to the Germans immediately. They would have been free to control the vital highways leading into Bastogne, free to smash their way west to create, perhaps, another "Bastogne" elsewhere in Belgium. The importance of Combat Command B's effort is already a matter of record in military history. For Combat Command B, the credit due the three task forces of Desobry-Hustead, Cherry and O'Hara cannot fully be measured. When the chips were down, those forces reacted magnificently.

Not to be overlooked is the first-rate support received from the sharpshooters of the 705th Tank Destroyer Battalion, the superb 420th Field Artillery, tough Ninth Armored fighters, the deadeye 609th Tank Destroyers, the tiny group of stragglers from many other units, and most of all, the help obtained from those rugged paratroopers of the 101st Airborne Division. Of the Troopers, Colonel Roberts had this to say,

Those 101st men were absolutely tops, they were taught to fight surrounded, and few divisions could have accomplished the same success. Their officers and particularly the staff of the division were superior in every respect. They didn't scare easily.

The heat of battle fused Tiger and Trooper into one great fighting machine. Friendships were made during Bastogne that were not forgotten after the war was over.

Most previous volumes, and some veteran recollections, state that Col. William L. Roberts's command post on Rue du Marche close to the center of Bastogne was destroyed by German shelling on December 30. It was actually the 3rd Tank Battalion command post that was hit, and five CCB officers were killed. While the 327th PIR's A Company, 1st Battalion, was relieved by its B Company, the S-2 and S-3 offices took a direct hit from German bombers. They were, however, no match for the Spitfires and P-47 Thunderbolts that were hitting German positions and harassing columns heading back to Bastogne from the west.

Remnants of the Luftwaffe had bombed Bastogne at around 7:00 pm the previous evening and again during the early morning; some observers claimed to have seen jets above Bastogne, but apart from that it was business as usual. In his customary magnanimous style, General Patton decided to personally inspect all the command posts around Bastogne. He must have presented quite a sight to the troops as he rode around in his jeep with his shiny helmet and mother-of-pearl-handled Colt pistols strapped to his belt. He took a lot of photos that day which he later published with his own personal narrative. He observed the low, purple cumulus clouds gathering in the east and it wasn't long before powerful blizzards and howling winds hit the whole area with tremendous force. Patton presented Distinguished Service Crosses to Brig. Gen. Anthony McAuliffe and Lt. Col. Steve Chappuis.

Sometime during the afternoon, on Patton's explicit orders, the 327th Glider Infantry Regiment's command post was moved a couple of miles south to Hemroulle, where 480 welcome reinforcements were received. The day also saw the introduction of a new rotation system for front-line troops which would allow them to take an occasional breather. With a new year fast approaching, every soldier that had fought in and around Bastogne would have had great difficulty forgetting the last few weeks of December 1944, while wondering what the new year would bring. They wouldn't have to wait long to discover something big was about to go down.

CHAPTER EIGHTEEN

No Prisoners

They got me here in my hand, it went through my leg muscles, my jaw and my right leg, the medic said that I would be a cripple all my life.

GEORGE HELLER, D COMPANY, 2ND BATTALION,
501ST PARACHUTE INFANTRY REGIMENT

On December 31, New Year's Eve, the opposing forces kept mostly to themselves. While the defense perimeter was being strengthened in preparation for the coming attack, the 327th Glider Infantry Regiment's (GIR) A Company was designated regimental reserve. For its actions in the defense of Bastogne, the 327th was given the moniker "Bastogne Bulldog." All paratroopers that had endured the siege were now provided with overshoes for their jump boots, and fleece-lined jackets. The real highlight of the day was the arrival of a mail truck from Mourmelon-le-Grand. It had been over two weeks since any of the Bastogne defenders had received any mail from home, so every unit was brimming with anticipation. All in all, it was a relatively peaceful day.

The Germans remained under cover in the woods and dug in as they shared their meager rations, and what provisions they had captured from the Americans. They had acquired some K-rations, and boxes of Lucky Strikes, which were far superior to the standard German Army issue cigarettes that some claimed were rolled from camel manure. K-rations were originally developed for paratroopers and usually consisted of 4 ounces of either meat, meat and egg product, or cheese spread, together with biscuits, confectionary, chewing gum, and beverages with sugar. A wooden spoon, cigarettes, toilet tissue, and salt tablets were also included. K-ration version IVb, which was issued to the troops in October 1944, wasn't that different from the original, although caramels replaced the chocolate bars. The 0.8-ounce sugar package was replaced by a 0.9-ounce compressed block of granulated sugar. As an alternative to the lemon and orange-juice powders, grape-juice powder was introduced. Most contained bouillon, and Nescafe-powdered coffee, which was infinitely better than the German ersatz coffee, ominously known to the German troops as "Muckefuck," that was usually made from acorns and must have tasted like it was named.

Most of the German tank crews were provisioned with cans of whitewash brought from home to camouflage their vehicles. It came in very handy because a heavy snowfall blanketed the whole area again on New Year's Eve. To replace the traditional New Year's fireworks and ticker tape at midnight, all American artillery units opened up with everything they had and pummeled every German position they could reach; and so the battle raged on.

Despite the immense collateral damage the battle for Bastogne inflicted on the population, most interaction between the defenders and the civilian population was extremely good, but there was one dissenter that paratrooper Private George Heller, D Company, 2nd Battalion, 501st Parachute Infantry Regiment (PIR), recalled. He also vividly remembered getting wounded:

> We got to Bastogne, we walked up to a town and people were all waving to us, and this woman up at a window, she started throwing hot water out on the soldiers, so our Captain shot her. Then we went over to an old farmhouse and we slept there. The snow was about two and a half foot deep and it was below zero. We were cold, we didn't have time to build fires, we was fighting. It was rough, shells were coming in and everything. They [the Germans] didn't take nobody alive, they'd kill them. So we'd go down fighting. It wasn't the general who said "Nuts" it was us. We said "Nuts" we was going to fight until the finish. So that's what happened. Two Germans were shot right above my foxhole. I came up and I asked, "What happened?" They musta fell asleep you know. January 3rd I got hit. An 88 went over, tree burst, it came down on me. The medic came over, but there was another guy [wounded] so I said, "Take care of him, he's worse than I am." So he went over there and came right back. I said, "Take care of him." He [the medic] said, "He's only got one hole in him," I didn't know that I had all this [extensive wounds]. They got me here in my hand, it went through my leg muscles, my jaw and my right leg, the medic said that I would be a cripple all my life. There was no pain or anything, I don't know why there was no pain, musta been shock or something. He said, "We'll send a truck for you." We were beside a railway bridge. I didn't know that I was so badly hit. So they put me in the back [of the truck] and that's the last I remember. I was in a field hospital in Bastogne. When I woke up the next morning the guy beside me said, "Boy they worked all night on you. They thought you were gonna die." Doctor came in and stuck a pin in my hand and asked if I could feel it, and if I could move my fingers? I said I could so he said, "We're going to save that hand." They took me back to the operating room and they sewed my hand [to my midriff] for twenty one days to make a skin graft. After we left, I came home on the *Queen Mary*.

The 506th PIR mentioned in its daily reports that it received considerable assistance from the air force on the previous day but, according to all reports, there wasn't a great deal of activity during the first few days of the new year. The artillery was now resupplied and ready for action, as noted in the 969th Field Artillery Battalion's after-action report:

> At the beginning of the New Year, 1 January 1945, the Battalion was still in position about a thousand yards north and west of Bastogne. The 101st Airborne Division was defending the city and the Battalion was attached to the Division in General Support. The Third Army was gradually widening the corridor in the south, the Division sector was being reduced and operations were daily becoming more normal. The enemy was still launching probing attacks from three sides, but he did not succeed in making any penetrations. The Battalion

was shooting harassing and interdiction missions as well as observed targets of opportunity. Considerable harassing fire was landing in the Battalion area and although some of it was heavy caliber, casualties were few.

Hitler gave orders to launch Operation *Nordwind* on December 31. According to reports, the entire area to the south of Bastogne was covered in thick fog when the attack commenced. The Americans were well dug in and had occupied some Maginot Line bunkers that were still intact. The Germans were ill informed and poorly prepared from the start; they had neither location maps nor knowledge of these bunkers. Moreover, they hadn't conducted any serious reconnaissance and were lacking concerted artillery support. More importantly, they didn't have enough boots on the ground at any given time to affect any serious breaches in the American Seventh Army and French 1st Army lines, although they did make a temporary 10-mile indentation in the American line. The only real result of this abortive offensive was the terrible collateral damage it inflicted on those centuries-old villages in the area, which were reduced to ruins, killing innumerable innocent civilians.

The initial purpose of this offensive, led by three corps of Army Group G, belonging to the German 1st Army, was overly ambitious from the offset, and although it was intended to weaken VI Corps, there was never any significant danger that it would draw Gen. George Patton's forces away from their positions in the Ardennes. After the Normandy breakout, Patton had initially placed his Third Army in the Alsace–Elzas area because he suspected that, if the Germans were going to launch a counteroffensive, this is where it would occur. It's true that this area was the location of the first attacks during the Franco-Prussian War in 1870, and it was heavily contested in World War I, but the general got it wrong on this occasion. Being an avid student of history, he should have known the Germans attacked through the Ardennes in 1870, 1914 and 1940.

The Battle of the Bulge witnessed the final serious air attack by what remained of the Luftwaffe. Reich Marshal Hermann Göring had promised Hitler 3,000 aircraft to provide support for the initial counteroffensive, but at that stage of the war he knew full well he had neither the machines nor the pilots.

General Dietrich Peltz, commander of Jagdkorps II, received instructions to execute an aerial attack with all available aircraft, codenamed Operation *Bodenplatte*, or "Baseplate." The target was Allied airfields and the purpose was to create conditions that would level the playing field aeronautically. The plan for the attack was to take British and American airfields by surprise. The by now traditional radio silence was to be observed for all German fighter formations that would fly at tree-top level to avoid detection.

The attack began just before sunrise on January 1, 1945, while the Allies were nursing massive hangovers after celebrating New Year's Day. German aircraft attacked 27 Anglo-American bases in France, Belgium, and the Netherlands in combined groups of between 50 to 70 aircraft. The first wave caused considerable destruction and devastation as they swooped in on airstrips and fuel depots. Allied command reported losses were significant: 200 aircraft destroyed on the ground and 400 damaged. These aircraft were rapidly replaced.

The main problem the Germans encountered was due to the unavoidable use of inexperienced pilots; around 200 of their aircraft were shot out of the sky by Allied fighters and antiaircraft defenses. Although *Bodenplatte* could be considered a tactical success, it accentuated a major strategic failure, further reducing the resources of an already decimated Luftwaffe. It was an effective strike, but it was too little too late to affect the inevitable outcome.

Bodenplatte was bad indeed but, on the ground, Patton's reinforcements had provided some relief for the embattled paratroopers and supporting units, but they also brought news of terrible German atrocities perpetrated by the SS on the northern shoulder. One story claimed the Germans were murdering American prisoners of war. This had happened on December 17 just east of the Belgian town of Malmedy in the north, at a diminutive farming village called Baugnez, but, as with all bad news, the numbers increased exponentially every time the story was retold and disseminated among the ranks. The 84 men killed soon became 100, then 200. Either way, the news had an understandably adverse effect on some American units, and not just those in the line around Bastogne.

Some troopers from the 82nd Airborne Division operating in the Amblève Valley, facing the wrath of the SS, also on the northern shoulder, made no secret of the fact they didn't take prisoners. Private First Class Bill Hannigen, H Company, 82nd Airborne, said quite openly, "We didn't take those SS men prisoner. We were paratroopers, where were we going to put them? We just took them into the woods and finished them off." The murder of SS prisoners had become commonplace for some American units, but the Germans captured in Chenogne, five miles west of Bastogne, were not SS.

Private First Class John Fague, B Company, 21st Armored Infantry Battalion, 11th Armored Division, went into action with his unit near Chenogne. He described how some German prisoners were executed by GIs from his company:

> Some of the boys had prisoners lined up. I knew they were going to shoot them, and I hated that business. They brought the prisoners back to assassinate them with the rest of the prisoners we had taken that morning. As we walked up the hill out of town, some of our boys lined up German prisoners in the fields on both sides of the road. There must have been 25 or 30 German boys in each group. Machine guns were set up as we prepared to commit the same crimes the Germans had been accused of.
>
> I didn't participate in these murders, but a little time later when I scanned the adjacent fields where the German boys had been killed I saw bloodied, lifeless forms lying prostrate in the snow.

The victims were identified as soldiers from the Führer-Begleit-Brigade (Führer Escort Brigade) and the 3rd Panzergrenadier Division. Eisenhower was informed sometime later and ordered an investigation, but the incident was conveniently erased from the records; by the time the war had concluded, most of the perpetrators had scattered to the four winds. Hence, no arrests were ever made, and no trial ever transpired. But another detail emerged from American soldiers taken prisoner during the Battle of the Bulge, indicating those of the Jewish persuasion were being singled out and separated from their comrades. They would receive very different treatment than their fellow soldiers. Prisoners of war would become "slave labor" as they were sent to Nazi labor camps and subjected to horrendous, inhumane treatment by their captors. Two of the GIs who were part of an 11th Armored tank crew suffered this fate.

In the corner of the main square (Place McAuliffe) in Bastogne, there's a lone Sherman tank with "Barracuda" written on the side; it belonged to the 11th Armored Division. Combat Command B of the 11th Armored successfully liberated the villages of Lavasalle and Houmont but suffered significant casualties. Early in the engagement, *Barracuda*, under the command of S/Sgt. Wallace Alexander, and a companion tank commanded by Capt. Robert L. Ameno, became separated from the rest of the company. They moved north into enemy held terrain, approaching the village of Renuamont, the command post of Col. Otto Ernst Remer, commander of Hitler's elite Führer-Begleit-Brigade. After being discovered by an astounded Col. Remer himself, they came under attack.

While attempting to turn and escape, *Barracuda* became mired in a snow-and-ice covered pond. It became a sitting duck for German tanks and panzerfaust (bazooka) fire. Alexander was mortally wounded; gunner Cpl. Cecil Peterman and loader Pfc. Dage Herbert were wounded and captured. Driver T/4 Andrew Urda and bow gunner Pfc. Ivan Goldstein were uninjured but also captured. Alexander died several days later in captivity. Peterman and Herbert received minimal treatment for their wounds, survived, and were incarcerated as prisoners of war in Stalag XIIA near Limburg, Germany. Urda and Goldstein also eventually made it to Stalag XIIA, but only after being treated as slave laborers. Goldstein had been identified as Jewish by his dog tags, and by a letter in his pocket from his mother reminding him to observe the Jewish holiday, Hanukkah. Goldstein and Urda had already made a pact, vowing to stay together in captivity. They narrowly escaped execution but were brutally overworked and starved. After their liberation near the end of the war, the two severely emaciated captives spent many months recovering in U.S. Army hospitals. Andrew Urda never fully recovered from his mistreatment in captivity. He died in 1979. Ivan Goldstein's health was eventually restored. He eventually settled in Jerusalem. Captain Ameno's tank was also destroyed, killing the crew. One of them was wounded but died in captivity a short time later.[1]

Out west, in support of the British 53rd (Welsh) Infantry Division, low-flying fighter planes were strafing the 2nd Panzer Division in the area between Hotton

---

[1] Information from http://www.11tharmoreddivision.com/news/barracuda/index.htm, accessed January 10, 2024.

and Marche. Simultaneously, the American 2nd Armored Division was arriving from the north and hitting the same Germans in the flank, who would be decimated. Meanwhile, in Bastogne, the new year got off to a resounding start. At noon, all American artillery units lashed out at German positions with the most powerful artillery barrage to date.

Clear weather on New Year's Day allowed P-47 Thunderbolt fighter-bombers to provide effective air support by strafing German positions with devastating effect throughout the day. Some pilots said it was like a turkey shoot. Now that all the commanding officers had collectively concurred Bastogne had been secured, over the coming days, Allied military strategy in the Ardennes moved from the defensive to the offensive. The first orders issued to 506th PIR were to clear the Bois Jacques, north of Bastogne between the villages of Foy and Bizory.

The German 5th Army's Gen. Hasso von Manteuffel was sounding pessimistic when he wrote in his diary:

> The German 2nd Panzer Division covered almost a hundred kilometers in a week, but although they didn't reach the River Meuse, on Christmas Day 1944 they were within 6 kilometers of their target. Three days earlier, Patton had begun his advance against the German left flank, which culminated in the raising of the siege on the afternoon of December 26. Allied High Command had been initially taken by surprise by the German offensive, but now they said that German Army Group B no longer posed a strategic threat. When the weather was conducive to Allied air forces, they orchestrated massive aerial bombardment and destroyed the German supply lines on the left bank of the Rhine in massive attacks. It has to be said that before the new year dawned Rundstedt's armies were a spent force.

Many of the soldiers serving under General von Manteuffel would have worn belts with metal belt buckles inscribed with "Gott Mit Uns" (God with Us) and the Swastika in the center. World War II challenged the beliefs of many people, but there were those whose faith was unshakeable. One of those was Father François L. Sampson.

One of the most revered and respected officers of the 101st Airborne Division was a man of the cloth. Regimental Chaplain François Sampson, better known as "Father Sam," made his first combat jump in Normandy, which saw him land in the middle of a flooded canal. Fumbling for his knife, he was able to free himself from his pack, but still could have drowned had it not been for a divine gust of wind filling his still-attached parachute, which pulled him to the canal bank. Then he repeatedly dove back into the canal to retrieve the tools of his trade, a mass kit and holy oils. He told one of his comrades that he was just unlucky when it came to jumping, "If I jumped into a desert, I'd probably land on a camel's hump."

When war reached the United States, Father Sampson was granted permission to join the Chaplain Corps of the U.S. Army. After enduring the harsh rigors of training, he volunteered for the Airborne, though he later admitted he did not know in advance that he would be required to jump. He was assigned to the 501st PIR as the regimental chaplain.

He was captured, while tending some wounded paratroopers during the Battle of the Bulge, and sent to a prison camp in Germany where he spent six days in an overcrowded boxcar, sustained only by snow scraped from the top of the train. At his own request, Father Sampson was confined with the enlisted men, rather than the officers. James D. Alger, a fellow prisoner who later became a lieutenant general, said, "Father Sampson's misfortune in being captured turned out to be a blessing for the men he served in Stalag II-A [*sic*]. God knew he was sorely needed there."

The 1st Battalion, 506th PIR, was being kept in reserve in the village of Savy until it was requested to provide cover for the 2nd Battalion about a mile away on the Foy–Bizory road. When the column reached Luzery, on the Bastogne–Houffalize road, it was strafed by around a dozen German aircraft. At about the same time, the remnants of Team Cherry and the 327th GIR's F Company prepared to attack Senonchamps. They once again displayed tremendous cooperation and cohesion. The 506th's 2nd Battalion attacked Foy but was repulsed after experiencing some stubborn resistance.

Field Marshal Walter Model presented a plan to Hitler that would, in his opinion, put the final nail in the coffin and capture Bastogne; the 9th and 12th SS Panzer Divisions (Hitler Youth) would strike from the north-east, and the Führer Grenadier Brigade from due east. Hitler readily agreed to this audacious plan, but no consideration was given to the terrible weather hitting the area at the time. Regardless, it was "Game on" again.

CHAPTER NINETEEN

The Seminal Month

There was a first sergeant that got killed by a 50 caliber bullet, by our own P-51s. One of them was still in his chest. We were that close together you know, the Germans and us.
AL MAMPRE, MEDIC, E COMPANY, 2ND BATTALION,
506TH PARACHUTE INFANTRY REGIMENT

Sources indicate that, by December 30, Gen. Anthony McAuliffe had left Bastogne and was in Luxembourg, awaiting his next assignment, which would be commanding general of the 103rd Infantry Division. He would return to Bastogne in time but only for ceremonial purposes.

By January, it must have been overtly apparent to all that Hitler's strategy for reaching Antwerp had been an abject failure and all that was left was a "limited objective strategy" designed to inflict as much damage as possible before the inevitable retreat. Bastogne had assumed a significance disproportionate to its actual military importance because of the powerful Allied propaganda generated by the siege and ensuing battles to facilitate its capture. Inside the perimeter, it represented and encapsulated a strategic microclimate, a pervasive spirit of defiance, and ultimately great courage, that affected absolutely everyone who was there.

January was going to be a seminal month in the history of the city where seven roads converged, and the 3rd was going to be a day of frenetic activity as the Germans attempted to dislodge the defenders for the umpteenth time. Some of the American soldiers would come to regard this as the toughest day yet, and those who had experienced the full brunt of the siege would concur. The 327th Glider Infantry Regiment's (GIR) S-3 (operations) journal for January 1945 read:

First Battalion patrols reconnoitred [*sic*] the main road to Mande St. Etienne on 3 January and reported it clear of enemy. At 1330 hours the First Battalion began a movement to relieve the First Battalion, 502d Parachute Infantry at Champs. Strong enemy pressure here and at Longchamps where a tank and infantry attack was launched by the 10th S Panzer Division at 1400 hours delayed completion of the relief until 2000 hours. The Second Battalion was attached to the 502d Parachute Infantry at 1410 hours and close into its assembly area at 533610 at 1630 hours. At 1530 hours this Regiment became part of a Task Force commanded by Brigadier General Higgins.

A heavy barrage fell on First Battalion positions beginning at 0430 hours on 4 January. At 0500 hours the enemy launched a regimental strength attack striking at both flanks and at the center of the First Battalion. The enemy unit, later identified as the 104 Panzer Grenadier Regiment, 15 Panzer Division, was preceded by an estimated total of eleven S.P. guns and tanks. Four tanks with infantry in support broke through in the vicinity of 514620 and drove to within 100 yards of the Battalion Command Post in Champs. Furious fighting continued until about 0845 hours.

Sometime around noon, the 2nd and 3rd Battalions of the 501st Parachute Infantry Regiment (PIR) began to advance through Bois Jacques to eradicate any German opposition. Meanwhile, covering the right flank, the 3rd Battalion moved out, supported by the 50th Armored Infantry Battalion, 5th Armored Division. They encountered heavy German resistance from the outset but continued to advance. At the same time, the 2nd Battalion progressed deep into the woods almost unimpeded. About an hour later, D and F Companies reached their target astride the Foy–Michamps road. Once there, they established a roadblock at the Bastogne–Bourcy railroad line that runs almost parallel to the road. Twenty minutes later, Sgt. Lawrence J. Silva, D Company, 502nd PIR, called the regimental command post to let it know he'd spotted around 20 tanks heading in his direction. Sadly, it would be his valedictory message because, moments later, he was crushed to death by a German tank in his foxhole.

The 502nd was still covering a line that extended south-west from Longchamps, through Champs to as far as Recogne, when an attack by what remained of the German 9th and 12th SS Divisions hit its positions hard. Recogne lies in a natural valley, covered by dense mist at the time, making it difficult for the defenders to determine the nature and strength of the opposition. This was very much a "déjà vu" situation for the Americans, who were largely unprepared when the assault commenced, but they quickly rallied and stepped up to do the job. They estimated they were being attacked by about 35 Mark IV tanks followed by a quite widely dispersed company of grenadiers. The 506th PIR war diary attests to the severity of the combat, with the entry for January 3, reading:

> The battle is raging at its highest peak all day. We had the worst shelling from the krauts we ever did through all our missions. We thought Carentan and Veghel was bad but nothing can compare with this. 501st was attacking across our front, and left us in the middle to receive all the dirt. Left that area and moved back to our old defense line. 501 controls the area we moved out. Snowed just about all day.

Six German tanks crossed the narrow road that leads from Bertogne to Longchamps and attacked D Company's antitank and machine-gun positions. Almost simultaneously, five more tanks were launched against E Company's positions. The combined fire from these tanks was so intense every single GI was pinned down in his foxhole. The 6th Armored Division's 50th Armored Infantry Battalion tried to move up to Bois Jacques to attempt to relieve some pressure on the right flank of the 501st PIR's 2nd Battalion. This move was prevented by the untimely arrival of eight Panzers and a company of grenadiers, forcing the 50th to withdraw to safer ground.

It became the zenith of the fight for Bastogne, the bloodiest and most excruciating test for all incumbents to date. Mortars, machine guns, artillery and armor exchanged fire unabated throughout the whole day. Pine trees were blasted and reduced to matchwood, while the ground was punctuated by bloodstains, and black earth from the constant earth-shuddering explosions. The ferocity and merciless pounding reduced even the strongest men to quivering heaps, as they heard their comrades screaming in agony, and saw limbs, entrails and torn flesh scattered in proximity to foxholes. Unrecognizable bodies laid where they were crushed like roadkill beneath the merciless tracks of tanks and mobile armor. While Team O'Hara sent in what remained of its tanks to provide armored support, Team Cherry was hauled in from regimental reserve and ordered to go to Longchamps.

The 101st Airborne Division's headquarters after-action report read:

> On the morning of 3 January, units on the line reported considerable activity to their front. This information was obtained from listening posts as the visibility was zero due to a heavy ground fog. At about 1300 hours, 3 January a concentrated attack consisting of about twenty-five tanks and a battalion of infantry hit the right flank of the 2nd Battalion. Four of the 57mm anti-tank guns were knocked out although only after inflicting considerable damage on the enemy's armor. A number of tanks penetrated the main line of resistance but our Infantry remained in position and succeeded in stopping all of the enemy Infantry and part of the tanks. A gap had been created between the 2nd and 3rd Battalions and the Reserve Company of the 2nd Battalion was committed to fill this gap. In moving up to the attack they were forced to cross open ground and received heavy casualties.
>
> One platoon became cut off by tanks and was captured. By 1630 hours the attack had been beaten off, and the main line of resistance restored. Team Cherry, part of the Divisional Reserve had been dispatched to support the 2nd Battalion but did not close into position in Longchamps until the battle was over. During the night of the 3rd of January, the 1st Battalion, on the left, was relieved by the 327th Infantry. A prisoner was captured about midnight and stated that there was to be another concentrated attack early in the morning of the 4th. From 0300 hours on the artillery concentration consisting of from one to nine battalions, was thrown on the area north of Longchamps. A prisoner that was later captured stated that the artillery fire had broken up a second "attack" to be launched at 0400 hours on the morning of the 4th. During the morning of the infantry and tank assaults, which penetrated their line of resistance, a simultaneous attack consisting mainly of tanks was thrown against the left flank of the 2nd Battalion. This was stopped only after quite heavy casualties from tank cannon fire. Division ordered the 1st Battalion, which had moved back into the Regimental Reserve to be committed to restore the main line of resistance in the 327th sector. By 1700 hours the 1st Battalion had succeeded in accomplishing their mission and were ordered back under control of the 502nd Parachute Infantry. On the 5th of January, readjustments were made shortening our lines. The 2nd Battalion was left in position at Longchamps and the 1st Battalion went into Regimental Reserve and the 3rd Battalion moved to Savy as Division Reserve. On 9 January, the 3rd Battalion returned to 502nd control and was ordered to make an attack on the right flank of the 2nd Battalion to protect the 506th Parachute Infantry which was attacking northeast toward Noville.

The 705th and 609th Tank Destroyer Battalions began hitting back at the German tanks and, by the afternoon, the 502nd PIR had restored its lines, but it was a costly affair that took a heavy toll on the regiment. Seventy-nine paratroopers were lost, including two officers and a company commander. In the process, the Germans captured an entire platoon, but it wasn't all bad news. The 81st Airborne Anti-Aircraft Battalion destroyed 10 Mark IV tanks. Sergeant Edward Ford, Battery C, was awarded the DSC for destroying seven German tanks:

> The President of the United States of America, authorized by Act of Congress, July 9, 1918, has awarded the Distinguished Service Cross to Sergeant Edward E. Ford, Battery C, 81st Airborne Antiaircraft Artillery, [who] distinguished himself by extraordinary heroism in connection with military operations against an armed enemy in Belgium. On 3 January 1945 when his anti-tank gun position was attacked by 14 German tanks near Longchamps, Belgium, Sergeant Ford fearlessly maintained his position in the face of devastating artillery, mortar and tank fire; and with cool, accurate fire, disabled seven of the hostile tanks. Although painfully wounded, he continued his aggressive actions until his gun was hit and rendered unserviceable. With heroic tenacity, he maintained fire against the approaching enemy with a rocket launcher and with a Browning Automatic Rifle. Refusing evacuation during the night, he directed the repair of his gun the next day and fought on until wounded again. Sergeant Ford's indomitable courage and unflinching devotion to duty exemplify the highest traditions of the military service, and reflect great credit on him, the 101st Airborne Division and the United States Army.

Later that night, thanks to the combined efforts of the 6th Armored Division and the 501st PIR, the 506th PIR's line was reestablished. Now it was time for both sides to take stock and prepare for the next round. During some of the melees, the situation became confused due to one prevailing factor. Many GIs had received winter clothing, which the majority of attacking Germans had been provisioned with since the beginning of the battle. However, this made it difficult to ascertain precisely who was fighting for who, and the situation was exacerbated by the punishing blizzard conditions. A German prisoner taken during the battle ominously informed his captors a new offensive was being prepared for the following day. It would be the culmination of weeks of hard combat but, according to everyone who was there, nothing exceeded the ferociousness of those couple of days.

There was no underestimating the determination and tenacity of the additional Waffen SS soldiers that had joined the fray; even though they'd been badly mauled on the northern shoulder, there was still a lot of fight in them. Now it was down to the numerical and material advantage of the defenders, who were just as determined and just as tenacious, if not more so.

Private First Class Thomas G. Erwin, Jr. of the 506th PIR recalled the events of early January 1945 in his memoir:

> Then came the biggest day of my army career. It was Sunday, around noon, the third day of January 1945. My assistant gunner and I were ordered to go further back in the forest and help get some of our men out that had been on a combat patrol and had not been heard from in some time. We did not know where or how far back in they were, we just had to look.

He and I had gone about one-half a mile when we found a dirt road. I guess it was a dirt road, it was covered in about two feet of snow. As we crossed over the road and got a few hundred feet back in the woods, I don't know how many, but more than two, Kraut tanks (Tigers to be exact), spotted two half frozen, half starved, dead tired, nearly lost American paratroopers. The first shell, an 88 mm, from one of the tanks almost got us. The tankers must have thought that we were leading in a large group or a large patrol and that was why they let us get across the road. When they realized that it was just the two of us they got mad and tried to waste us. They almost succeeded. By knocking us out, we could not give away their location. We did not have a radio, but they did not know this. Every time one of their shells landed it would blow me up in the air. I knew that the end was near. They poured in one shell right after the other and it seemed like each one hit me. I could feel the shrapnel going through my clothes and my pack and knew that the next one would hit me somewhere; and it did. My helmet went flying off of my head and I thought my head was still in it.

We were lying flat in the snow and didn't even realize it. I was praying so fast that I didn't even know what I was saying. The Good Lord must have known what I was saying because he let us both get out of that mess alive. Then I realized that I was hit; my legs, especially my right one, went numb. Blood was coming out of my nose and ears. I could not hear. My vision was blurred. I felt sick all over; I wanted to throw up, but there was nothing in my stomach. I lay there a few minutes and realized that I was still alive but was afraid to move or make a sound. The tanks thought that they had killed us and withdrew because their firing on us alerted our people of their location.

I was thankful that there was no infantry with them because they would have finished us off. After a minute or two I heard my buddy moan and when I looked over in his direction I could see that he had been wounded also. A piece of shrapnel had torn a huge hole in his left arm and he was in great pain. His name was Franco, and he knew that I had been hit and started over to me to see what he could do to help. He asked if I could get up and try to walk with his help; but when I got to my feet I fell down. He tried to hold me up but it was no use. We had to get out of there before the Krauts came back, or it turned dark, or we froze or bled to death.

I had no alternative but to get my shot-up butt out of there and to try to get back to our base. My bazooka and carbine were destroyed when I got hit and the only weapons we had was Franco's carbine and a few hand grenades. With his help, which was not very much due to his wound, I crawled back to the other side of the road. This was as far as I could go, my hands were almost frozen, my knees were bleeding, and my legs were hurting so badly I just could not go another yard. He found an abandoned foxhole with a cover over it and helped me get into it. Then he went back to the base camp and tried to get some help for me. That was the last time I saw him for three months. It seemed like I was in that hole for a year before anyone came to help me. I heard two American paratroopers outside my hole, Franco had seen them on his way back to get me help and had asked if they could get me out. They were from another company and were on a similar patrol to the one we had been on.

All they could do for me was administer first aid. They cut my pants leg up to my knee and I heard one of them grunt. I knew then that I had a lulu of a wound. Then he said, it looks like a clean wound, it went in one side and came out the other. This really made me feel good. They put a dressing on my legs and tried to give me a shot from my morphine syrette, but the needle broke. Then one of them said that there was a dead trooper a little ways back and he would go get his. When he came back I asked him the name of the dead man, but he didn't know him. I was afraid it was Franco. They hurriedly patched my wounds and gave me a shot of morphine that lasted about ten minutes; told me the best of luck; and that was the last of them I ever saw. I hope they made it.

Due to the extremely cold weather, my wounds didn't bleed as much as usual so I quit using a tourniquet. I noticed that it was getting dark and I started to wonder if I was going to be out there all alone and all night. My mind started playing tricks on me. I knew that I would freeze to death without a blanket, especially with my pants legs cut all the way to my knees. Then the thought entered my head. "What would the reaction of my family be when they received the telegram from the War Department saying 'Regret to inform you that PFC Thomas G. Erwin, Jr. has been killed due to enemy action in Belgium.'"

While I was waiting to die, I heard the sweetest noise on earth, the sound of a medic and a rifleman coming to my rescue. Franco had gotten back to our area OK and had sent these two to get me out. I knew the medic real well and the first thing I asked of him was, "Is Franco OK?" The second thing, in the same breath, was, "Give me some morphine, now!" They didn't have a stretcher, so I sat on a M1 rifle they were holding between them, with my arms around their necks. I fell off a couple of times, but they got me back up. By now I was completely drained. All the way back, I was cursing my platoon leader, Lieutenant Throughkill, for not sending someone to rescue me sooner.

I was mad at my sergeants for leaving me up there to get out the best way I could. I was mad for getting set up in an ambush and getting my butt shot off. I was mad at everybody and everything.

The dead trooper the paratroopers had seen was Lieutenant Throughkill.

January 4 began with a fierce American artillery barrage that commenced at 3:00 am and received a German reply roughly an hour later. After some ferocious hand-to-hand street fighting with the 327th GIR's 1st Battalion, many of whom were killed or taken prisoner, the Germans actually succeeded in capturing Champs. Later that morning, the 327th's 2nd Battalion repulsed a tank attack that didn't appear to be supported by infantry. Fifteen panzers moved in for the kill and hit out at Longchamps again, but there was no encroachment into the line on this occasion and they were decisively beaten back by intense artillery fire.

Staff Sergeant Al Mampre, a medic with E Company, 2nd Battalion, 506th PIR, 101st Airborne Division, attested to the caliber of the men in his unit in an interview:

I was right across from McAuliffe's HQ in Bastogne. There was a situation, some guy was putting a wire up on a wall from division to some regiment out there. A shell hit the bottom of the wall, knocked him right off the wall, it was a pretty good sized wall [it's still there] and right back up he goes, he's going to have to put that wire up. A shell hits the wall again, bang! Down he goes again, and then right back up that wall. They didn't fire the third time, maybe somebody silenced that gun, or they gave up, I don't know what, but he got that wire up. Looking at it objectively he was a hero right? But actually he was mission oriented. His job was to put that thing up, people are depending on him, he had to do this, and he did it. He accomplished it. I have to give him credit for that you know; who wouldn't?

[In the woods at Bois Jacques] There was a first sergeant that got killed by a 50 caliber bullet by our own P-51s. One of them was still in his chest. We were that close together you know, the Germans and us.

I met a guy here in Arlington Park, who owns the Arlington race track, a tank destroyer guy and he was with us at Foy, with the 101st, with E Company right there. Some of us even came into their tanks and he saved our sorry butts. They destroyed tanks, some of them were destroyed, and I met him there, he is the nicest guy. We were just plain ordinary guys. A shell came in through a wall. I was in a room, just a room right there in that location, and a shell came in and it fell apart with big pieces. I looked down and I said, "My, that was a good sized shell." It wasn't until 75 years later, that's really how slow I am. I could have been on Jupiter or some place now if that would've exploded. But it must have been built by one of their forced laborers or something, that I found out later. I never thought I'd die, during my whole time in the service, never thought I'd die. That's partly youth and partly stupidity you know.

General George Patton frequently argued that a static defense was the worst form of defense, and he didn't hold sway with such extended fortifications such as the Siegfried and Maginot Lines. But the defense of Bastogne was the antithesis of this. The defenders had all the advantages at their disposal. Even the inclement weather worked in their favor on several occasions. Granted, clear weather allowed for close air support, of the type that had devastated German units in Normandy, but methodical, coherent movement of troops to places where they were needed greatly hampered German attempts to capitalize on any minor, temporary encroachments into American perimeter lines. Constantly relying on mass attacks, as opposed to small unit assaults, both restricted and hindered their capacity to deploy to advantageous positions. This had been very much the case during the ferocious exchange in and around Champs. The nature of the terrain in this sector is considerably hillier than to the west of Bastogne. Steep, narrow roads and large wooded areas were inevitably detrimental to the movement of German armor and favored the defenders considerably.

Brigadier General Gerald J. Higgins, the deputy division commander who led the eponymous task force, mentioned that Col. Joseph H. Harper, the 327th GIR's commanding officer, had furnished him with a blow-by-blow account of the fight at Champs, on the northwest perimeter between Monaville and Longchamps, which had already witnessed some savage fighting. German tanks, hitting the south of the town, had succeeded in driving right up to within 100 yards of American positions. They fired directly at the men huddled in their foxholes, which offered scant protection from such direct fire.

Successive deployments by American armor and tank destroyers managed to neutralize the attack and prevent the Germans from capitalizing on a situation that could have inflicted considerably more casualties than it did. The paratroopers would have been largely oblivious to the fact they were being hit by seasoned, battle-hardened German veterans that had served on the Eastern Front, where conditions had been just as harsh, if not more so. At Champs and Longchamps, concentric attacks in the 501st PIR's sector on the northeast perimeter were executed by elements of the 12th SS Panzer Division (Hitler Youth), augmented by the 9th SS Division's 19th SS Panzergrenadier Regiment.

Higgins described, in some detail, how he walked the field after the battle had ended and discovered an American and a German locked in each other's arms, both stone dead and frozen in their final position. The German had been stabbed and the American strangled.

The after-action report of the 502nd PIR accurately testifies to the fluidity and scale of the German attacks during those early days of January 1945. The numbers, as in previous reports, refer to map coordinates:

> At 0855 the 1st Battalion received orders to send on officer patrol to Mande St. Etienne and contact and ret the situation of friendly troops in that area. The patrol returned at 0100 and reported no enemy on main road to Mande St. Etienne. At 0930 the 1st Battalion sent an officer patrol to Mande St. Etienne, which returned at 1130 with information of disposition of friendly troops to the west. At 1330 the Battalion began moving to the vicinity of Champs and at 1450 Company A [1st Bn] had gone into position as shown on overlay. Due to a fight in the sector Company B [1st Bn] was to occupy, Company B was placed in the woods at 1540. At 2000 Company B [1st Bn] moved into positions as on overlay, relieving a company of the 1st Battalion 502nd Parachute infantry. Due to the tank attack followed by infantry at 1400 on Longchamps, the 2nd Battalion was attached to the 502 Parachute Infantry at 1410 and immediately began to move to Longchamps. Four TDs [tank destroyers] from the 1st Battalion were sent to the support, of the 502nd. The 2nd Battalion closed into its assembly area at 533610 at 1630 then moved to position as shown on overlay in Regimental reserve for the 502nd.
>
> At 1530 this Regiment became a part of Task Force commanded by General Higgins. At 1640 company C [3rd Bn] established strong points at 503593, 511597 and 509601 as tie in with the friends on the west.

> JANUARY 4TH
> At 0430 the enemy laid down on artillery barrage, which fell to the rear of Company A [1st Bn]. At 0500 the enemy struck at the 1st Battalion at three places; the right and left flanks of Company A and also at Company B. It was estimated a Battalion of enemy attacked at each position supported by a total of about 20 tanks. Some tanks and infantry penetrated our lines and went into the town of Champs. At 0700 the 1st Battalion [502nd Parachute Infantry] was attached to this Regiment but was not committed. At 0900 the attack had quieted down. The enemy had caused many casualties in Company A [1st Bn] by direct fire from tanks and SP guns. As it became daylight the tanks and SP Guns withdrew back across the hill. At 0900 Company B [3rd Bn] was moved from its sector on the line to the woods at 533609 as protection for a road block in that vicinity. At 1400 Company A was attached to the 1st Battalion and at 1430 moved into the line in the same sector held by Company A [1st Bn]. At 1400 the 1st Battalion [502nd] reverted back to the 502nd and 2nd Battalion [327th] became Regimental reserve for this regiment.
>
> At 1600 the 2nd Battalion made a reconnaissance to move into the woods at 533609. This move was completed at 1900 and the 2nd Battalion CP [command post] was set up in Hemroulle. The 3rd Battalion received orders at 2100 to send a reinforced squad to 507609 to make contact with 2nd Battalion 513th Parachute Infantry on our left. Contact was made and a strong point was established.

These descriptions of attack and defense become intrinsically repetitive, which is testament to the nature of the fighting, and indubitable lack of imagination on behalf of the German forces. This, combined with battlefield leadership that had almost completely lost confidence in the higher echelons of their command, and the continual directives, which held little or no compliance with the reality of the situation on the ground, was only ever going to culminate in a lack of motivation and lack of innovation among the troops doing the fighting.

Staff Sergeant Larry Michaelis, C Company, 327th GIR, was not in Champs right after Christmas with the rest of his unit. He was pulling guard duty at Isle-la-Hesse where General McAuliffe was holed up during the nights when Heintz Barracks was being bombed. He said the guard duty probably saved his life because most of C Company was in Champs and was badly mauled. Hence, A and C Companies were put together as "ACE" Company for the attack on January 13.

The 1st and 2nd Battalions remained in their positions until 4:00 am when they began the move towards the line of deployment. From 8:23 to 9:00 am, a preparatory artillery barrage was laid down but the jump off was delayed until 9:15. The attack jumped off with the 1st Battalion on the right and the 2nd Battalion on the left. The 3rd Battalion was in the northeast in reserve, east of the road to Noville. The 1st Battalion received artillery, mortar and small-arms fire just after the jump off but was able to proceed slowly. The 2nd Battalion was temporarily held up by heavy artillery. At 2:15 pm, the attack in both sectors was staggered due to enemy infiltration on the open right flank to the rear. The 502nd PIR failed to keep abreast and, at 4:00 pm, the 3rd Battalion was ordered to move forward to close the exposed flank; it was in position by 6:00 pm. The lines were consolidated and held throughout the night against small-arms and artillery fire. At 5:00 pm, the regimental commander received orders and passed them on at a battalion commanders' meeting that the attack would continue the next day. According to Larry Michaelis:

> We were going through the 501st Infantry and attacking so we had a full load of ammo. On the path going up there they had a couple guys from the Division Quartermasters with case after case of ammo. You want any extra ammo, they asked. I had a belt full and two bandoliers but I put on two more bandoliers and we went through a company of the 501st. In something like that [attacking] everyone would fire all the same time. Even the guys carrying machine guns would cradle it in their arms and keep firing continuously. We hit a German out post; they had dugouts there with shelter-halves over the door and dirt all over them. It wasn't very smart to look in one. You'd go by one and you'd just throw a grenade in the hole and keep going. Then a bunch of surrendering Germans came out of there and we weren't too far in front of the 501st so we just motioned them back to them and kept moving. It was a bunch that I think thought it was about time to get out of the war. We didn't go too much farther and a mortar shell exploded in the trees above us and that's when I got hit. Standing up one second and the next second my face was in the snow. I got hit in the chest-wall. Just a hole like that [indicating a hole with his fingers about an-inch-and-a-half in diameter] and over about that far I guess and it came out. It didn't really hurt, just stung like heck. I didn't know if I had a big hole or a little hole or what. I knew there was something there. Medic came running up and said he can't rip that jacket, take it off if you can. He ripped my shirt away and said, "Awe, it isn't too bad." I said, "I suppose I could stick around." He said, "You damn fool, get the hell out of here, there's an aide [sic] station right back there a way."

He lost Edward Pinneke, one of his good friends during the attack. Most American troops that took part in the fight were visibly shaken by the devastating experience of enduring sustained shell, mortar, and bullet fire. Some would never mention the name of Champs, or Longchamps, ever again, while others would become very emotional when relating their experiences. It's easy to venerate the courage of these men, but they were just men, not the superhumans often depicted. The first few days of that bitterly cold January would remain in the hearts and minds of those who were there. Many felt there was no end in sight, but there was; it just needed one last effort.

CHAPTER TWENTY

Ashes and Collateral

Gorey glory, what a helluva way to die!
THE HYMN OF THE 101ST AIRBORNE DIVISION

Sergeant Dan McBride, F Company, 502nd Parachute Infantry Regiment (PIR), vividly recalled the intensity of the fighting at Champs in an interview:

> I was going through ammunition like you wouldn't believe. Tracers were going in all directions, I think all the rifling was shot out of the barrel. All of a sudden everything stopped, it was then that I started crying like a baby. I was trying to light a cigarette and I almost stuck it in my ear, you know, nervous reaction. Shaking like a leaf. There was a tank right in front of me and somebody screaming, and it was a German someone had hit with a bazooka. It was only, not more than thirty yards away. I didn't realize how close it was until I went back in 2009. They have a marker where that tank was, only thirty yards from my hand.
>
> But I'm most proud of being in the 101st Airborne Division. In my opinion it's the best division in the army. We were the first division in the United States Army to get a Presidential citation for the whole division. We got that for Bastogne. I got a lot of things that I'm happy to remember, and a lot of things that I wish I could forget, but I can't. You gotta put it behind you and just live your life. They always told me, "Cheer up, things could be worse." So I cheered up and things got worse. That's the way it was. The way I looked at it was, if you could look at yourself when you were shaving you were alright. I don't think I've done anything I'm ashamed of. I've done a lot that I'm proud of. I never tried to be something I wasn't. I'm not going to say I'm a real good church goer coz [*sic*] I'm not.
>
> We (my girlfriend and I) went to a show and they had a newsreel showing experimental parachute troops. They showed the French doing it, the Russians doing it, and then they showed Americans doing it, and my girl said, "Man they must be so brave," and I said, "They gotta be so stupid," because I was afraid of heights. But the idea stuck with me and I said "If they can do it, there's no reason why I can't do it." My dad said, "Fear is nature's safety valve, but if you let it get the best of you, you're beat," you see. So when I was standing at the door of a C-47 at Ft. Benning I was getting more natural all the time. We're required to sing this song when we went through jump school, because they tried to make us quit.

He sang the first verse and chorus of the 101st anthem:

> "Is everybody happy!" cried the sergeant looking up, Our HERO meekly answered, "Yes" and then they stood him up. He leaped right out into the blast, his static line unhooked, AND HE AIN'T GONNA JUMP NO MORE!

> GOREY GLORY, WHAT A HELLUVA WAY TO DIE!
> GOREY GLORY, WHAT A HELLUVA WAY TO DIE!
> GOREY GLORY, WHAT A HELLUVA WAY TO DIE!
> AND HE AIN'T GONNA JUMP NO MORE!

The rest of the song explains a lot about the general ethos in the 101st Airborne Division:

> He counted loud he counted long and waited for the shock. He felt the wind and felt the cold, he felt that awful drop. The silk spilled out and wrapped about his legs,
> AND HE AIN'T GONNA JUMP NO MORE!
> CHORUS
> The risers wrapped around his neck, connectors cracked his dome, The suspension lines were snarled and tied in knots around his skinny bones. His canopy became his shroud, he hurtled to the ground,
> AND HE AIN'T GONNA JUMP NO MORE!
> CHORUS
> The days he lived and loved and laughed kept running through his mind, He thought about the girl back home, the one he'd left behind. He thought about the Medics and he wondered what they'd find,
> AND HE AIN'T GONNA JUMP NO MORE!
> The ambulance was on the spot and jeeps were running wild, The Medics jumped and screamed with glee as they rolled up their sleeves and smiled. For it had been a week or so since last a chute had failed,
> AND HE AIN'T GONNA JUMP NO MORE!
> CHORUS
> He hit the ground the sound of "SPLAT!" The blood went spurting high, His comrades then were heard to say: "What a helluva way to die!" He lay there rolling around in the welter of his gore.
> AND HE AIN'T GONNA JUMP NO MORE!
> CHORUS
> There was blood upon the risers, there was brains upon the chute, Intestines were a-danglin' from his Paratrooper's suite. They poured him from his chute and poured him from his boots,
> AND HE AIN'T GONNA JUMP NO MORE!!!
> Beautiful streamer please open for me, blue skies above me and no canopy. I counted 10 thousand, waited too long, reached for my ripcord the handle was gone.
> GOREY GLORY, WHAT A HELLUVA WAY TO DIE!
> CHORUS ad infinitum.

In a letter to a friend, Captain Morton, C and Headquarters Company, 502nd PIR, related the horrors of those final days of fighting in quite graphic detail.

> On January 9 we began a big attack to reduce the German bulge. We attacked all day. Headquarters Third was caught in a woods by a mortar barrage, and my men dropped at every quarter. Webb went out of his mind. Beard, now a lieutenant, was shot in the arm. Lundquist was killed. Kopeisk, my runner, was hit at my side. A mortar shell hit the trees above us. Fragments wounded Kopala severely but I was unscathed. I was blown off my feet twice, a most unpleasant experience. That night, as we were digging in on the objective, Tiger tanks came through the snow and shelled the woods. I was hit by the first round. It nearly severed my ankle. I bled like a stuck hog. Gibson, the medic, raced to my assistance and got hit by

the next round. I, too, was wounded again. Barney Ryan has written to me that 156 men were killed and wounded that terrible night. The next morning, says Ryan, there were fifteen dead bodies sprawled about the aid set up. Blood trails, he said, marked in the snow where our wounded had dragged themselves in a futile effort to find shelter or medical aid. Ryan writes, "Never have I lived through such a nightmare. All night long shells screamed into the woods, direct fire from tanks. It was nearly impossible to evacuate the wounded. They were dying like flies. Through the whole night we heard the screams of the wounded and moans of the dying." Barney Ryan got two burp gun slugs through the left chest on January 17, four days after I was hit. Joe Madonna a sergeant in I Company, was standing beside Ryan and caught the same burst in the head. He fell stone dead.

A particularly maligned character from the TV series *Band of Brothers* was Capt. Norman Dike. In late 1944, Lieutenant Dike, as he was then, was selected as the temporary commander of E Company, 506th PIR, a position he was to hold throughout the defense of Bastogne up until the attack on Foy. Many who saw the mini-series saw how, according to the producers, Dike bungled the attack into Foy in January, for which he was relieved of command. Some claimed he froze because he was wounded, but there's no written evidence to support this. Another version says he panicked because he couldn't see his friend Lt. Jack Foley. Either way, it became blatantly obvious he wasn't the right man for that particular job.

January 12, at 9:00 am, the attack to retake Foy began when E and I Company of the 3rd Battalion, 506th PIR, moved out of the woods. The rest of the 2nd Battalion remained in reserve and provided suppressing fire to support the assault. They were able to secure Foy by 11:00 am. Lieutenant Dike froze near a haystack during the approach to Foy and the attack almost ground to a halt. Dike later claimed he was confused about the situation on the battlefield. He panicked because he lost sight of 1st Platoon. Stopping in the middle of an open field made the paratroopers extremely vulnerable.

Captain Richard Winters grabbed a rifle and started to head down to take command of the situation and get the unit moving again. He stopped and reminded himself he was responsible for the entire battalion, not just E Company. He turned to look for someone to send in to relieve Dike and saw Lt. Ronald Speirs. Dick Winters would later say he did not select him, "he was just there." Lieutenant Speirs was the perfect man to take over E Company. He, like Winters, was able to quickly assess the situation and make quick and accurate decisions. Despite the ignominious display by Lieutenant Dike, surprisingly enough, he was still considered for other positions in the 101st Airborne.

The celebration for the capture of Foy was short lived. The Germans counterattacked and, by 4:15 am, January 13, the Germans retook the town. Their success was equally short lived, because the 506th immediately counterattacked and captured the town for good by 9:30 am.

The division's combat journal, maintained by Col. Ned Moore, the chief of staff, recorded the following entry on January 24: Dike was among three candidates recommended by Colonel Sink from his unit as aide-de-camp, with the addendum: Lt. Dike is a graduate of Yale University (note: this was incorrect, he was a Brown Univ. alumni). He hailed from a privileged and auspicious background. His father was a New York based Supreme Court Justice. Lt. Dike was a Co Commander but his removal from command was due to calling in an artillery request on the wrong location. Colonel Sink thought Dike was the best man for the job. Hence, he was chosen and spent the remainder of his World War II service as the aide to Major General Taylor. The implication here is that, thanks to his somewhat ignominious track record, Dike was not considered as a battlefield commander, rather someone who was probably more suitable for desk work. It's a little strange Dike was chosen to be Taylor's aide even though other candidates for the job appear to have been better qualified. It could have been something to do with his masonic father's connections. Taylor was a notoriously ambitious man and having an aide with serious family connections could have been his reason for choosing Dike. .

Although the exact date of his selection as General Taylor's aide is not recorded, by February 1945 the journal records him executing the routine duties of a general's aide: processing the evaluation reports of senior officers; receiving issue of medal sets for later presentation by General Taylor; tracking paperwork for battlefield commissions; and following up on recommendations for non-judicial punishments.

Captain Dike appears in photographs taken of the reviewing stand at the Distinguished Unit Citation presentation ceremony on March 15, 1945. Norman S. Dike Jr. was active in numerous fraternal organizations, among them Yale University Club, the Society of Cincinnati, the Society of Colonial Wars and the Society of Descendants of the Mayflower. He also served on the board of the World Wildlife Fund and the National Council of the Boy Scouts of America.

After the war, Dike continued his military service by joining the U.S. Army Reserves, ultimately reaching the rank of lieutenant colonel before resigning in 1957, just four years short of retirement.

Dike's name came to prominence on January 13, 1945, when the 506th's E and I Companies launched their third concerted attempt to capture Foy, which was at that time still held by Generalmajor Kokott's 26th Volksgrenadier Division, supported by tanks from the 1st Tank Battalion, 12th SS Armored Division. During the previous day, while the members of E Company were being hammered by German artillery, a group of 10th Armored Division tankers and 101st Airborne paratroopers were clearing the woods east of Bastogne in the vicinity of Bizory. E Company was given the task of leading the assault on Foy. As soon as sufficient covering fire had been laid down allowing the American units to reach Foy, fierce hand to hand fighting ensued. Despite the urban-fighting scenario, which required units having to go house-to-house to clear out snipers, this innocuous little hamlet was successfully captured with dozens of German soldiers taken prisoner. The next day the 506th's 1st and 2nd Battalions were ordered to advance north and northwest towards Noville and Cobru respectively.

German forces counterattacked. But, despite being exchanged a number of times, Foy ultimately remained in American hands, and there were no civilian casualties incurred throughout the whole period, just massive collateral damage, which would take decades to repair. The same applied to Bastogne, which capitalized from its own devastation by selling collections of postcards showing the extent of the damage. Over the next few days, with the support from elements of the 11th Armored Division, the 101st Airborne gradually helped to liberate the territories north of Bastogne, as far as Houffalize, which was also virtually destroyed. Foy never entirely recovered from the battering it received in 1945, and today the community is smaller than it was back then; reminders of the battle are everywhere.

After the fighting around Bastogne had dissipated, the 506th PIR was ordered onto some troublesome trucks and told to head south to Alsace. The final diary entry by the 506th from the Bulge, January 20, reads:

> Rolled our rolls and packed equipment, to move out. Moved out in 40 cattle trucks. Left Rosiere about 1030. Very cold day and ice on the roads. Had to get out three times to push the truck up the hills. Convoy was together until we hit Nancy, France. Somehow back truck lost contact with each other and took off by themselves. Rode in trucks all day and all night.
>
> Still riding the trucks still very cold. Early in the morning we made contact with other trucks of the convoy but lost them again when we had to get out again to push the truck up another hill. We arrived at Walhambach, Alsace Lorraine, about 1430, just about 10 hours more than we should have made the trip. Our truck was about the first to arrive. Trucks still coming in the rest of the day and way last into the night. Billeted in houses in the village, we are in reserve, just waiting to be taken out, back or up to the front lines. Snowing all day long, it's quite deep where we are.

A temporary cemetery was established at Foy in 1945 that contained 2,701 corpses of American soldiers killed during the Battle of the Bulge. A few years after the war, in 1948, the bodies were exhumed, and some were placed in the American cemetery at Hamm, where Gen. George Patton's remains were interned. The rest were transported to Antwerp and repatriated in accordance with the wishes of the next of kin. During the exhumation, specialists examined some 267 unknown remains and positively identified, coincidentally, all but 101 of them.

MEMORANDUM: 28 December 1944

Message from the Division Commander:

At the time of the recent German breakthrough on the front of the First Army, I was on temporary duty in Washington where I saw the effect of the event on our Country. As the breakthroughs developed, the importance of the communication center of BASTOGNE to the success or failure of the German effort became apparent to everyone. On December 21 the situation map of the War Department first showed the 101st assigned to the defense of this key point and since that time, the eyes of the Nation have been fixed on the action of this Division. On returning I passed through every senior American Headquarters of the chain of command and received the comments of the senior American Commanders upon the recent work of the 101st.

Everyone from the Secretary of War, Mr. Stimson, sends his congratulations. The Chief of Staff, General Marshall, General Eisenhower, Chief of Staff, General Smith, General Bradley

and General Patton join in commending the 101st for its magnificent defense of BASTOGNE. To the soldiers of this Division who have lived through the day to day fighting in this area it is not possible to fully appreciate just what has been accomplished, but every senior Commander knows the American people know what the retention of BASTONE meant in checking the German drive. BASTOGNE joins Normandy and Holland as a brilliant feat of arms performed by the 101st Air-borne Division. I wish to congratulate Brigadier General A. C. McAuliffe, and every officer and man for this job so well done. Your defense has beaten off the German. The time will soon be here to resume the attack and finish him off with a decisive blow.
Maxwell Taylor
Major. General., U.S. Commanding

The siege of Bastogne was a battle with no precedent in the Western Theater. The incredible hardship and deprivations shared by defending soldiers and civilians alike remain the most poignant legacy of the battle to this day. Bastogne is the home of the largest American battle monument outside the United States and every year on or near December 16 (the beginning of the Battle of the Bulge), the "Bastognards" and multitudinous visitors commemorate the siege with "NUTS DAY."

Epilogue

It's all about the Veterans

Not all the veteran stories here are from the 101st, but they all experienced the battle, and they all endured the same hardships. The shared adversity created lifelong friendships and enduring allegiances. We have loved every one of them and listened attentively to their incredible experiences with great reverence and respect.

There's nothing obsequious or sycophantic about this admiration. We're just a small group of guys who care deeply about veterans of all wars. It was never a case of "Thanks for the interview, take care." We kept in touch with every single one of them and, in most cases, Mike Collins, Ronald Stassen and I became firm friends with them and their families.

I vividly recall inviting Medal of Honor (MOH) recipient Francis S. Currey to join Mike and I at our lecture at Siena College in Albany, New York. Francis's wife was at the hairdresser so he politely asked my wife Freya if she could attach the light-blue ribbon behind his neck, which she did with great veneration. It's not every day a Belgian nurse gets asked to help a war veteran to put on his MOH.

It's all been a genuine labor of love, and it's more than worth it just to have known them. Bless 'em all, the long and the short and the tall.

Although there are some other Battle of the Bulge veterans here, I'll never forget the 101st Airborne Division veterans. They had an esprit de corps that far exceeded their remit of just being a member of this illustrious division. I did a podcast some years ago with 101st veteran Vinnie Speranza, and decorated Vietnam veteran Dale Dye. Dale had been the historical consultant on numerous blockbusters such as *Last of the Mohicans*, *Saving Private Ryan*, *Band of Brothers*, *Platoon*, *The Pacific* and many more, and he's Hollywood royalty, but it was Vinnie who really got my attention on the day.

We were in an ad hoc studio, which had been set up in the excellent Airborne Museum in Bastogne. My dear friends, the charmingly effervescent Helen Ayer Patton (granddaughter of the famous general) and Hans van Kessel (one of the museum proprietors), were there. Helen did a great job as always; she really cares about veterans too, and has worked both with them, and for them, for many years.

I was sitting beside Vinnie and I noticed he was getting a little bored and drifting a little off topic. He told me the "Beer in the helmet" story in great detail three times. Then he said, "You're not Belgian, are you?"

"No," I replied, "I'm British, from the far north, where the men are men and the sheep take Prozac."

"I once stole a bottle of whiskey up there," he said with a wry smile.

"I hope it was a good one."

He shrugged his shoulders, "I think it was, anyway I need a drink and a smoke."

He took a sizable cigar from the top pocket of his dress uniform and lit it before we left the building.

"That's bad for your health," I quipped. I couldn't expand on that because I'm a fan of tobacco too. Then, with that devilish twinkle in his eye, he sagaciously imparted, "Bullshit, if I don't get my cigar when I want, it's bad for everybody's health," and then he asked me if I would like a drink. I replied in the positive, so we decided to go AWOL, and hit a bar on McAuliffe Square. The landlord of the Nuts café will not win any awards for being jolly. Fact is, he's a miserable bugger and he knows it. The only time I've ever seen him crack a half smile was when he saw Vinnie approaching. It was "Nuts" weekend in Bastogne, the place was heaving, and the re-enactors were out in force wearing their 101st Airborne uniforms and regalia.

When they saw Vinnie wearing his Airborne cap, a scene reminiscent of Moses parting the Red Sea occurred. The re-enactors just stood aside as Vinnie walked straight up to the bar and ordered his "Beer in the ceramic helmet." Naturally, I joined him for a few. I can confirm it's a rather powerful brew. Six of these later, the only audible voice in the café was Vinnie's and, while I was inadvertently becoming incapacitated, and losing all sensation in my lower limbs, he was knocking it back like there was a train to catch. I have no recollection of leaving the premises. That was the last time I saw him in person, but his legacy, and his legend, will remain for decades to come. Helen had a statue of him made that is on display at the 101st Airborne Museum in Bastogne.

Another notable encounter with a veteran occurred at the Pentagon. Mike Collins and I had been invited there to present our book, the sister volume to this one, *The Tigers of Bastogne*. For the occasion, we invited our mutual friend, Battle of the Bulge veteran John Schaffner. My wife and I loved John dearly. He was just so wonderfully unpredictable, and he had the most incisive wit of any veteran I met. Mike and I kept our introduction short so John could get the limelight; he really enjoyed public speaking.

He related various stories about the inhumane cold, facing the SS and all the while desperately longing for a change of underwear. "The SS can do that to you," he said. When he was almost finished, a general approached him and asked, "Mr. Schaffner, you have done so many things in your life. Do you still have any ambitions?"

John eyed him up and down and said, "Sure, I have at least one ambition left, one thing I have to do, before the great spirit calls me home."

"And what would that be, sir?" asked the general respectfully.

"I wanna get shot by a jealous lover."

John was 96 years young at the time. Every time he said something untoward, which, to my amusement was quite frequently, he would add with a wicked grin, "The devil made me do it."

John was a high-ranking freemason, Concordia Lodge, Baltimore. The front of his white car had a huge masonic symbol attached. When he became ill some years ago, my wife and I flew to Baltimore to see him one last time. We both held his hand as his dear life ebbed away. He left us before we left the building.

When that legendary double act of "Babe" Heffron and "Wild Bill" Guarnere visited Bois Jacques in Bastogne, there were two film crews on hand recording the event for the evening news. Born 18 days apart, they grew up blocks from one another in South Philadelphia, but met for the first time thousands of miles from home. On the day of the filming, Babe said to Bill, "Watch that filthy mouth of yours, Bill, don't embarrass me."

"Aw, shut up," Bill retorted, "I'm from Philly, we cuss."

"Not today."

Bill didn't use a prosthetic limb, he preferred to walk with a stick to support himself. They were already deep in the woods when Bill stopped and looked at both cameras to make sure they were filming him. Then he smiled, winked at Babe, and bellowed at the top of his voice, "If any of you fuckers finds a leg, it's mine."

The item was the lead story on the evening news in two European countries. But the clip shown in the *Band of Brothers* series of them standing, looking down on Foy, is not the view they would have had on the day, and it isn't the location where their foxhole would have been.

Some years ago, I accompanied veteran James W. Hanney Jr. and some members of his family back to where he had fought during the Battle of the Bulge. James served with the 168th Engineer Combat Battalion, which had the job of protecting the other important town on the Bulge, Sankt Vith. We walked up to the ridge where he had been and even managed to locate, what we believed to be, the actual foxhole he dug back in 1944. The soldiers of the battalion were ordered to dig in on this ridge just to the east of Sankt Vith and hold their positions until they received further orders. For six long days and nights, James and the rest of the 168th resisted sustained attacks from the 18th Volksgrenadier Regiment in the most inhumanely cold conditions.

It was −28° Celsius up there, and they had to contend with a scythe-like wind that skimmed across the icy hills of the Schnee Eifel. James was eventually wounded and helped down from the ridge by his best friend Frank Galligan.

It was a gloriously warm summer's day as we stood together on the ridge looking out between the trees. He did not actually say much, but he was obviously deep in thought, and his eyes said everything. I recall James telling me he was a Boston man and not afraid of the cold, but what he endured in 1944 was unlike anything he'd ever experienced. Some years after he had returned to the States, he and his wife moved to Florida to escape the cold north. Nevertheless, decades after the battle, he still wore three pairs of socks, even in the middle of a sweltering summer because, according to him, "My feet haven't been warm since the longest week of my life back in 1944."

Sadly, most of the World War II veterans have left us now, but thankfully some of their stories will be around for a long time to come. I have dedicated 30 fruitful years of my life to them and never regretted a second. Americans, British, Germans, and innumerable civilians have enriched my life and given me so much more than what I could have ever given them. My books are all about them. We can't see what they saw, we can't hear what they heard, we can't feel what they felt, but we can remember what they did, and we can be proud of them. Their like will never pass this way again.

The DIY Tour Guide to Bastogne

Martin King and Bob Allen

If you plan to visit Bastogne, it really isn't difficult to find your own way around. Below is a list of the sites, memorials, and museums, complete with their corresponding GPS coordinates. If you prefer the analog approach, maps are usually available at the Visitor's Information Center to the right of McAuliffe Square (Place McAuliffe), but be warned, they don't always have English-speaking staff there. When all else fails, try frenetic pointing; this usually works.

There are still traces of foxholes in the woods at Bois Jacques, but you need to visit the Bastogne War Museum first and pay an entrance fee to gain access. The team who assembled this volume are rather dubious regarding the authenticity of these foxholes. Firstly, one monument to "Easy Company" in proximity to the woods states unequivocally that these foxholes are precisely that, but according to original battlefield maps, the location of E Company was further north. There are also foxhole remnants, to the right and on the opposite side of those woods.

The coordinates provided here are separated by a comma, and can be transcribed directly into an internet browser or map app and used to generate directions, or a map for printing:

Information Center	50.000831°N, 5.714792°E
10th Armored Division Command Post	50.001298°N, 5.713861°E
Renée Lemaire Plaque	49.999826°N, 5.714328°E
101st Airborne Museum	49.999143°N, 5.712096°E
Pays d'Ardenne Museum	49.999826°N, 5.714328°E
Patton Memorial	49.998321°N, 5.715481°E
St. James Church	50.005143°N, 5.721167°E
Memorial to WWI/WWII	50.005432°N, 5.721948°E
101st Aid Station Entrance	50.006536°N, 5.721049°E
101st Command Post	50.00818°N, 5.718394°E
Cady Memorial	50.008825°N, 5.731405°E
10th Armored Memorial	50.008553°N, 5.729315°E

Bastogne Military Museum	50.010528°N, 5.734664°E
Mardasson Memorial	50.00934°N, 5.73901°E
Easy Company Memorial	50.028848°N, 5.756527°E
Entrance to Foxholes	50.033336°N, 5.752987°E
Sniper House in Foy	50.044409°N, 5.749379°E
Temporary Cemetery	50.049174°N, 5.743972°E
German Cemetery	50.049389°N, 5.741187°E
American Indian Memorial	50.045157°N, 5.732312°E
Turn to Noville	50.051945°N, 5.736469°E
Rachamps Church	50.083568°N, 5.787853°E
Glessener Memorial	49.995009°N, 5.706407°E
Turn to Pillbox	49.987587°N, 5.69424°E
Pillbox	49.983558°N, 5.698982°E
Nurses of Bastogne Memorial	50.0085°N, 5.7287°E
Bastogne Barracks Museum	50.0091°N, 5.7175°E

All Bastogne museums and memorials are within easy walking distance of the information center at McAuliffe Square, where there are usually ample parking facilities if you start early enough. You can start your tour at the information center. It is the circular building located near the Sherman tank and bust of Brig. Gen. Anthony C. McAuliffe. At the far left of the square is Rue Docteur Chiwy. The first house on the left of that street is where Nurse Augusta Chiwy lived with her father. The Bastogne War Museum and Mardasson Memorial are roughly 15 minutes away. There's a car park there that requires a small entrance fee to use it.

A plaque to the left of the 11th Armored Division Sherman tank *Barracuda* at McAuliffe Square reads:

IN HONOR
OF THE VALIANT MEN
OF THE 10th US ARMORED DIVISION
WHO GAVE THEIR LIVES FOR FREEDOM
IN THE 1944–1945 ARDENNES CAMPAIGN
AND IN THE BASTOGNE AREA

The plaque at the front of the tank reads:

This tank, knocked out in December 1944, recalls the sacrifice of all the fighters for the liberation of Bastogne and Belgium.

When one stands beside the information center with the building on your right and the road on your left, about 130 yards up the east road is the site of the former Hotel LeBrun. This is where Colonel Roberts, commander of Combat Command B, 10th Armored Division, had his command post. Almost directly opposite, there is a shop beside a large garage door. This was the collection point for Team

SNAFU, but there's no memorial plaque there. Now turn 180 degrees. You will see the traffic lights just past the information center on McAuliffe Square where you started. Walk toward these traffic lights with the square on your left. The next stop will be the plaque dedicated to Reneé Lemaire, the nurse who was depicted in *Band of Brothers*. Go to the corner where the traffic light is located and turn right, this is Rue de Neufchâteau heading away from McAuliffe Square. At the time of writing, the plaque dedicated to Reneé and the 30 wounded men who died in the Christmas Eve bombing raid is located on the front of a restaurant roughly 140 yards from the traffic light.

The text on the plaque reads:

IN MEMORIAM
SITE OF THE AID STATION
OF THE 20th A.I.B. 10th
ARMORED DIVISION WHERE
OVER THIRTY U.S. WOUNDED
AND 1 VOLUNTEER BELGIAN
NURSE (RENEE LEMAIRE)
WERE INSTANTLY KILLED
BY A GERMAN BOMB
DECEMBER 24, 1944

Reneé Bernadette Emilie Lemaire was born April 10, 1914, in Bastogne. She was a registered nurse who worked at the Brugmann Hospital in Brussels and was visiting her family in Bastogne when she volunteered to assist Dr. John Prior, 20th Armored Infantry Battalion, 10th Armored Division, in the Sarma grocery store. The aid station had to be moved twice during the battle. It was first located in Noville when Team Desobry from Combat Command B was there trying to stop the German advance. It was moved to Rue du Vivier and then finally to the store on Rue de Neufchâteau. Reneé worked exclusively for the 10th Armored Division.

The next place really worth a visit is the 101st Airborne Museum. Continue down the Rue de Neufchâteau, past the Renée Lemaire memorial plaque for about 220 yards to the Avenue de la Gare. Fifty yards up that street on your right you will find the 101st Airborne Division Museum. The displays are spread over three floors with a combination of show cases and dioramas. There is a small gift shop on the first floor. You can find more information about the 101st Airborne Museum at the following website: http://www.101airbornemuseumbastogne.com/.

The Patton Memorial is located in a parking lot approximately 400 yards from the main square. When you leave the Airborne Museum, turn left and go back to the Rue de Neufchâteau. At the top of the street, just before the main square, turn right at the traffic light into Rue Joseph-Renquin. There is a large parking lot almost 200 yards from the traffic light on the right side of the street. When you approach the parking lot, you will see the Patton Memorial relief at the far end.

Return to McAuliffe Square and then head down Rue du Sablon. Just over one hundred yards on your right is the old Notre-Dame School. The cellars beneath this school were used by both civilian and military personnel during the siege; it's almost directly opposite the town hall. Augusta Chiwy attended this school. Continue down this street to the end.

This short walk will take you through the old Latin quarter that was largely destroyed in 1944–45. On your right is St. Peter's Church, often misrepresented as the aid station of the 101st Airborne Division. The church dates from 893 AD. The tower is 33 feet wide and 60 feet high. The interior of the church has a vaulted ceiling painted in 1536 AD with scenes from the Old and New Testaments and effigies of patron saints. There is an old city entrance gate located behind the church known as the "Treves" or "Trier" Gate. The gate, along with the rest of the city walls, was built in 1336 AD by order of John the Blind. He was the Count of Luxembourg, King of Bohemia and Poland.

As you walk past the church with the building on your right, you will see a small red, white, and blue bollard that stands about three feet high. This is marker number 1,146 on the Liberty Road. The final marker is at the entrance to the parking lot of the Bastogne War Museum. They follow the circuitous route that General Patton took to reach Bastogne with his Third Army, starting in Normandy, from Sainte-Mère-Eglise to Cherbourg, then through France from Cherbourg to Avranches, Avranches to Metz, and then finally from Metz over the border to Luxembourg and on to Bastogne. On the white part of the bollard, there are various indications such as mileage, terminal number, and directional information.

The last milestone on the Liberty Road, number 1,147, was installed on July 5, 1947, at the foot of the Mardasson hill. It is only a few steps from the Mardasson Memorial, which was inaugurated three years later.

From the front of the church, one can see the former seminary building that is home to two museums about Bastogne; a steeple, clearly visible from the road, indicates the chapel. This is the place where the 101st established an aid station. On the same side of the roundabout is the Bastogne War Memorial dedicated to the citizens of Bastogne who gave their lives during the two world wars.

The closest war museum is the Bastogne Barracks. From the roundabout, follow Rue de La-Roche. The Bastogne Barracks Museum is at Number 40 on that street. It's directly opposite the cemetery where Renée Lemaire and Augusta Chiwy are buried. The open ground beyond that is where the Airborne pathfinders placed their flares for the C-47s and gliders that began arriving on the morning of December 23, 1944. The Bastogne Barracks Museum is a museum at its very best. There are no snack or souvenir shops, just good old, honest, fantastic museum exhibits. The museum staff are extremely knowledgeable and friendly (https://bastognebarracks. be/en). The collection is a definite "must see" with arguably one of the best tank collections in mainland Europe. It's also the location of the cellar where General McAuliffe made his famous "NUTS!" riposte to the German surrender ultimatum.

Now you have the option to walk or take your car to see a memorial dedicated to Combat Command B of the 10th Armored Division, which is on Rue Gustave-Delperdange. Two of the authors of this volume were responsible for raising the funds and organizing this memorial. The plaque at the base of the tank turret reads:

The U.S. 10th Armored Division's Combat Command B, the first major combat unit to defend Bastogne, arrived on the evening of December 18, 1944. Colonel William L. Roberts deployed his Combat Command in three teams:
Team Desobry at Noville
Team Cherry at Neffe and Longvilly
Team O'Hara at Wardin and Marvie

Now you're on the right road to get to the Bastogne War Museum and Mardasson Memorial. Drive or walk a little over one hundred fifty yards and turn left at the Cady Memorial on the corner of Rue de Clervaux. This is a bunker and memorial dedicated to Cpl. Emile Cady, Premier Chasseur Ardennais (Premier Light Infantry Ardennes). This unit was based near Bastogne. Corporal Cady is recorded as the first Belgian to die in the defense of Bastogne. The plaque on the memorial reads:

STOP IF YOU ARE PASSING
Here on the 10th May 1940 the hero
Corporal Cady died
First Ardennes Chasseurs
Fell for the defense of Bastogne

He was killed during the initial blitzkrieg in May 1940 when Belgium fell to the Germans.

The entrance to the Bastogne War Museum and the Mardasson Memorial is almost four hundred fifty yards up the road on the righthand side. It's the location of a gift shop, cafeteria, bathroom facilities, and a museum. When you reach the parking lot and walk toward the museum, which will be on your right, you will see the Landing Eagle Memorial on your left. This memorial was sculpted by talented local artist and dear friend, Robert Remacle, and is dedicated to the 101st Airborne by the city of Bastogne.

The plaque on the front reads:

May this eagle always symbolize the sacrifices and heroism of the 101st Airborne Division and all its attached units.

There's another plaque/marker opposite the eagle. This one, on the right side as you face the memorial, gives thanks and recognizes the other units that fought at Bastogne.

The Mardasson Memorial is dedicated to the 76,890 Americans who were wounded or killed during the Battle of the Bulge. The star-shaped structure is 36 feet high and has a side width of 93 feet. The open area in the center of the structure is 60 feet. The monument was finally completed and dedicated on July 16, 1950.

On the inside of the pillars are inscriptions recounting the story of the Battle of the Bulge. The names of all 48 American states that were in the union during World War II are engraved around the top of the memorial. There are also engravings on the outsides of the pillars of all the American units that fought in the battle.

As you face the memorial, look to the right and you will see signs that lead to the crypt. There are three altars dedicated to the Protestant, Catholic, and Jewish faiths in the crypt. The Protestant altar is directly across from the entrance with the Jewish altar on the left and the Catholic altar on the right. This is where the people and dignitaries of Bastogne commemorate Memorial Day. The crypt was carved and decorated by a French artist named Fernand Leger. The inscription on the memorial stone is in Latin; it reads:

> LIBERATORIBVS
> AMERICANIS
> POPVLVS BELGICVS
> MEMOR
> IV.VII.MCMXLVI

"The Belgian people remember their American liberators, 4 July 1946." The current "Bastogne War Museum" was initially created thanks to the efforts of one man—Guy Franz Arend. Originally, it was called the "Bastogne NUTS Museum," which opened its doors for the first time in 1950. Arend had many supporters, including Generalmajor Hasso von Manteuffel, commander of the 5th Army tasked with capturing Bastogne.

After the Mardasson Memorial, you can continue your journey as you exit the parking lot of the Bastogne War Museum, and turn right onto Chemin de Marvie/ Route de Bizory. Follow the road for just over a mile and then turn left at the base of the valley toward Foy. Continue down the road another 850 yards to the Easy Company Memorial. The memorial is across the road from where the old train station used to be, which is now used as a private residence. The area to the left of the old railroad track as you face the memorial was the responsibility of the 501st Parachute Infantry Regiment (PIR) and the wooded area on the right, the Bois Jacques, was partially garrisoned by the 506th PIR.

The memorial was dedicated on June 10, 2005, and attended by some of the surviving members of E Company. The panel on the left side of the memorial lists the names of the 14 men who died in the defense of Bastogne. The panel on the right reads:

> In the wood behind this monument, on 18 December 1944 "E" Company of the 506th P.I.R 101st Airborne Division U.S. Army dug their foxholes in the Bois Jacques Woods as part of the defence [sic] perimeter of Bastogne City that was soon to be surrounded by several enemy divisions. The circumstances were dreadful with constant mortar, rocket and artillery fire, snow fall, temperatures below –28 Celsius at night with little food and ammunition. The field hospital had

been captured so little medical help was available. On December 24th the "E" Company position was attacked at dawn by about 45 enemy soldiers. The attack failed and "E" Company held their position with 1 casualty against 23 of the enemy. The position of "E" Company was twice bombed and strafed by American P47's [sic]. During the periods of January 9th and January 13th "E" Company suffered its most casualties ending with the attack and capture of Foy on January 13th. 8 were killed in Foy and 6 earlier. During the whole period 32 were wounded and another 21 were evacuated with cold weather illnesses. In many units involved in the defence [sic] of Bastogne the casualties were even greater. This monument is dedicated to all that fought and symbolic of what happened to other units during the Battle of the Bulge.

The Bastogne–Gouvy railroad ran through the area during the war. The rail tracks acted as a kind of demarcation line between the 501st PIR and 506th PIR during the battle.

If you follow the small road beside the woods, you will arrive in the small village of Foy. Turn right at the end of the road towards the traffic lights and then look at the last house on your left. It's completely pock marked with bullet holes from the battle to take Foy. This is the house where "Shifty" Powers killed the German sniper as depicted in *Band of Brothers*. The sniper was in an upstairs window of the house.

Continue through the intersection toward Recogne. Approximately six hundred fifty yards up the road you will see an American flag and a Belgian flag on a ridge to the right. This is the location of the temporary American Cemetery. The engraving under the American and Belgian flag reads:

Here lies the site of the
FOY AMERICAN TEMPORARY CEMETERY
From 1945 to 1948
It served as a temporary resting field for
2,701 Americans killed in action during
THE BATTLE OF THE BULGE
12–16–1944 1–28–1945

The poem in the lower center portion of the memorial reads:

We have only died in vain if you believe so;
You have to decide the wisdom of our choice,
By the world which you shall build upon our headstones,
And the everlasting truth, in which you have your voice.
Though dead, we are not heroes yet, nor can be,
'Til the living by their lives which are the tools,
Carve us the epitaph of wise men,
And give us not the epitaph of fools.
David F. Phillips, 506th PIR 101st Airborne

Many of the remains that were not repatriated after the war were reinterred in one of the American cemeteries in Hamm, Luxembourg, Margraten in the Netherlands, or the largest, Henri-Chapelle in Belgium.

Return to the small crossroads and continue toward Recogne. On your left, about three hundred thirty yards down the road, you will see the German cemetery.

This is where many of the German soldiers killed in the battle for Bastogne were buried. Unlike the Americans, the Germans do not repatriate their war dead. The cemetery at Recogne contains 6,809 remains. Once the Volksbund Deutsche Kriegsgräberfürsorge, the German War Graves Commission, took control of the cemetery, they were able to identify 1,121 of the discovered remains. The crosses are gray sandstone and each has the names of six dead, three on each side.

Return to the intersection on the main road and turn left to go to Noville. This was the location of Team Desobry/Hustead and the 506th PIR. As you proceed, look to your left and you will see a ridge that runs parallel to the road a little way in the distance. This is Vaux Ridge where Captain Winters led 2nd Battalion during its attack on Noville. On the right side of the road in the direction of Houffalize, just a few yards down from the church, there is a memorial to some of the men of Noville who were murdered by the Gestapo. The memorial cemetery is dedicated to Father (Abbe) Louis Delvaux and seven others executed by the Germans after they were accused of aiding the Americans during the battle.

A little over a mile to the north, in the direction of Houffalize, is the tiny hamlet of Rachamps. One can clearly see the white church from the main road on the right. E Company spent its last night in the Belgian Ardennes in this church listening to a girls' choir.

With a good map and this book, it's relatively easy to locate the other teams at Longvilly and Marvie, and the positions of other Airborne units at places such as Champs and Longchamps (Château Rolley is still there).

Cemeteries

Luxembourg American Cemetery
    Website: http://www.abmc.gov/cemeteries/cemeteries/lx.php

Ardennes American Cemetery
    Website: http://www.abmc.gov/cemeteries/cemeteries/ar.php

Henri-Chapelle American Cemetery
    Website: http://www.abmc.gov/cemeteries/cemeteries/hc.php

Bastogne: The Gaming Guide

Alex Khan, "Prince of Macedon"

World War II was undoubtedly the biggest world event to impact our planet. This devastating period in modern history inspired countless tales of heroism, bloodshed, and sorrow around the globe. A vast majority of people can relate to some episode of World War II because a not-too-distant ancestor passed down oral stories. My own grandfather fought in World War II as a local defender against Imperial soldiers in the Philippines. The distant memory of the war is kept alive to this day not just through oral history, but also through literature, television, movies, and now the most peculiar medium of all: computer gaming. I have been tasked by esteemed military historian Martin King to utilize my passion of gaming to recommend some titles related to the 101st Airborne Division in World War II as well as some games related to Bastogne.

The "Greatest Generation" were asked to serve their country. Today's World War II enthusiasts revisit this conflict because they are fascinated that something so devastating could have happened in modern times. Today's World War II gaming culture has access to a multitude of video-game titles that allow the player to be transported to digital battlefields without facing the real-world dangers of life and death. I will only mention my absolute favorite gaming titles that relate to the 101st Airborne and their involvement with the events surrounding the Ardennes Offensive. The titles I will mention are all available for the PC. Some games (like *Hell Let Loose*) are also available on gaming consoles.

Close Combat: Wacht am Rhein (2008)

The first game worth mentioning is *Close Combat IV: The Battle of the Bulge*, which was initially released in 1999 by Atomic Games and then remade into *Close Combat: Wacht am Rhein*, developed by Strategy 3 Tactics (published by Slitherine Ltd) in 2008. "Wacht am Rhein" was the initial German codename for the Ardennes Offensive. The Allies referred to the campaign as the Battle of the Bulge. *Close Combat: Wacht am Rhein* improved the pathfinding of units from the 1999 game and made a number of other improvements (such as increasing the number of battle groups and expanding the strategy map). The graphics were slightly improved but are now incredibly dated. However, the gameplay of *Close Combat:* Wacht am Rhein is where this game shines. It is a tactics game (with the option to pause) where players fight their battles in real-time but plan their strategic moves between battles on a larger strategic map. On the map, players have access to historic battle groups such as the 501st, 502nd, and 505th Parachute Infantry Regiments to name a few. Players have the option of also fighting the Battle of the Bulge from the German side.

One of the unique features of this game (and one which many real-time games lack) is a morale feature placed on units. Prolonged exposure to gunfire can result in units panicking and fleeing the battlefield. Battle conditions can also have adverse effects on units, such as an individual soldier going berserk in the middle of a gunfight. The combined audio effects of the gunfire, explosions, and soldiers yelling create a haunting battlefield atmosphere. The biggest drawbacks to *Close Combat:* Wacht am Rhein are the outdated graphics and the smaller-sized battlefields compared to other war games of this genre.

Men of War: Assault Squad 2 (2014)

As far as World War II real-time tactical games are concerned, the very best title I have played is from the *Men of War* series, which was developed by Digitalmindsoft in 2014. This title is mostly about the multiplayer experience, but also features a single player "Campaign" aspect that includes a "Bastogne" mission as well as a "Battle of the Bulge" mission.

There is also a fantastic Airborne-specific mission for "Normandy" where you parachute behind enemy lines and take out enemy shore batteries ahead of an impending naval assault. I would rather call these "missions" because of how quick it is to complete them.

The multiplayer feature of the *Men of War* series is the biggest draw to this game, in conjunction with the superior battle system compared to its World War II-themed competitors. The multiplayer aspect features 65 different maps, five different game modes, and five playable factions (Germany, the Soviet Union, United States, the Commonwealth, and Japan). It should be noted the United States has access to some special units such as the Airborne infantry. There is a variety of ways to play this game online, whether it be 1-vs-1 battles, team battles, or cooperative modes. One of the most unique features is "Direct Control" where players can take control of a specific unit on the battlefield and utilize it directly in a "Third Person" mode. This feature has an infinite number of advantages. One of the biggest advantages comes with tank duels. The artificial intelligence will not always target the weakest part of a tank for a player, so I have found it advantageous to take "Direct Control" over my tanks and fire into the most vulnerable point of an enemy tank. Players can also change the fuze times of grenades when lobbing them against opposing infantry units.

Another dynamic feature of the game is the ability to capture enemy equipment and vehicles. This means players can pick up enemy weapons from the battlefield.

Players can also repair damaged enemy vehicles and turn these armored units against the other player. I have launched many successful covert missions behind the other player's lines with the sole purpose of commandeering enemy tanks taken out of action. I have also lost many memorable battles when my opponents did the same cunning trick to me. *Men of War: Assault Squad 2* lacks a strategic map where you can move your unit formations around a regional map, but the amazing in-depth gameplay compensates for this deficiency. Another feature lacking is morale. Your troops can get suppressed by enemy fire, but they will not run away in fear. Even your conscripts can tell the elite German units "Nuts" if they get surrounded. All of your units will fight to the bitter end.

Hell Let Loose (2021)

Moving away from the real-time tactical command games, it is very pertinent to talk about my favorite World War II first-person shooter available. This is a massive World War II online game featuring battles of 50-vs-50 players on massive maps. This online multiplayer game was officially released in 2021. The game was created by multiple developers, but ultimately fell into the hands of Team17.

The massively detailed maps in this game were created with satellite imagery in addition to the usage of archival photos showing what these battlefields would have looked like during the war. There is even a battlefield set in Foy, Belgium, where the 101st Airborne retook the town from the Germans during the Ardennes Offensive. Added to this game is another town in the Ardennes region—Marvie (where the 327th Glider Infantry Regiment acquitted themselves against the German Panzergrenadiers). Some other significant maps in this game (where Airborne units were utilized) are "Carentan" and "Purple Heart Lane." Teamwork is essential in winning these large-scale multiplayer battles. Investing in a microphone is a good idea when playing "Hell Let Loose" so you can properly coordinate your tactics with random teammates. Learning how to properly utilize the different player classes effectively will help your team tremendously. Running off solo in your own direction in search of glory and kills will not benefit your team's efforts. This is the most immersive World War II game currently available and you can spend hours a day imagining you are part of the "Greatest Generation."

Post Scriptum (2018)

I will mention this title with a slight disclaimer: this game does not take place during the Ardennes Offensive, but rather during Operation *Market Garden*. However, the 101st Airborne does make an appearance in this massive first-person shooter that was made for multiplayer online gameplay. Battles can accommodate teams of 40 players competing against 40 other players on large historical battlefields. There are over 70 authentic weapons to be seen throughout the game as well as over 50 vehicles.

Uniforms are historically accurate (based on original sources). *Post Scriptum* offers a steeper learning curve than *Hell Let Loose* which is a blessing in disguise for players looking for an even more realistic and accurate World War II experience. Just as in *Hell Let Loose*, using a microphone is crucial for communicating with your teammates. This adds to the realism and immersion factor that truly puts you in a chaotic battlefield situation. This is a game that relies more on teamwork over individual actions. When it comes to individual movement, this game offers a slightly superior experience than *Hell Let Loose* where movement over objects is restrictive. Players are able to surmount nearly every obstacle; furthermore, every building can be entered, which allows for more depth in movement and tactical possibilities.

Brothers in Arms: Hell's Highway (2008)

Brothers in Arms: Hell's Highway is another title that features the 101st Airborne Division but takes place during Operation *Market Garden*. This is a single-player, story driven game that focuses on a fictional character (S/Sgt. Matthew Baker of the 101st). It is predominantly a first-person shooter with some elements of third-person views when your character is taking cover and shooting around a corner. This game features a tactical element of gameplay where you command a squad of infantry to assist your character during missions. The squad aspect separates the game from other first-person shooters. Love it or hate it, the fictional story is a dominant aspect of this game. For dramatic effect, some of your shots will include slow-motion cinematics to highlight the action. This game is very graphic with much blood and gore added to the special effects. I felt the need to include this game because you will absolutely get attached to your character as he makes his way through the Netherlands along with his squad from the 101st Airborne Division.

Conclusion

The "Greatest Generation" might not understand our modern fascination with re-enacting World War II, but the plethora of games available from this time period are hard to ignore and offers an immersive outlet for fans of historical gaming. Video games are always evolving. Some of the titles, such as *Close Combat:* Wacht am Rhein and *Brothers in Arms: Hell's Highway* are classic games but are close to being obsolete in the face of more modern games such as *Hell Let Loose*. Future titles are always in development and gamers are always waiting for that next title that takes historical gameplay to the next level. Historical gaming is a great tool to help foster passion in learning more about an historical period. It is my hope that playing these games, and strapping on the virtual boots of a 101st paratrooper, will help gamers in further educating themselves about the history and actions of the 101st Airborne Division during World War II.

Unit Strengths

Army Group—400,000 or more with several armies typically commanded by a full general.

Army—50,000 or more with several corps typically commanded by a lieutenant general.

Corps—20,000–45,000 with 2–5 divisions typically commanded by a lieutenant general.

Division—10,000–15,000 with three brigade or regiment-sized elements typically commanded by a major general.

Brigade—3,000–5,000 with 2–5 battalions typically commanded by a colonel.

Regiment—1,500–3,000 with 2–3 battalions typically commanded by a colonel or lieutenant colonel.

Battalion—300–1,000 with 4–6 companies typically commanded by a lieutenant colonel.

Company—62–190 with 3–5 platoons typically commanded by a captain.

Platoon—16–44 typically commanded by a lieutenant with a noncommissioned officer as second in command.

Squad—9–10 typically commanded by a sergeant or staff sergeant.

APPENDIX FOUR

Military Abbreviations

AA—Antiaircraft; weapons used to shoot down aircraft.

AWOL—Absent Without Leave.

CC—Combat Command; a major tactical unit made up of a headquarters, headquarters company, and attached units such as armor, infantry, and artillery.

D-Day—A generic term to mark the beginning of a military operation. Since the landings on June 6, 1944, it has been directly connected to this event.

GI—American soldier.

KIA—Killed in Action.

MLR—Major Line of Resistance.

NCO—Noncommissioned officer; sergeants and corporals in the grade of E-3 and above.

PIR—Parachute Infantry Regiment.

POW—Prisoner of War.

R&R—Rest and Relaxation.

SNAFU—Situation Normal All "Fouled" Up.

VE-Day—Victory in Europe.

VG—Volksgrenadier; German infantry made up of individuals who would normally not qualify to serve because of age, physical requirements, or other issues.

American Army Rank Structure

Officers

General of the Army—Five stars

General (Gen.)—Four stars

Lieutenant General (Lt. Gen.)—Three stars

Major General (Maj. Gen.)—Two stars

Brigadier General (Brig. Gen.)—One star

Colonel (Col.)—Eagle

Lieutenant Colonel (Lt. Col.)—Silver oak leaf

Major (Maj.)—Gold oak leaf

Captain (Capt.)—Two silver bars

1st Lieutenant (1Lt.)—One silver bar

2nd Lieutenant (2Lt.)—One gold bar

Enlisted 1942–48

E-7 Master Sergeant (M/Sgt.)—Six stripes

E-7 First Sergeant (1Sgt.)—Six stripes with a diamond in the center

E-6 Technical Sergeant (T/Sgt.)—Five stripes

E-5 Staff Sergeant (S/Sgt.)—Four stripes

E-5 Technician Third Grade (T/3)—Four stripes with a T

E-4 Sergeant (Sgt.)—Three Stripes

E-4 Technician Fourth Grade (T/4)—Three stripes with a T

E-3 Corporal (Cpl.)—Two Stripes

E-3 Technician Fifth Grade (T/5)—Two stripes with a T

E-2 Private First Class (Pfc.)—One stripe

E-1 Private—No Insignia (Pvt.)

Technicians were addressed as the equivalent grade. A T/3 would be referred to as staff sergeant. Technicians did not normally have the authority to issue orders unless specifically granted the authority by a noncommissioned officer.

German Army Rank Structure

Army Officer Ranks	American Equivalent
Leutnant	2nd Lieutenant
Oberleutnant	1st Lieutenant
Hauptmann	Captain
Major	Major
Oberstleutnant	Lieutenant Colonel
Oberst	Colonel
Generalmajor	Brigadier General
Generalleutnant	Major General
General	Lieutenant General
Generaloberst	General
Generalfeldmarshall	General of the Army

The Germans also had variations for different positions, but this is the basic rank structure.

Army Enlisted Ranks	American Equivalent
Obersoldat	Private
Gefreiter	Private First Class
Unteroffizier	Corporal
Unterfeldwebel	Sergeant
Feldwebel	Staff Sergeant
Oberfeldwebel	Master Sergeant
Stabsfeldwebel	Sergeant Major

SS Officer Ranks	American Equivalent
Untersturmführer	2nd Lieutenant
Obersturmführer	1st Lieutenant
Hauptsturmführer	Captain
Sturmbannführer	Major
Obersturmbannführer	Lieutenant Colonel
Standartenführer	Colonel
Brigadeführer	Brigadier General
Gruppenführer	Major General
Obergruppenführer	Lieutenant General
Oberstgruppenführer	General
Reichsführer-SS	General of the Army

In the SS, the Führer designation simply meant leader. Although the SS had officer ranks, the separation between the officer and enlisted corps wasn't as strict. The men were bound by duty and would follow orders as necessary.

SS Enlisted Ranks	American Equivalent
Schütze	Private
Sturmmann	Private First Class
Rottenführer	Corporal
Untersharführer	Sergeant
Sharführer	Staff Sergeant
Obersharführer	Sergeant First Class
Hauptsharführer	Master Sergeant
Sturmsharführer	Sergeant Major

There were a couple of different ranks in the administration portion of the SS. These are the enlisted ranks for the Waffen (armed) SS, the portion of the SS that fought during the war.

Bastogne Cakes

Patrick Seeling

Just before the 78th anniversary of Bastogne, I was inspired to make pancakes for my coworkers at the Don F. Pratt Museum as a tribute to Bastogne. The reason for this is the 101st Airborne Division was fortunate in discovering an abandoned Army bakery in Bastogne with a large supply of flour and lard. Using these supplies, many soldiers within the Bastogne perimeter were able to supplement their diet with flapjacks. The following recipe was sent to me in response by my friend Shaunessey Scott who, despite my best efforts, remains a far better cook than me. Please note this is intended as a tribute to be enjoyed, not as an historically accurate recipe.

Ingredients

Amounts are based on your preference:
- Pancake batter (your choice of using a mix or making it from scratch, Shaunessey uses Kodiak Cakes mix with one egg, water, and whole milk)
- Bacon
- Nuts
- Chocolate chips (optional)
- Fruit Compote and whipped cream (optional)
- Powdered sugar (optional)

Directions

1. Preheat the oven and a 10" cast-iron skillet to 420° F. Once the pan is up to temperature, add enough bacon to cover the bottom (about four pieces) and return to the oven. This may seem like too much bacon, but that is the point.
2. Make your pancake batter and chop the nuts. Time is of the essence!
3. Once the bacon begins to crisp around the edges (three-quarters done), drain the fat and arrange the pieces in a circle around the pan.

4. Add a tablespoon of butter to the center and pour the pancake batter until it reaches the bacon.

5. From head height above the pan, paradrop the nuts and chocolate chips onto the pancake batter. A good drop will land them evenly dispersed around the batter.

6. Place the pan back in the oven and bake until everything is done (about ten minutes).

7. Remove the pan, drain off any excess fat, then plate and garnish. I recommend a cranberry-apple compote and whipped cream or powdered sugar. Merry Christmas!

Bibliography

Books

Ambrose, Stephen E. *Band Of Brothers: E Company, 506th Regiment, 101st Airborne From Normandy To Hitler's Eagle's Nest.* New York: Simon & Schuster, 2001.

Killblane, Richard E., and Jake McNiece. *The Filthy Thirteen: From the Dustbowl to Hitler's Eagle's Nest—The True Story of the 101st Airborne's Most Legendary Squad of Combat Paratroopers.* Havertown, PA: Casemate, 2003.

King, Martin, and Michael Collins. *Voices of the Bulge: Untold Stories from Veterans of the Battle of the Bulge.* Minneapolis, MN: Zenith Press, 2011.

King, Martin, and Michael Collins. *The Tigers of Bastogne: Voices of the 10th Armored Division in the Battle of the Bulge.* Havertown, Pennsylvania: Casemate, 2013.

King, Martin. *Searching for Augusta: The Forgotten Angel of Bastogne.* Guilford, Connecticut: Lyons Press, 2017.

King, Martin. *The Battle of the Bulge: The Allies' Greatest Conflict on the Western Front.* London: Arcturus Publishing Limited, 2019.

Koskimaki, George E. *Battered Bastards Of Bastogne The 101st Airborne In The Battle Of The Bulge, December 19, 1944–January 17, 1945.* New York: Presidio Press, 2007.

Mullins, G. K. *Foxhole.* Memoir Books, 2021.

Rapport, L., and A. Northwood. *Rendezvous with destiny: A history of the 101st Airborne Division.* Old Saybrook, CT: Konecky & Konecky, 2001.

Sterne, Gary. *The Americans and Germans at Bastogne: First-Hand Accounts of the Commanders Who Fought,* Pen and Sword Military, 2020.

Articles

Chen, C. P. "Hasso von Manteuffel." *World War II Database,* January 12, 2013. https://ww2db.com/.

General Kokott, "United States Army in World War II," Stetson Conn (Editor), The European Theatre of Operations, The Ardennes: Battle of the Bulge by Hugh M. Cole, 1965. The Third Samy Offensive.

Killblane, Richard E. "World War II: Pathfinders Resupply 101st Airborne Division In Bastogne Via Daring Parachute Drop." *Weider History Group,* 2006. https://www.historynet.com.

Archives

Bundesarchiv, Potsdamer Str. 1, 56075 Koblenz, Germany.

Don F. Pratt Museum Archives, Fort Campbell Kentucky.

Mike Collins, Personal Archive.

Martin King, Personal Archive.

Ronald Stassen, Personal Archive.
The National Archives, Washington, D.C.

Websites

"Freiherr von Lüttwitz, Heinrich Georg Diepold." *Lexikon der Wehrmacht*, January 11, 2013. http://www.lexikon-der-wehrmacht.de/Personenregister/L/LuttwitzHFv-R.htm.
General Fritz Bayerlein, January 10, 2024. https://www.feldgrau.com/ww2-german-130th-panzer-lehr-division/
"Panzer-Lehr-Division." *Lexikon der Wehrmacht*, January 10, 2024. https://www.lexikon-der-wehrmacht.de/Gliederungen/Panzerdivisionen/PzLPD.htm
Sgt. Lee Weaver (text only). "Interview of Lee Weaver Transcript Number 198," August 21, 2002. https://library.uncw.edu/capefearww2/voices/lee_weaver198.html
"Lauchert, Meienrad von." *Lexikon der Wehrmacht*, January 11, 2013. http://www.lexikon-der-wehrmacht.de/Personenregister/L/LauchertM-R.htm
Selected veteran interviews provided by The West Point Center for Oral History, January 10, 2024. https://www.westpointcoh.org/
Albert Mampre
Vincent Speranza
James Megellas
George Heller
Ed Hallo

Index